Talking to a Brick Wall

Talking to a Brick Wall

HOW NEW LABOUR STOPPED LISTENING TO THE VOTER
AND WHY WE NEED A NEW POLITICS

Deborah Mattinson

First published in Great Britain in 2010 by
Biteback Publishing Ltd
Heal House
375 Kennington Lane
London
SE11 5QY

ISBN 978-1-84954-056-8

10 9 8 7 6 5 4 3 2 1

A CIP catalogue record for this book is available from the British Library.
Set in Jenson by SoapBox
Printed and bound in Great Britain by TJ International Ltd, Padstow, Cornwall

For my parents, with love and thanks

Contents

Acknowledgements

This book was written in a few weeks but draws on the work of twenty-five years and more. I owe thanks to so many people...

To my father, Dick Mattinson, for nurturing my interest in, and enthusiasm for, politics, and to my mother, Jo, and brother, Robert, for putting up with our often heated debates.

To the many colleagues who have worked with me on Labour Party projects over the years: at Ayer Barker back in the beginning, then at Gould Mattinson Associates, at Opinion Leader Research after 1992, and finally at Brand Democracy. Many of you have been involved in this book directly and all of you have helped me along the way. Special thanks are due to Natalie Read, Mark Bunting, Graeme Trayner, James Morris, Ben Shimshon and Des Bezuidenhout.

To Viki Cooke, my long-standing and long-suffering business partner, whose wise counsel made the work better and good humour made it fun.

To everyone who contributed to the Shadow Communications Agency polling and focus group programme: Leslie Butterfield, Jane Bigham, Tim Mills, Kay Scorah, Peter Kellner, Nick Moon and especially Roddy Glen, who played such a vital role, and who allowed me to read his amazing notes from all that time ago.

To my sister in law, Kiki McFarlane, and friend Sarah Webb who listened while I ran through early thoughts on the book and brainstormed the Peter Pan politics idea with me.

To many friends who generously gave their time and advice, including Fiona Reynolds, Laura Vincent, Patricia Hewitt, Spencer Livermore and Roger Williams.

To Iain Dale, James Stephens, Jonathan Wadman and Sam Carter at Biteback, and Caroline Michel and Nelle Andrew at PFD, who have all been terrific to work with.

To Dan Hancox, who provided background research and helped organise and manage the Harlow panel, and to Sue Matthias, whose clear-sighted, creative, advice and superb editing skills were completely invaluable.

To all the Harlow panel, whose insights were brilliant, and to everyone who has ever been in one of my focus groups – I have tried my best to convey what you have told me to people who have the power to make a difference.

To all the politicians that I have worked with, over the years, many of whom have become good friends. I hope you think this book is fair even though its message is sometimes not what you would want to hear.

To my kids – I have noticed that people often apologise to their offspring for their absence when writing – I apologise instead for my annoying presence. Clara was able to escape on her gap year travels only after carefully transcribing many hours of focus group tapes for me, for which I am grateful. Theo and Francis, working for A-levels and GCSEs, had to put up with my hovering around when the solitary task of writing got too much – which was quite often.

And most of all to Dave, who tolerated my descent into über-sluttishness as the piles of paper grew and grew around my desk and absolutely nothing else got done. Thank you so much for your constant support and for just making everything possible.

Foreword

When I first stood for Parliament, a lady in Handsworth in Birmingham asked me a difficult question. She was by then the only white face in her street, and she wanted to know when she had had the opportunity to vote for or against a multiracial society. The incident drifted back into my mind when, during the last election, Gordon Brown described Gillian Duffy as a bigot, after she raised the question of immigration. Many voters feel that the biggest political issues are never presented to them, and that raising delicate questions with politicians – capital punishment or leaving the European Union would be other examples – will simply get them labelled, as Mrs Duffy was, and dismissed.

National politics sits unhappily between the local and the global. It is hard for parliamentarians to convince the voter that they can really accomplish anything against forces that sweep the planet: recession, climate change, terrorism or pandemics. Yet they are equally unconvincing about how their national policies can make a difference in the local school or A&E. To make matters worse, local politicians have been stripped of most of their powers. They receive most of what they spend from central government, and abide by its diktats.

It is not hard to understand why people feel disillusioned. The three main parties crowd together on the centre ground, so most voters find it hard at election time to know what choice they are being offered. They rely on habit, or they deduce from the parties' histories where their real instincts lie, or they vote for a change of government when they have grown tired of the incumbents.

In the last election, the three parties avoided debating the true nature of the deficit. But as soon as the coalition took office it made clear that austerity lay ahead. Voters may ask why that could not have been clearly explained before the votes were cast. The distrust is mutual. Politicians would respond that they could not tell the electorate the truth because it clearly did not understand the gravity of the economic situation. Voters found it hard to believe that the nation could be in a mess if they personally felt perfectly solvent.

Deborah Mattinson examines in this book how the gulf between voters and MPs has grown. She traces how New Labour sought to track public sentiment through focus groups and to listen to those voices, but how, over time, it ceased to listen. But she also points out that voters infantilise themselves. Too many believe that politics is what politicians do, and that democracy is only about voting. In fact, politics and democracy should involve everyone in the country. If the present set of MPs is venal and self-seeking, let a new wave of volunteers step forward. Even those who would not wish to stand for election should reflect that it has always been possible for people outside Parliament to start movements and to set the agenda, and that is especially possible in the age of the internet.

My own view of the New Labour experience is not that it listened too little, but that it led too little, especially at the beginning. Voters have plenty to say, of course, but they do not wish to take the time to understand every issue They cast their votes in the hope that their government will lead. Sometimes they will hate it for where it takes them. Many grew to dislike Margaret Thatcher and then, after the Iraq War, Tony Blair. But at least voters understood their characters. They gave them credit for not being insipid.

This book comes at an interesting moment in British political history. Politicians from two different parties have set their disputes aside in order to govern together: the sort of action that many voters have apparently been clamouring for. It seems that the country is to be led firmly – albeit into the valley of austerity. Citizens will be asked to shoulder more responsibility and play a bigger role in shaping the places where they live. In the pages that follow, you will often read that voters demand to be told the truth. The period ahead may test whether they can handle it; or it may prove that voters are more grown-up than politicians have assumed.

Michael Portillo
June 2010

1. 'Only Tory voters drive Jags' – learning to listen

My first experience of a political focus group was in a small terraced house in Balham, south London in 1985. I had been invited along by Colin, a research and polling professional and prominent member of the Breakfast Group – a collection of experts advising Labour. We arrived early and arranged the room, dragging the sofa, armchairs and dining chairs in the sitting room/diner into a semi circle. Colin perched on a chair in front of the fireplace as the eight voters – male, lapsed Labour – arrived. I sat at the back with tape recorder and notepad.

Colin was an outspoken, larger than life Brummie. He was also a very successful entrepreneur with a Jaguar car and beautiful house overlooking Clapham Common. He was passionate about his successful consultancy business and passionate about the Labour Party, which he had joined as a sixteen-year-old. He was eager for others to share this enthusiasm. He tried in vain to engage those eight voters in conversation about our new slogans and policy ideas, but they remained unmoved.

I had often observed focus groups before, while working for one of the UK's leading ad agencies. I had seen people much more animated than this when talking about antiseptic cream, fried chicken, shampoo and even stain remover. So had Colin.

Eventually, utterly frustrated, he resorted to shock tactics. 'Have you seen my Jag outside? Guess how much I earn!' he demanded, startling the slightly bored group of men lounging before him on the sofa and in easy chairs by leaping up from his seat and pacing around.

A little nonplussed, one or two guessed figures that must have seemed high, although were, I imagined, in reality much lower than his actual salary. 'Thirty-five grand?', 'Forty?'

'Now guess how I vote!' he urged.

'Tory?' suggested Geoff, a minicab driver, hesitantly, already beginning to sense that this might be a trick question.

At that point Colin lost it. 'I'm a Labour voter!' he yelled. 'Labour! Labour! People like me vote Labour and you should too!'

All eight men watched him open mouthed. It was a very unorthodox approach to focus group research, but the dismissive views of Labour held by these voters were typical. Labour was not the political party for people like them, and had nothing to say to them. At least Colin had made these swing voters sit up and listen. Maybe if he could have focus-grouped every voter in Britain, changing Labour's fortunes would not have taken so long. But as it was, it would be almost twelve long years before swing voters like these would be interested enough to notice much of what Labour was up to, let alone like it.

GETTING STARTED

I joined the Labour Party the day after its humiliating defeat at the 1983 general election. I was depressed at the prospect of five more years of Mrs Thatcher. I worked in advertising, and had been horrified by Labour's amateurish communications. It was hard to pick a campaign low, but the poster featuring a badly photographed image of shrieking young people sliding into a gutter, alongside a headline urging voters to 'Think positive, act positive, vote Labour' had the ad industry, and, I daresay, many voters too, hooting with derision. How could Labour fail so badly to get through to people? It was a cruel contrast with the Tories' slick presentation masterminded by Tim Bell at Saatchi and Saatchi. I desperately wanted to make a difference and felt that I had real expertise to offer: expertise that was clearly needed. I called up my local party headquarters on Lavender Hill in Battersea.

Battersea Labour Party was set to become famous – after the '97 election, John O'Farrell told its story in his bestselling book *Things Can Only Get Better*. Even in the mid-1980s the members list was studded with stars, including Prunella Scales, Timothy West and Jude Kelly, and future politicians, such as Fiona MacTaggart, Martin Linton and Tamsin Dunwoody. Most of the local ward stalwarts came from more ordinary backgrounds, though. They were mainly public sector workers: teachers, college lecturers, council workers. Some eyed me, with my advertising background, and my flatmate Jenny, who worked for an investment bank, with slight suspicion when we turned up for our first meeting.

Alf Dubs, the local MP, was immediately warm and welcoming, however, and so were many of the other members. Alf was eager to get his message out there and asked me to help him to design and draft a mailer. It included a distinctive drawing of him, which he initially rejected on the grounds that it made him look too old and too lined. We tippexed out a few wrinkles and persuaded him that the look was distinguished rather than elderly. The leaflet ran and was well received. On the back of this, Alf introduced me to his old House of Commons room mate, Robin Cook, who was working with a collection of Labour sympathisers from the communications industries.

Known as the Breakfast Group, as it met over coffee and croissants, this comprised some of the most senior and respected people in the business. I was puzzled that they had not had more impact on Labour's fortunes. Sitting through my first meeting the reason became clear. The problem was that they didn't actually do anything other than talk. . . There was a lot of eminence grise in the room, spending a good deal of time analysing where Labour was going wrong, but it stopped short of actually offering concrete help in fixing the problems. Labour had been unable to translate this often sensible, strategic advice, offered in the stylish board room of a London ad agency, into practical solutions.

Luckily, this was about to change. Labour had just appointed a bright young TV producer named Peter Mandelson as its communications director. He had commissioned another adman, Philip Gould, who would soon become my business partner, to conduct a review of Labour's communications. One of Philip's first recommendations was that a 'Shadow Communications Agency' be formed: a virtual agency drawn from communications experts who would be willing to *do* as well as *talk*. The agency had to be virtual because Labour would struggle to hire a decent ad agency – having put out soundings in the industry it was clear that top agencies feared that their commercial clients would desert them if they were known to be working for Labour. Peter asked Philip and me to establish and run the SCA and in 1986 I took a deep breath and resigned my job as an ad agency account director to do this.

Philip and I set to work starting up a number of specific and practical projects that drew on the talents of a wide group of Labour sympathising communications experts. We both worked from home initially, then took a tiny office in a mews courtyard off Greek Street in Soho. We knew our first task was to understand how the voters we needed to win back felt really about Labour, to better shape and test out some of the early communications ideas that the group had been developing.

PINSTRIPED SUITS AND CHAMPAGNE

Stereotypes were hard wired. In focus groups we asked voters to describe a typical politician by scribbling words down on cards and cutting pictures out of magazines: What did they wear? Where did they live? What did they drink and smoke? (it was the 1980s...) Which newspaper did they read? Which car did they drive? Where did they go on holiday? What kind of personality did they tend to have? In 1986, in a front room in Roehampton, swing voters produced a very clear pen portrait:

- Upper class
- Male
- Pinstriped suit
- Drinks champagne
- Rich
- Drives a Rolls-Royce
- Worked in the City
- Reads *The Times*
- Went to Eton
- Holidays in Barbados
- Lives in a mansion
- Confident
- Arrogant
- Good speaker
- Southern

What is striking is that this collection of generic politician images was almost identical to the pen portraits supplied to a more specific brief: a Conservative politician. If the general image of a politician matched that of a Conservative so closely, then the mountain Labour had to climb to gain electoral credibility was even greater than the polls suggested. Especially if you considered the pen portrait produced by the same target voters for a Labour politician:

- Working class
- Cloth cap
- Drinks pale ale
- Smokes a pipe
- Factory worker
- Holidays in Blackpool
- Takes the bus
- Lives in a council house
- Trade unionist
- Argumentative
- Protesting
- Poor
- Reads the *Mirror*
- Northern

Which would they rather spend time with? Neither! Who would represent them better? Neither! Who would be best at running the country? Well, neither party type matched voters' own lives and aspirations very closely, but at least the Conservatives were used to running things, they reasoned, and led by the new breed of 'non-posh' politicians like Thatcher and Tebbit they might just make a fist of it. Labour, by contrast, was at best backward looking, old fashioned and argumentative. Voters found it hard to imagine Labour politicians running anything.

There was another, even more sinister, problem that was particularly pronounced in London and the South East. Here Labour was not always old fashioned and down at heel, sometimes it was youthful and vigorous but maybe a little unhinged. The so called 'loony left', particularly pronounced in London (which had the greatest density of marginal seats), produced a different and more damning description of Labour:

- Bonkers
- Loony
- Lesbian
- CND
- Militant
- Dungarees
- Dirty hippy clothes
- Lefty
- Mad
- Feminist
- Smokes pot
- Lives in a squat
- Weird

STILL LIVING WITH MUM

That image of weirdness was something that cut through the party at every level. It had the ring of truth because it was, in part, truthful. It matched my own experience as a member. I now know how lucky

I was to start out in Battersea, where the members were friendly and there was an appetite for getting involved with the local community. A highlight was the Labour Party pensioners' Christmas dinner – old folk throughout the constituency would be invited to a festive knees up and cooked a meal by local members. It was fun, useful and connected the party to local people.

The meetings, honestly, were dreadful. I found them very hard going. Jenny, my banker flatmate, soon dropped out, preferring to spend Wednesday evenings at home watching *Dallas*. She would occasionally drop back in for the best bit of the evening – the pub afterwards. I persevered, but often found both the format and the vocabulary a little intimidating. They took place in the basement of a Victorian terraced house rented as party HQ. We all kept our coats on. The ward 'officers', chair and secretary, would preside at the front behind a large desk while the rest of the members sat in a wide semi-circle on hard metal stacking chairs. A lot of cigarettes were smoked.

It took me some time to dare to speak, and I never could bring myself to adopt the usual meeting etiquette – some members always contributed by 'proposing motions', reading out stiff and formally worded propositions, circulated in advance, so that equally formal responses could be prepared, rather than introducing their ideas more conversationally. They referred to each other as 'comrades', and sometimes ended their statements with a dramatic flourish: 'Brothers and sisters, I move. . .' We would then vote and the officers at the front would solemnly count our show of hands, and record the result in the minutes: 'Motion carried'. The meeting usually ended with two or three very lengthy and detailed councillors' reports.

The debates were not usually very gripping. Very often discussion would focus on minute aspects of the Labour Party constitution.

My eyes glazed over as we argued about whether the process created to agree composite motions for the annual Labour Party conference (known simply as 'Conference') was the correct one. My mum had called me from Manchester after watching the Labour Party conference that year to ask 'what on earth are these composite thingies that they keep going on about?'

On one occasion Martin Linton, who was to be MP for Battersea from 1997 to 2010, but was then a *Guardian* journalist and chair of the local ward, became exasperated with the abstract nature of our discussions: 'Imagine if a member of the public walked in here from the street and heard us all? What on earth would they think? They could be forgiven for thinking that they'd landed on another planet.' On another occasion, after the final councillor's report droned to its conclusion, Martin gave thanks saying, 'We probably have time for a question or two, but I'm afraid we don't have time for the answer so I declare this meeting closed!'

Knowing how vital it would be to involve the party itself in bringing about change, the SCA decided to commission some focus groups to better understand the party members' mindset. We knew from a recent survey that members were overwhelmingly male, older and rather well qualified – a very high proportion of graduates and post graduates, and, matching my own experience in Battersea, predominantly working in the public sector. Beyond that we knew little about what they were like or cared about.

We brought in a very experienced SCA qualitative researcher, committed to the cause. She went off enthusiastically and talked to members all around the country. She returned to the debrief meeting in London a little downcast. The members' political views were a patchwork quilt from placidly middle of the road to, in each locality, a handful of die-hard lefties. The 'loony left' profile that was causing so much grief in London was evident throughout Britain. Labour activists were a cobbled-together coalition of a wide range of views, many of which would have been unrecognisable to most ordinary voters. Debate was frequently passionate. She was struck that, while often well meaning, all this talk rarely resulted in anything practical. She saved her descriptions of the party members themselves until last. She explained how she had been struggling to pinpoint what it was that united these diverse people in Leeds, Brighton, Glasgow or Birmingham and at last she had found it.

'Basically they were all a bit weird,' she explained. 'I mean what they had in common wasn't their political opinions – those covered the whole spectrum from centre-left to far left – they weren't united by any ideology or political belief. No, it was that that they were all slightly strange people. . . strange personally I mean.' She added as we all looked at her expectantly. 'I mean they were people who really did want to spend their evenings sitting in church halls or community centres agonising over quite arcane points of detail. And they weren't just doing it that night, but *every* night – the committee for this, the committee for that, the council, whatever. They were sort of lonely and socially odd. They were the kids who wouldn't be members of any gang in the playground. They were outsiders. Just weird – I can't think of any other way to put it. . .' she trailed off.

Sometime after this I read a piece that Julia Langdon, a journalist then writing for the *Telegraph*, had written along similar lines. She described her own experience of joining the Labour Party and turning up to her first meeting. She too found most of her fellow party members somewhat unusual. In the end she latched on to the most seemingly 'normal' member of the group to discover over a post-meeting drink that this 43-year-old man – by far the most regular bloke there – still lived at home with his mum.

So what might have been the politician's most powerful weapon in reaching out to the public – the party members living in their local communities – too often turned out to be part of the problem instead. Unusual people doing unusual things, with the rare exception like Battersea's Christmas dinner, there was almost no link between local people and party. That Labour often selected candidates from this gene pool did not bode well for creating politicians who could speak 'human'. It was clear that part of the battle was going to be to attract a wider selection of, well, normal people to join the party.

It would also be important to change the Labour 'draughty church hall meeting' culture. The SCA researcher who conducted the study compared the people she had met when researching party members with the people who had been in her local, very prominent, Conservative Party at the time: 'It seemed to be that the local Conservatives were people who would turn up and make a rice salad or turn up and get involved with the PTA. They were joiners and doers, while Labour people were joiners and talkers.'

SYMBOLS OF CAMPAIGN SUCCESS

Understanding the problem was the first step to solving it. The next challenge was to persuade the politicians themselves to listen. Peter Mandelson, completely on side, was the SCA's main ally as he championed the thinking through the party. Neil Kinnock 'got it' too. The first big breakthrough came in September 1985 at Labour's party conference in Bournemouth where Neil made his now famous speech calling for the expulsion of hard left 'militants' from local parties. Top qualitative researcher Roddy Glen and senior ad agency planner Leslie Butterfield conducted focus groups either side of this speech and the difference in people's reactions to Neil Kinnock before and after seeing it was extraordinary. He had cut though and won people's attention. He had taken on his own party and positioned himself against the 'loony' left and on the side of common sense. There was some way to go but it was a start.

We developed the idea of the 'symbolic policy', a policy which symbolised a political party's vision. The theory was based on the premise that a party's 'promise' had three components: its vision, its programme to achieve the vision, and specific policies to illustrate the clear offer. Too often recently Labour had been stuck, like the local party meeting agendas, at the programmatic level. It was obsessing about the mechanics of how it operated, forgetting both the 'higher purpose' – the party's overall aims – and, crucially from the public's point of view, the policies that might illustrate that vision, bringing it to life and making that vital connection by improving their lives.

The Tories could boast what I believe remains to this day the most effective example of a symbolic policy: giving tenants the right to buy their own council house. It meant that voters had a clear and accurate view of what they believed in because their vision was translated into a simple tangible idea, and one that delivered a clear benefit to the voter. It has stood the test of time. Focus groups more than twenty years later still name-check council house sales as the best thing the Conservative Party has ever done. The downside of reducing the availability of housing stock to those unable to buy their own home simply faded into the background. Swing voters in Harlow in March 2010, some of whom were children during Mrs Thatcher's premiership, were all able to attribute this to her: her big achievement and proof that she was in touch with what people cared about.

The Freedom and Fairness campaign, launched in April 1986,

was the first that I worked on at a national level. Devised by Peter Mandelson to aim directly at the voter, rather than at the party, it led with the line 'putting people first' and boasted specific policies to spearhead each theme. True, we lacked anything with the punch of council house sales, but at least the party had accepted the need to highlight tangible policies that held real appeal to voters. The focus was on cervical cancer screening, on nurseries and on lead-free petrol, anticipating the celebrated Pledge Card that was to follow more than ten years later.

The launch also heralded an end to the ineffectual communications that had characterised the 1983 general election campaign. The campaign was the last thing I did before leaving my job in an ad agency and I was able to recruit two Labour-supporting 'creatives' from the agency to help out: Kaarl Hollis and Trevor Beattie. (Trevor would go on to work with Labour for many years, designing, amongst others, the award-winning 'Wiggy': Mrs Thatcher's hairdo on William Hague.)

Although Freedom and Fairness went unnoticed by the public, the Westminster Village was bowled over. Even the *Telegraph* noted that the new campaign was a sign of Labour 'shedding its weary cloth cap image'. So if voters were a little unmoved we still felt that we had achieved something important. Peter wrote me a warm thank-you letter, saying, 'Together, we may just have made a little bit of history'. I loved the letter and keep it to this day, but wonder with hindsight if this reaction was an early lapse into the bad habit of believing headlines rather than voter reaction.

A year later, the 1987 general election boasted advertising that was the talk of the industry, party election broadcasts by world class directors like '*Chariots of Fire*' Hugh Hudson, and much more polished media performances. But a smart new look was not enough to gloss over the Labour's shortcomings, especially in the policy areas. Our private polling, conducted by MORI and a growing group of volunteer researchers, included nightly focus groups and twice-weekly polls. It showed that we were not making the connection we needed to. Although the media continued to be impressed, voters still saw Labour as old fashioned, out of touch and not on their side. The transformation had been too superficial to correct the deep rooted alienation the electorate felt.

The campaign had achieved one important electoral objective, though, and one that hits home to me writing this, as I am, more than two decades later in 2010. It is often forgotten that Labour began the 1987 campaign polling in third place to the SDP/Liberal Alliance. By the end of the campaign the SDP had dropped back to 23 per cent – the mark around which they would hover over the coming years and exactly what the Lib Dems would poll in 2010.

In 1987 the Tories won a decisive victory. Chris Powell, then head of ad agency BMP and a key figure in the SCA, often observed that there are really only two election campaign themes: 'Steady as we go' or 'Time for a change'. Our much admired election posters all carried the emotive strap line 'The country's crying out for change'. The only problem, as the election result proved, was that it wasn't.

2. Meet the swing voter

Worcester Woman, Mondeo Man, Pebbledash People, NetMums, Mr Motorway, even Mr Bored – over the years the Westminster Village has endlessly reinvented voters. Like zoological specimens, they have been counted and recounted, categorised, observed and labelled. Swing voters have been under particular scrutiny. These are not necessarily homogenous. What unites them is that they have not yet heard anything from any party to make up their mind. They do not feel represented by anyone so it is vital for parties to find ways of connecting with them.

As long ago as 1949, reeling in the aftermath of the Conservative defeat in the 1945 general election, Tory grandee Lord Poole hired ad agency Colman Prentis Varley, and, through them, commissioned the first ever study of swing voters. 'The Floating Vote', as it was called, cost £1,180 – the price of a typical swing voter's house at the time. It analysed the newspaper-reading habits, occupation, recreations, age and gender of undecided voters, concluding that the Conservatives' key targets were women, young people, shopkeepers and Liberals. The resulting change of strategy would help the Tories to regain power in 1951.

Understanding the profile and attitudes of undecided voters is now an essential feature of modern political campaigning. Psephologists, pollsters and strategists all have their own favoured models for deciding who are the most persuadable. Calling this correctly is vital for electoral success. In large scale polls a series of questions will determine how wedded each voter is to their party of choice, and how likely they are to stray. This information is then used to form groups clustered by political preference. By examining the demographics, lifestyle and views of each group, politicians can define the electoral battleground, and get to know those sought-after swing voters.

In 2009, analysis for Labour divided the population up like this:

15.1m   *Out of reach* – people who would never vote Labour
3.2m   *Loyal vote* – people who would always vote Labour
2.7m   *Vulnerable* – Labour voters who might go elsewhere
2.3m   *Within reach* – Other voters who might shift to Labour
2.4m   *Winnable* (Labour in 2005)
4.3m   *Winnable* (not Labour in 2005).

Examining the demographic make up of these groups added further information:

- *Out of reach* was Labour's traditional opposition: older, and upper/middle class.
- *Loyal vote* was Labour's traditional support: again older but more working class, a tendency to be male.
- *Vulnerable* was middle aged, with kids, working, better off, with no strong gender bias.
- *Within Reach* was also younger, Lib Dem leaning, more affluent.
- *Winnable (Labour in 2005)* was middle aged, less affluent, less well educated and with kids.

- *Winnable (not Labour in 2005)* was younger, better off, better educated and single.

Both 'winnable' groups were more likely to be female.

Choosing which group or groups to target will shape a party's campaign. Getting this right is a matter not just of mathematics but also of judgement. Over the years, an enduring debate in the Labour Party has been whether it is more fruitful to focus on its core vote, with a strategy devised to motivate and maximise turnout, or whether the party would be more successful by appealing more widely to a middle class vote.

In the run-up to 2010 Labour politicians were bitterly divided on this point. Choosing the 'core vote' route had led to the Tory 'toff bashing' blamed for losing the Crewe & Nantwich by-election as campaigners donned top hat and tails to mock the upmarket Conservative candidate. The 'middle class' strategy demanded a more positive, aspirational and wealth-tolerant message, although perhaps not going as far as Peter Mandelson in 1998 when he said he was 'intensely relaxed about the filthy rich'.

This is not a new debate. After the First World War, Labour produced a pamphlet entitled *Why Brain Workers Should Join the Labour Party*. In the 1920s, Herbert Morrison, Peter Mandelson's grandfather and personal inspiration, produced a detailed evaluation of London's vote, asking 'Can Labour win London without the Middle Classes?'. His conclusion, based on analysis of 1921 census data, was that it could not, partly because the number of middle class voters in the capital was so great and partly because Labour needed to attract some middle class voters to compensate for the working class votes that it had already and irrevocably lost to the Conservatives.

ANGER NOT APATHY

In 1997 Labour won by making a direct appeal to the middle ground voters that had eluded them in the previous three elections. The resulting coalition of Labour's core working class vote and more well-to-do swing voters was electorally successful but not without problems. In 2001, turnout dropped from the fairly consistent 70 odd percent achieved since the 1970s to 59.4 per cent. In some seats, notably those that were working class Labour strongholds the turnout dropped up to 20 per cent. Barking in East London was one such seat. Margaret Hodge, Barking's MP and I ran a series of focus groups after the election to discover why.

Our report, entitled 'Anger not Apathy', outlined how Labour's core vote felt neglected with its focus on Middle England. Barking voters told us how New Labour neglect had led to a problem that stemmed directly from the Conservatives' triumphant council house sales policy: the demise of the public housing stock. We described the appalling conditions that many Labour voters were living in, and how public housing had become a 'Cinderella' issue. We presented this work to the party and to No. 10, where it was met with solemn agreement but I'm not sure much was actually done.

My own view is that any government has a moral imperative to ensure that its poorest live in adequate conditions. Given Labour's values and traditions this is deep in the party's DNA. Yet, while getting the core vote out is critical for all political parties, especially in a period where turnout has been low, Labour can only succeed electorally and thus be in a position to help the most vulnerable by extending its appeal beyond the working class vote. Spencer Livermore, Gordon Brown's Director of Strategy until 2008 puts it like this 'You're in politics to change things and to do that you have to be in power. You have to win.'

Just like the 1920s London that Morrison described, it is the middle class vote that populates marginal seats up and down the country. So these voters have taken on iconic status, becoming the battleground voters for any election. In Morrison's day the term 'middle class' implied well-to-do professional classes – any relevant definition of 'middle class' nowadays would be very different. These voters would increasingly not identify with the description 'middle class'; instead they recognised themselves in a term which I began to use in the run-up to the 2005 election: 'the squeezed middle'. These are people who see themselves as a neglected minority: too poor to manage easily without government hand outs, yet too well off to qualify for that help. I usually refer to them as 'middle ground voters'.

INTRODUCING THE SWING VOTER

If the large scale polls can identify which swing voters matter, it is the qualitative research that can best help us to understand them. This means carefully selected, small scale and in-depth sessions, of which the focus group is the best known. In spring 2010, I set up a panel of twelve typical uncommitted voters, all living in Harlow, Essex. At that time Harlow was Britain's fifth most marginal seat, and held by Labour since 1997. The contest in 2005 was so close that there were three recounts and the eventual result was not declared until 11.40 a.m. on the Saturday after Election Day. The Labour MP, Bill Rammell, had a majority of less than 100.

My aim was to get an up-to-date picture of middle ground voters' lives, their take on politics and their reactions to the general election campaign itself. I also wanted to review the eventual result with them afterwards.

I first met everyone on a chilly March evening in a comfortable semi in Old Harlow. I arranged the session as two separate groups, first meeting the women, then the men. We gathered at the home of Donna, the focus group hostess, and assembled in her airy living room, as she ran backwards and forwards back to scoop up and remove her yappy chihuahua and huge and very persistent tabby.

As a warm up, I suggested that everyone should chat to the person sitting next to them and then introduce them to the rest of the group. The group of women fizzed with energy straight away. They talked intently in their pairs, quizzing one another, as I had asked them to, on work, on family life, and on their hobbies. I requested that they try to unearth one surprising fact about each other. The room filled with chatter and laughter. After a few minutes I hushed them all and, going round the room, each person described their neighbour.

Lorna, a slim, dark-haired, serious young woman in track suit

The Harlow focus group. Left to right: Denis, Paul, Tracey, Michael,Danny, the author (in front), Scott, Sadia, Natasha, Alicia, John,Lorna (not pictured: Angela).

and trainers introduced Tracey, middle aged, with a neat grey bob, in a smart red top.

'This is Tracey. She's lived in Harlow for twenty years and is married with a fifteen-year-old doing GCSEs so it's very stressful in her house at the moment. She's worked in PR at Pearsons for eighteen years – and knows my sister-in-law, who works there too. She enjoys gardening and reading, and her surprising fact is that she likes watching cricket. She goes and watches local teams every Saturday and Sunday and she's been to see Essex a couple of times too.'

Lorna herself, Harlow born, was a strategic buyer at ITT, living on her own but close by her mum, dad and brother. Her surprising fact was that she was a jujitsu black belt who has represented Great Britain in competition.

We also met Sadia, a City executive assistant with a mane of thick, curly black hair. Married to a policeman she confessed to a liking for singing and luxury holidays. Surprising fact: the youngest of nine children. Sadia introduced Angela, small and blonde, who apologised that she was wearing a blood pressure monitor which was going to bleep at us every half an hour.

'This is Angela, she's a finance manager in Hainault. She has a girl and a boy and is taking them to Orlando on Christmas Eve this year. She's lived in Harlow since she was five. She likes running and ran the Marathon last year—'

'No!' interrupted Angela, 'I haven't done it yet – it's this year!'

'Her surprising fact is that she has walked the Great Wall of China.'

Alicia sat nearest to me, the chair everyone avoids in focus groups as it's a bit like sitting in the front row at school, but she arrived last and had no choice. Alicia was small and lively with a dry sense of humour. Walking with a perceptible limp she explained that she suffers from arthritis. Surprising fact: 'I have two new hips and two new knees.' Mum to two grown-up 'well-behaved boys' of twenty and twenty-nine, not being fit enough to work does not stop her from keeping busy volunteering for charity caring for rescued animals. A passionate dog lover, she has an Alsatian, a blind retriever and a sheltie. She introduced Natasha.

'Natasha is thirty years old and young, free and single, with a seven-year-old daughter. She works for BT and is originally from the Midlands but her family moved here when she was fourteen. You haven't got any accent at all, have you?'

'No, I got rid of that as quickly as I could,' said Natasha.

'Natasha's weekends are busy with her daughter's activities: her daughter dances and she's on at the Playhouse next week. She last holidayed in Thailand and likes kick boxing. Oh, and her surprising fact is that she's a natural blonde.'

This was a showstopper and we all gazed in amazement as Natasha peered bashfully from behind her glossy brunette curtain.

The men approached the introductions in a less matey, more matter-of-fact way. One of the men had got lost en route, leaving Scott, now pair-less, to introduce himself.

'My name is Scott and I work in sales at BT. I have two young boys aged three and one and live with my partner – we're getting married in September. I like football and hanging out with the family. My surprising fact is that in 2000 I was the furthest easterly person in Australia. I mean I stood at the most easterly point. Although I can't actually prove it but that's what they said. . .'

John and Michael had made a labour saving pact to not bother 'interviewing' each other but instead to each write down their personal details and simply give them to the other to read out. They wrote in silence, then Michael read:

'This is John, aged forty-eight. He has been married twice and has daughters aged eighteen and sixteen and a stepson aged thirteen. He was made redundant from his job as a graphic designer in November 2008 and now works as a PAT test engineer – that's testing plugs apparently. His hobbies are golf and football – watching, not playing – and his surprising fact is that he likes opera and classical music.'

'Not many people do, I find,' added John, who then introduced Michael.

'This is Michael, aged fifty, divorced with two boys. He works at Stansted Airport. He coached Under 14s for Marquis and likes to go on holiday to any place that Ryanair will take him. His surprising fact is that. . . er, he has no surprising fact.'

The 'surprising lack of surprise' was a formula that Denis and Danny, sitting together in the middle of the wall-to-wall seating, chose to adopt too. Denis, somewhat reticent at first, was, we learned, married with three kids – a girl of fourteen, a boy of thirteen and a boy of nine. He likes the outdoors life and enjoys football and golf. He then introduced Danny, more confident, well built and friendly.

'This is Danny. He has two very young girls – nine and six – and works in print. He likes cycling and rugby and used to play with Saracens in their academy. He now sticks to the more, ahem, social side at Chingford. He has a four-berth camper van and for his holidays he likes to travel all over Europe with the kids.'

The twelfth member of the group missed the first session and arrived a couple of weeks in just after the start of the general election campaign: Paul, who introduced himself.

'I'm a telecoms engineer, and I've recently been made redundant. I've got a partner who's got a couple of children, twelve and sixteen. I enjoy outside things like walking in the fresh air and DIY at home.'

Paul had an unusual interest: 'I'm finding myself more interested in politics recently – I've got more time.'

WHO ARE THE SWING VOTERS IN THE ELECTORAL BATTLE GROUND?

My Harlow panel members are typical of the Middle England voters that I have met over many years. They are lively, smart and perceptive. They are busy, working hard, looking after their families, pursuing their hobbies. They want politicians to make a difference to their lives but doubt that they will. Much of the Westminster Village buzz passes them by, yet they notice a lot – often picking up the non-verbal clues that politicians might prefer them to miss.

In 2007 I wrote a note for Gordon Brown's team as they approached his transition to PM entitled 'Who are the battle ground voters' and subtitled – 'understanding the people that we need to win back to win.' Having spent at least an evening a week over the past twenty-five years in the company of voters like these I knew them well. I also knew how much they mattered and believed that it was vital that Team GB had them in mind at every turn. I wrote:

> They are C1C2 social class: skilled manual workers or office workers – plumbers, decorators, hairdressers, secretaries, computer operators or accounts clerks. They are unlikely to be graduates and probably left school at 16. They work in retail, in financial services, or telecoms, in local government or in the NHS. The older ones may have served an apprenticeship. If a couple, they may not be married, and both partners will be economically active, although if children are small the women may take a break or work part time. They will be the first or second generation in their family to own their own home. They go abroad for their holidays, and enjoy weekend breaks away. They eat out regularly and may own two cars.
>
> They may no longer buy a daily newspaper, but if they do it

will probably be a tabloid, most likely the *Daily Mail*. Otherwise news is accessed from TV or, increasingly, the internet. They are less interested in current affairs than they are in things that directly impact on their own families, so ages and life stages of their children/grandchildren/parents are central to their concerns.

Those with older children worry that their kids will not be able to maintain the lifestyle that they currently enjoy: they are anxious about house prices, and about the demise of skilled labour. They do not particularly aim for their children to be university educated, and, although they will certainly be proud if they do, they have a deep rooted suspicion that university is probably an expensive waste of time. They would prefer to see a return to 'old fashioned' apprenticeships where you are paid to participate, maybe gain formal qualifications at the same time, and then have a guaranteed job.

For those with younger children, concerns focus on choice of school, especially secondary school. They are worried about lack of discipline and order. Scornful about 'political correctness' – a fundamentally Labour trait – they believe government's attempts to address problems like discipline are undermined and teacher, police and parent power diminished. They bemoan threats to British culture and tradition e.g. banning Christmas. Older voters will also be worried about their own elderly parents, especially as, with increasing geographical mobility, they may no longer live nearby.

They do not feel that society is 'broken' but do feel that it is breaking down: they have a general anxiety about social unrest, which may mean kids hanging around on street corners or may mean crime which they believe to be on the increase and of a different order than in the past (guns and knives rather than fists and twelve-year-olds rather than seventeen-year-olds). They also regret that communities are less cohesive than they were: partly because people work harder, have less time, and aren't out and about on the street so much; this is partly because more people have moved away from their families; and partly because there are more immigrants who do not integrate and 'keep themselves to themselves'.

They argue that institutions that once were reliable such as the NHS, schools and the police are now prone to let you down. Symbols of failure would include hospital bug MRSA, unruly youth and CCTV cameras. These institutions are also undermined by immigrants, they believe, putting resources under pressure with sheer numbers and their own particular needs, such as language support in schools.

They question the sustainability of the economy and its impact on them. This is a powerful underlying anxiety. Many remember Black Wednesday and the period around that vividly and dread a similar threat.

They feel vulnerable and believe that government is unfair to people like them – they describe themselves as 'caught in the middle', hardworking ordinary families who lack long term financial security and are the first to feel the pinch but get no break from a government which is focused on looking after the 'undeserving poor': immigrants, teenage mums and benefit cheats. The rich/poor or middle class/ working class dichotomy where less well off are victims of social injustice is not a reality they recognise. Instead they identify a tripartite grouping of the rich, themselves and the undeserving poor.

Like most people in Britain, these people don't much care about the cut and thrust of politics. They aren't moved by process stories, and don't much care who is up and who is down. Their main test for political ideas is whether they affect them or their family. They believe Labour looks after the poor (and is a soft touch for the undeserving), and the Conservatives look after the rich and that no one looks out for people like them.

Their central belief about politicians of any hue is that they are in it for themselves, and are constantly trying to hoodwink people into believing something that is not untrue, but is a distortion of reality.

Convinced that political parties are trying to game them, they heavily discount claims by perceived plausibility. Promising the earth earns no points. Similarly, they judge leaders at least as much on whether they believe they can get things done as on the things that the leaders promise to do. It is both a problem and an opportunity that this group of voters do not closely identify with either party, believing that Labour and the Conservatives both have a core audience that leaves, them, 'the voters in the middle', disenfranchised.

AN EMPTY BOX OF PROMISES

When I run focus groups I often ask the people who come along to do a bit of homework first. In this instance I asked Chris, who had recruited the panel for me to ring around and ask everyone to bring an object or a word that best summed up how they felt about politics. Each explained what they had brought along and why:

ALICIA: I've got Robert Halfon's [Conservative candidate] piece that's just come through the door. It's fantastic. It's got everything we want … jobs, houses, roads. It's all what they're going to do. And I've no doubt at all that Labour will say the same thing. But they'll have all these debts and won't be able to. It's a miracle cure. They all say the same thing. They know what's needed but in the end they can't do it.

ANGELA: My object was a hairdryer, because politicians are full of hot air. The things they say don't mean an awful lot – it's just waffle.

Evasive is the word. They do everything but answer the direct question when they are being interviewed.

DANNY: My object is a big fat question mark. None of them are getting it right. They all say they're trying to improve the country but they can never justify what they actually do. They're all at each other's throats. Why don't they all sit down together and stop beating each other up?

DENIS: I was going to bring along a jar of pickled onions, but I couldn't find any pickled onions, because politicians have such old fashioned ideas – they're not with the global world. So I've brought along an empty bottle instead. In my view politics is empty. Empty to the fact that they're not aware of what's going on, empty to the fact that they can't do what they say they'll do, empty to the fact that their hands are tied given the country's burden with debt.

JOHN: I've brought along a box that I made – it says 'promises'. But [*opens box*] you can see it's empty. The pot of money is empty. They can't promise you tax cuts or more money 'cos the money isn't there.

LORNA: My object is a dice. It faces in lots of different directions, to suit the fashion and the changing climate. Politicians change at a moment's notice to suit themselves. They change their minds and they change direction.

MICHAEL: It's a word: 'scandalous'. It's scandalous that we haven't been told the truth about the war in Afghanistan. Scandalous that young men are being killed and we're not told why. It's scandalous about their expenses too.

NATASHA: My object would be Pinocchio and my word would be 'dishonest'. The obvious example is expenses – claiming on moats and suchlike. And they never follow through what they say they'll do.

SADIA: I drew this question mark. It sums up what I think – it's always a big question mark. One question leads to a barrage of new ones. That's how politics is going. You can't put your thumb on anyone any more. They don't go down traditional routes any more – you know, your traditional Labour or your Conservatives.

SCOTT: If I'd had one to bring along, my object would have been a duck house. It's all about those expenses. They just don't seem to understand the need to say sorry.

TRACEY: My word is 'slippery'. I thought long and hard about it. I'm being literal here.

It is hard to overstate the levels of cynicism, loathing, even disgust that politicians currently inspire in voters like these. Their overwhelming view confirms the problems set out in my 2007 note: politicians don't care about people like them and, at best, issue empty promises that will not be delivered. At worst they are simply 'out for themselves'. Since 2007 we have seen economic crises and the unprecedented expenses scandal. Small wonder, then, that the Harlow panel, chosen for their importance as 'persuadable voters' set out on their journey towards the general election feeling somewhat unpersuaded.

3. 'We're all New Labour now' – the early euphoria

On Friday 2 May 1997, the day after Labour's landslide general election victory, I arrived to collect my kids from school a bit early. A few parents were already sitting on the low wall around the playground squinting into the bright afternoon sunlight. As we waited, a teacher walked from one building to another in front of us. Halfway across she stopped suddenly and leapt in the air, tossing her bag up, and letting out a joyous whoop. She then walked briskly on to the classroom. I didn't know any of the other parents but we all smiled at her and at each other. There was even a small scattering of applause. We enjoyed sharing the moment. We all knew how she felt. We were all New Labour now.

The middle of the following week found me in Edgware running focus groups. For the first time we had recruited people who matched our new, post-'97-election, definition of swing voters: they had voted Labour last week but had previously voted Conservative. The mood was extraordinary. Everyone had their own election story to tell. One of them was Claire, the kind of woman who, back in the 1980s, I would have struggled to get along to a focus group if I'd confessed that the subject was politics: 'You should invite my husband; he's more interested than I am' would have been the typical response. Claire had been so moved by the moment that she and a friend had called a mini cab to take them to the South Bank where they waited, as the sun came up over the river, to cheer Tony Blair when he arrived at the Labour celebrations at Festival Hall.

> We just did it – we said 'Let's go to the Festival Hall' and it was a fantastic atmosphere, like a pop concert or something. Hundreds of people were there, all cheering and waving. It's like a fresh start for the whole country.

'Yes, it feels like a real break with the past,' said Anita, a receptionist, going on to say how disillusioned she had been with the Conservatives, with politics overall. But this felt different.

'It's different because it might actually make a difference to me – I really feel for the first time ever that politicians might help me out, might do something for my family,' agreed Suzanne, a part time dental nurse.

'He's so young and lovely – a real family man,' said Christina, a housewife, bright eyed as she described how touched she had been to see the youthful Blair and his family waving on the steps of No. 10.

The contrast with those early focus groups where I could hardly get voters to speak at all could hardly have been greater. As we sat talking on that warm May night, French windows open onto the neat suburban garden, these women were bubbling with excitement at what had happened and full of anticipation about what would come next. Tony Blair and New Labour spoke to them and for them. They were expecting a lot to happen. Expectations could not have been higher. They had no doubts at all.

MOVING ON FROM DEFEAT IN 1992

I had always planned to move on from political work after the 1992 general election. Some months before, I had signed all the papers setting up a new business, Opinion Leader Research, with my talented colleague and old friend from advertising days, Viki Cooke. When I first started working with Labour I had genuinely felt I had something real to offer: expertise from a different world. In the early days, I had been privately critical of some of the Labour Party team. These were people whose commitment to the cause was unquestionable, but, in my view, their skills were sometimes not up to scratch and they wouldn't have survived in a more competitive commercial environment. Had I become one of those people myself, after six years of working on little else? I needed to know. Viki and I decided to launch the business immediately after the election, whenever that might be and whatever the outcome.

My three children had a habit of arriving in politically newsworthy times. Clara, my eldest, was born just before Mrs Thatcher's dramatic resignation, while Francis, my youngest, appeared just before Tony Blair was elected Labour leader. Theo, my second baby, had arrived three weeks before the 1992 election was called. He accompanied me to Labour HQ at Smith Square every day of the campaign, where I was leading a team of polling experts analysing our own and published polling, as well as reviewing the qualitative research from our focus groups. He became the team's mascot, sitting in his bouncy chair by my desk as I worked, either in the office during the day or at home each evening.

There was of course no internet back in 1992 and late every night headlines from the polls and focus groups were phoned or faxed to me at home. I would sit down after the nighttime feed at about 1 a.m. poring over scribbled notes and reams of fax printout preparing a summary note for the 8 a.m. daily strategy meeting. The polls were pretty positive, and we did not yet know that they would all prove to be so wrong – overstating Labour's share of the vote. The focus groups proved a more reliable weathervane and remained relentlessly negative, especially about Labour's economic policies and its leader, Neil Kinnock.

Neil Kinnock is an extraordinary man: clever, passionate and courageous, he is also warm and kind. His office was a happy and productive place, despite the stresses and strains that leading Her Majesty's Opposition inevitably causes. Neil knew everyone and treated everyone with the same friendly, teasing manner. Because of my longish red hair and his balding pate he always enquired whether I was the hair transplant that he had ordered. He kept his good humour even in the harassed environment of an election campaign, shortening everyone's names in a matey way. I was, naturally, Debbie, while Peter Mandelson was Pete: even then it seemed hilarious.

A favourite question of pollsters in the 1980s compared Neil Kinnock and Margaret Thatcher: who would you rather live next door to? Who would you prefer to have a drink with? Neil won hands down. He was normal (for a politician). However, this striking advantage sat alongside a major and crippling weakness – voters struggled to rate him as highly as a leader or potential Prime Minister as they rated him as a human being. Perhaps he was *too* normal.

The SCA research that had fed into Labour's post-'87 review, 'Labour and Britain in the 1990s', recognised this. Many unpalatable facts were presented to the party's Shadow Cabinet and National Executive. We had told them how voters had adopted what some in the Labour Party would describe as 'Tory' aspirations such as home ownership, and how the Labour Party brand was seen as outdated, male and aggressive. However, the polling and focus groups that highlighted attitudes towards Neil Kinnock's leadership as a barrier to voting Labour were not shared at the presentation. This was for reasons that I well understood, then and now, looking back. How could Neil Kinnock have won his management team's blessing to make the changes needed if his own vulnerabilities were exposed to them?

Patricia Hewitt, Neil's press secretary, knew only too well how voters saw him: as a decent, idealistic, but emotional man whom they struggled to envisage as a leader. She had focused on Neil's personal presentation during the '87 campaign, drawing on voter research feedback. She had developed the brief that became the blueprint for the brilliant Hugh Hudson election broadcast which painstakingly addressed the issues raised by voters. Too weak?. . . 'There's steel at the heart of that young man' growled veteran MEP Barbara Castle. Too lefty?. . .'Traitor' snarled left-wing council leader Derek Hatton as he was expelled. Lacking in vision?. . .'Why am I the first Kinnock in a thousand years to go to university?' (In fact, Neil's own words about social mobility were so visionary that Joe Biden, now US Vice President, plagiarised them.) The Hudson broadcast also showcased his strengths: a loving family man passionate about his politics and his party. Neil's rating rose by 16 per cent overnight after one showing of the broadcast.

After John Major replaced Mrs Thatcher in 1990, Labour's poll ratings fell into decline. Neil Kinnock's personal ratings slumped too, and a team from the SCA set out to discover why. They came back with a penetrating study that suggested that the voters' problem was that Neil's positioning was oppositional not constructive. . . that he was wedded to the 'language of protest, the language of the valleys'. Neil saw inequality and it made him angry. He was 'always protesting *and railing against something*. But voters did not want a leader who was angry – they could do anger perfectly well themselves. As SCA researcher Roddy Glen put it, 'the country doesn't want a man *of* the people. It wants a man *for* the people.' Instead he was Mr Opposition – on the wrong side of the barricades.

Charles Clarke, running Kinnock's office during this period, received this work with a 'chilly silence'. 'It felt like he was thinking, I don't want this researcher dissing my boss,' Roddy reflected. Clarke sternly rejected both the debrief and the proposed action points drawn from it. He later demanded that all SCA polling feedback was edited to remove any mention of voter response to NK himself, unless, of course, it was positive – which it rarely was, at that time. Only then could research be shown to Neil or indeed anyone else. We argued, but knew that the pressures of the job combined with relentlessly negative media brought Neil down. What good could it do, we were asked? Increasingly I stopped writing up voters' comments. Later I even stopped asking the questions. There was simply no point. We had to get beyond 'there's an issue with Neil'.

I have dwelt upon this when reviewing my role in linking politician and voter at the time and since. Of course, the party leader is crucial to electoral success. A leader must do three things: firstly, provide vision and secondly translate that vision into action. He must then convey that vision to a wider audience and inspire them to share it. In my view, Neil did the first two so successfully that the Labour Party must forever be in his debt. I strongly believe the work that he did as leader, paving the way for victory in 1997, has not been recognised enough. However, he did not achieve the last objective. He was not able to convey his vision and inspire people to share it. As one member of his 1980s team observed sadly, 'he made the party electable but he didn't make himself electable'.

In my heart I knew we had not made it in 1992 and when the exit polls started to come in I was disappointed but not surprised. It was time to move on and start building my new business. One of the last things I did was to help organise some post-campaign focus groups, conducted again by the brilliant team of Leslie Butterfield and Roddy Glen. Their debrief made grim listening. They ran through a sober evaluation of voters' reasons for rejecting Labour. They talked about the problems with Neil, symbolised by his ebullience at the eve-of-poll Sheffield rally and the problems with tax – how badly the Conservatives' attacking 'double whammy' ads had hurt us.

What struck me most of all was how little progress we had made in changing voters' views of Labour from that list of tired and negative traits that spilled out of the first focus groups I sat through back in the mid-1980s. Roddy had asked voters to do a 'personification' exercise – if the Labour Party were a person, what kind of person would they be? The answer was depressingly like the answer back in 1985: Labour was old man in a cloth cap, holding a placard in front of a factory with smoking chimney stacks. He played us a tape of men describing the party. It could have been recorded back in 1985, so little had changed. The final conclusion was that the Labour brand was irretrievably tainted: the only way to succeed was to effectively create a new party. 'Change the name?' suggested Roddy, half joking. 'Change everything!' several of us chorused.

A DIFFERENT WAY OF DOING POLITICS

Over the next five years, that is almost what happened. Labour went into the 1997 election with a new name and a new leader – and at last the voting public felt that the party was talking to them. During this time I stepped back from full time political research, just working on ad hoc projects such as the Fabian Society 'Southern Discomfort' series. Instead, my energies went on building my new business, Opinion Leader Research, and dealing with the increasing demands of my three small kids, up until the '97 election.

My job in the '97 campaign was to organise a huge team of volunteers to conduct focus groups in key marginal constituencies around the country. We were out there every night, usually in several locations simultaneously. I ran many of the groups myself, which I had been unable to do in 1992 with a newborn baby and toddler to care for. It was a very different and much more rewarding experience. This time people in Stourbridge, Bolton, Slough and even Hove were really listening.

The backdrop to the campaign was the death throes of Major's leadership. The words 'Tory' and 'sleaze' had become inseparable by Election Day. Over a period of many months it seemed as if every day brought new stories of sex scandals, cash for questions, even criminal convictions. It was politicians being caught abusing their position of trust with the public and the damage was long term. (Over a decade later, our Harlow panel, shown a photograph of Neil and Christine Hamilton, drowned out my questions with howls of sarcastic laughter.) People had been unclear about what politicians actually did with their time, beyond shouting at each other in Prime Minister's Questions, or handing out leaflets at election time. Now they felt that they knew. It wasn't a pretty sight.

Labour resisted the temptation to feature the misdemeanours of sleazy Conservative politicians in its election campaign, instead choosing to set out its stall in a positive way. The ad agency BMP (by now Labour was rehabilitated sufficiently to be able to hire a proper agency) produced ads that summed up Labour's optimistic tone. In fluorescent pinks, greens and oranges each giant poster revealed one of five policies quoted on the innovative pledge card: smaller class sizes, fast track punishment, shorter hospital waiting lists, guaranteed youth employment and a strong economy with low interest rates.

These were tangible promises that we knew would be popular, for each of them had been rigorously tested to be the most appealing offer in its policy area. I had often observed that the Holy Grail for Labour – indeed for any political party – would be that you could stop people in the street, at the supermarket queue, in the pub, taking their kids to football, and ask them what Labour would do and find a ready answer – an answer that they found motivating. We had reached that point. By halfway through the campaign, voters in focus groups could list all five of those pledges unprompted.

These messages were memorable because they hit the spot so accurately. It's easy to forget that in 1997 public services seemed to be on the point of collapse. Focus group discussion was of primary school class sizes of forty or even fifty – and of kids leaving school completely unable to read and write. Voters told me about elderly relatives suffering waiting times for a hip operation that might leave someone in pain for several years, and of hanging around Accident and Emergency Wards with injured or sick children for twelve hours or more. There was a real sense of urgency about the need for change. The pledges were precise and clear. In the end though, the pledge card success was about much more than these specific public services. Its effect was to underpin Tony Blair's Labour Party as a party people could trust. And by now, it was definitely Blair's Labour – or, to be precise, Blair's New Labour.

Tony Blair was initially dismissed by voters and media alike as weak: his first nickname was Bambi. Yet he soon established his credentials for taking the modernisation work started so effectively by Neil Kinnock on to the next stage. It has become a Westminster Village cliché to talk about a 'Clause Four' moment, but the symbolic importance of publicly ditching the part of the Labour Party constitution that committed it to widespread nationalisation was immense. However, from the voters' point of view, an earlier section of the same conference speech may have mattered more, where Blair asserted that Labour was back as the party for the 'majority of British people' – 'the people's party'.

Scepticism about political parties and politicians had been huge in the dying days of Major's last government. What little faith voters had left in politics had been eroded. By offering a short and clear set of promises designed specifically to appeal to Middle England, understanding for their concerns, and addressing them, Blair was saying 'trust me, I'll do what I say. Vote for me and this is what you'll get' and vote for him they did, voting with huge enthusiasm for smaller class sizes and shorter hospital waiting lists. But most of all they were voting for a completely new way of doing politics.

THE PEOPLE'S POLITICIAN

On the first day Parliament assembled after the election, Tony Blair summoned all his new MPs to a briefing session. There were so many that a special hall had to be hired to house them. Blair chose the Great Hall at Church House in Westminster, usually reserved for meetings of the Church of England Synod. He told the MPs, 'We are not the masters now. The people are the masters. We are the servants of the people. We will never forget that.' Focus groups the following week recalled this, and some voters were quite emotional as they talked about it. Blair was the personification of New Labour.

Voters' pen portraits of the party now featured a smiley, youthful, family man, recognisably a member of the human race; he was almost someone that you might know, perhaps a little earnest, but truthful and trusted.

This feeling, strong in the aftermath of the May election, built up over the summer and reached a crescendo with the death of the Princess of Wales in September. Voters I spoke to after the events of that week were sombre. They could talk of nothing else. It was as if Princess Diana's death had jogged a collective memory of grief deep in the British psyche. This death was losing a close friend, it was a death in all our families. Several of the women cried as they talked about it. Some recalled their own family bereavements. There was anger, too, especially directed at what was seen as the callous reaction of the Queen and the wider Royal Family. Just one person seemed able to accurately articulate the nation's mood: new Prime Minster Tony Blair. He summed up how everyone felt about Diana, the 'People's Princess'. He was at that point the People's Politician, perfectly sensing the mood, perfectly shaping his response.

This was to be the peak of Blair's personal popularity, with MORI showing his positive ratings rising to an unprecedented 75 per cent the following week. For the first time in a long time voters felt that they had a government that was on their side, embodied by a leader who understood them and cared about them. Blair did not just empathise with people's problems. He did not just offer a solution. He *was* the solution. It was like the early courtship days of a love affair.

Of course, there were rational reasons for voting Labour too. Thanks to Neil Kinnock the party had ditched the strongest negatives from its past, and now looked modern, positive and representative (representative of Middle England as well as the poor, representative of women as well as men). It also provided tangible proof of intent, especially with the health and education pledges. 'I heard their promises on waiting lists and class sizes and thought – at last! Someone has listened to me!' said one swing voting woman who switched.

But swing voters recognised that Tony Blair's promise extended beyond smaller class sizes and shorter waiting lists. His was a new approach that was fundamentally different from what had gone before as it uniquely spoke to them and to their interests.

> It felt like they were giving government a new lease of life – people running the country would be different – of a different generation – more like us really. It was going to be an exciting time ahead.

> You feel that he understands how the likes of us live and what we care about.

It was fun to do focus groups in those first days and weeks of New Labour. Recruiting people to come along, we now found it impossible to find anyone who would admit to having voted Conservative on 1 May 1997. Everyone was New Labour now. Politics spoke to voters in a way that it had not done before. They were engaged. It was easy to persuade people to turn up. They even liked the idea of government running focus groups to find out what people thought.

> This is democracy – much more so than just voting every four or five years.

> It's the kind of conversations that you have in your own house with your family or partner. Government should hear those conversations.

The mood was positive, full of anticipation. With hindsight, of course, now would have been the moment to manage expectations more carefully. People had voted New Labour for better health and education, but, more than that, they had voted for a different way of doing politics. Seizing that opportunity to open a real conversation with the electorate could have changed politics for good. But it might have risked some of the good will that was washing over the new government. It was not just the voters who had hope in their hearts.

4. It was women wot won it

'Thank you, young lady. Well, that covers the social issues. Let's now move on to the meat of the meeting.' It was 1988 and I had been giving a presentation to the TUC General Council at Congress House on women's attitudes to work and politics. Using demographic data, polling and focus group work, I had set out to show how crucial women would be to the movement in the future, and how their issues and approach differed from the agenda of their male colleagues. The council members at the meeting, all men bar one, sat back in their chairs in the oak panelled board room and guffawed noisily at each others' jokes as I ran through the data. At the end, the TUC President moved the agenda on, dismissing me with a wave of his hand. There was no discussion about what I had presented at all, no action points, no follow up.

Since the 1950s women had increased as a proportion of the workforce, yet still the trade union leadership remained doggedly male. The unions themselves were also struggling with image problems of their own. Given their longstanding relationship with Labour, these problems were not contained and risked spilling over, contaminating the party's image. As Labour began to update its marketing effort, so did many trade unions. In 1990 I ran some focus groups for Britain's then biggest trade union: the Transport and General Workers' Union. The aim was to discover why so few women members were joining up.

The women in my focus groups were all manual public sector workers, mainly cleaners. I gave them pads of paper and crayons and asked them to sketch out what a trade union meant to them. They chose not to draw the many benefits derived from trade unionism: job security, better pay, flexible working or a safer work place. Instead, they all drew pictures of angry shouting men, with banners aloft and fists clenched. Several also drew logos of the Labour Party showing how interconnected the two organisations were. A word association game showed that the word most frequently associated with 'trade union' was 'trouble'. The same problem we had encountered when marketing Labour was evident here too: people could only see the process rather than the benefit to them. In this case the process was seen as extremely hostile.

If Labour's links with the trade union movement were to continue to be so close, clearly it would be difficult for Labour to transform its own reputation unless the reputation of trade unions improved also. This was a particular problem with women voters.

WHY WORRY ABOUT WOMEN?

Labour's electoral triumph in 1997 was an enormous achievement, and wooing the women's vote was perhaps its greatest success of all. Historically, women voters had been so against Labour that, had the suffragettes failed and women never won the right to vote, the mathematics of an all-male electorate would have resulted in a Labour victory in every election since the Second World War. Put another way, Labour's performance amongst women voters was so bad that it condemned Labour to the opposition benches, despite an often reasonable and sometimes good performance amongst men.

In early 1989, Patricia Hewitt, by then head of policy in Neil

Kinnock's office, and I wrote a pamphlet for the Fabian Society entitled *Women's Votes: The Key to Winning*. In the focus groups that Patricia and I ran to gather information for this, women told us what mattered to them. Dominated by their roles as family managers, social policy agenda was to the forefront: healthcare, education, social services, and public transport were issues that they grappled with every day. In short, women viewed politics through the eyes of their family. This was even true for young, pre-family women who anticipated that life stage in all their responses, and it was certainly true of older women who still identified strongly with that role through their children and grandchildren.

Despite protesting that politics was not for them, women were very much more likely than men to be involved in 'quasi political activity': parent–teacher associations, housing and tenants' organisations. They were experts. Yet they tended to discount this experience, not regarding it as 'proper politics'. Politics, they believed, were the abstract matters discussed by their male partners in pubs and trade union meetings. Small wonder that these swing voter women felt that politics was not for them, and that no political party was 'on my side':

There are too many men in this country making plans that affect our lives.

These politicians don't know what it's like for us – they send their kids to posh schools and they've got private health. And they've got wives who sort it all out for them.

A big issue emerging from these focus groups was that Labour, despite having more attractive policies and a strong heritage for 'caring', and despite having more women MPs than any other party at the time, was nevertheless thought to be more male. Again, this was partly derived from its traditional, trade union background. It was also because, although the Conservatives had fewer women, theirs were more high profile, obviously Mrs Thatcher, but also Edwina Currie and, at the time, Shirley Porter. Women voters said of Labour:

It's all blokes, isn't it? You see them on the telly at their conference.

My husband's in the union and he and his mates go to all the meetings. I think they're in very thick with Labour. I'm not bothered myself.

To get under the skin of how women saw politicians we showed them lots of photographs of different men and women, covering a wide range of ages, styles of dress, occupations and settings. They were told that, of the fifty or so pictures, eight were politicians, and were asked to pick them out. They all picked men wearing suits. We then asked them to pick who would make the best politician and this time the results were less predictable. They selected pictures of people who were aspirational versions of themselves: the older women chose smartly dressed older women, while the young chose 'well turned out' younger women, often with families mirroring their own.

The general view amongst women was that women would make better politicians than men. Women were felt to be more practical, more down to earth, more understanding and more compassionate. But, we learned, being caring was not enough. It was important for a woman politician, indeed any politician, to have courage in order to be effective:

You've got to be pretty tough.

They only survive if they are fighters.

Only the strong ones stand up for themselves and get things done.

Barbara Castle was quoted again and again by women of all ages as their ideal. She was practical and caring, but also brave and tough.

It's a pity that Barbara Castle isn't in it any more. She was really good. Very down to earth. Knew what she was talking about.

By contrast Mrs Thatcher, although brave and tough, but now nearing the end of her premiership and at her least popular, was felt to be too out of touch to be practical. . . and she certainly wasn't caring.

She's like one of those top business ladies – she can't remember what it was like before she was so successful.

She's had to be ruthless – more like a man to get as far as she's got.

Another technique that we used in this research was a 'word sort', where we showed each group dozens of descriptive words written up on cards and asked them to sort these into sections: essential qualities for a politician, ideal and undesirable.

Essential qualities were:

- Management
- Intelligent
- Strong
- Energetic

Ideal were:

- Charismatic
- Common sense
- Trustworthy
- Caring
- Inspirational
- Effective
- Understanding
- Independent
- Witty
- Generous
- Fair
- Practical

Qualities that they did not like were:

- Ambitious
- Condescending
- Greedy
- Dogmatic
- Pompous
- Expedient

In discussion, the essential qualities were felt to be likely to be found in either men or women, while the negative attributes were mainly male and the ideal were mainly female!

A DAY OUT IN EASTBOURNE

Patricia and I also used this material for a presentation on 'The Gender Gap' prepared for a special awayday held for the Shadow Cabinet. The venue was a wintry and deserted holiday hotel in Eastbourne, where two places had been reserved for us at the end of a long rectangular table in a gloomy, artificially lit room.

We showed how in the UK, unlike the US or Australia, women tended to be instinctively more supportive of the Conservatives, while men were more strongly Labour. Yet women tended to share Labour's broader values: supporting the idea of an 'enabling state' (a favourite Neil Kinnock term meaning a government prepared to intervene to provide higher quality public services, regulate business and industry, and promote equality between men and women). Tested blind, women in focus groups preferred Labour policies. Arguably, women were Labour's natural constituency. Our research showed that the long-held image of Labour as male, old fashioned, and somewhat aggressive was profoundly offputting.

Patricia and I had struggled to convey this to our male colleagues. Once again it was an all-male audience, with the exception of Jo Richardson, the women's minister. The men were not noisy but some read papers as we spoke. We had expected this and decided that an appeal to self interest was the only thing that would work. We had to persuade male politicians that their own futures depended on persuading women voters. Using an old-fashioned overhead projector and acetate slides we outlined our case. We showed the grim gender gap story of previous elections and how the Conservatives' stranglehold on women voters had led them to victory.

We outlined how the small improvement that Labour had seen in 1987 was due almost entirely to women shifting towards the party. But we also showed that this shift had substantially come from younger women (18–24s), a small and declining group, estimated to shrink by 1.2 million by 1995. This group were also significantly less likely to turn out to vote. Meanwhile the Conservatives enjoyed a lead of 20 per cent amongst 35–54-year-olds and 15 per cent amongst women of 55-plus – the latter group representing one fifth of the whole population. They were also the most likely demographic to turn out. Our conclusions were clear: the Conservatives had won by winning women's votes.

We went on to review how women's lives had changed and were set to change more. By the mid-1990s, women would form half of the workforce, and almost half of working women would have young children at home. A third of women with children under five would be working by the next election. These were shocking figures for a party traditionally dominated by male workers. We also highlighted the changing lives of those all important older women, many of whom would still be working into their sixties or active in other ways: caring for a grandchild or an elderly parent, or volunteering.

We made the point over again that women did not see politics as an interesting pursuit or even a spectator sport, but were family focused, viewing political success or failure through the prism of their own lives. Women were very much less likely to join a political party, talk about politics, even watch politics on the television. We reiterated that women felt that politics was *for* men, and that no political party was really on their side.

We also looked at the success of centre-left parties abroad: at that time, in West Germany the SPD had set a target that women should fill 40 per cent of all elected and appointed places by 1996. The Norwegian Labour Party and the Danish SDP also both had quotas set of 40 per cent. Norway's female PM at the time presided over a cabinet that was almost half women. The Spanish and Portuguese socialist parties had both recently adopted quotas of 25 per cent and the French and Italians had both set quotas at 20 per cent.

This and the voter research spurred us on. We suggested that, if Labour truly wanted to appeal to women, then it must change dramatically and become more representative. Emboldened, we made two radical proposals: one was that the party should also set a target of 40 per cent (helpfully, Bryan Gould, Labour's campaign co-ordinator, had recently proposed this himself to the NEC). All-women shortlists were to be voted in at the 1993 Labour conference (they were later used in 50 per cent of target seats in 1997).

We also pointed out that there was only one woman, Jo Richardson, in the Shadow Cabinet, which was elected by the 90 per cent male Parliamentary Labour Party. We recommended that to raise the profile of Labour's women, Labour should reserve three Shadow Cabinet places for women; cunningly we had agreed before with NK that this should be three *additional* places, thus not threatening the men's existing places. This was introduced later that year.

In the presentation, we stopped short of adding our third proposal from the Fabian pamphlet: that gender balance was important in the party leadership, and that Labour should consider 'changing the constitution to create two Deputy Leader posts, one of which would be held by a woman'. This would have to wait until Harriet Harman, one of the first women to be elected to the Shadow Cabinet in the reserved places scheme, was elected deputy to Gordon Brown in 2007.

WHAT DID MEN THINK?

Patricia Hewitt, reflecting on that time, says: 'I did think we could win, both the argument and the positive action – partly because we'd got Neil's support, partly because it was such a compelling case and partly because we weren't asking the men to give anything up!' My own recollection is that the Shadow Cabinet reaction to addressing the gender gap was certainly more positive than the Trade Union Congress Council's reaction the year before. In some ways, it became regarded as part and parcel of the modernising programme that Labour knew it must embark upon, and, given that men were not being asked to give anything up, what was there not to like?

Still, in the wider Parliamentary Labour Party some did not like it, and many men jumped through hoops to find ways of not electing a woman Shadow Cabinet member. For some this meant simply refusing to cast those votes; for others it meant using their votes on 'unelectable' female candidates. For example, the late Mildred Gordon, a hard left firebrand from east London, found herself the surprised recipient of votes from several right-wing backbenchers. She was not elected, but that she received their support at all shows the depth of anti-women reaction: some men were prepared to vote for a woman whose politics they despised in an attempt to keep the Shadow Cabinet as male as possible.

It took longer to achieve the all-women shortlists. This was brought about by a coalition of women drawn from organisations like Labour Women's Network and Emily's List, cutting across political divides. The trade unions were also crucial in delivering this, finally seeing the need to appeal to women as their traditional male industrial recruiting grounds dried up.

THE FOUR PS

Seven years later, in 1996, Patricia and I again made a presentation to another Shadow Cabinet awayday, now under Tony Blair's leadership. This time we called it 'Winning Words' and it was intended to remind the top team of campaigners and politicians of the fight they faced to get their message over to women. The fundamental problem was still there. Although Labour had upped its game, women voters remained resolutely uninterested in politics.

Women's disenchantment had grown following the televising of Parliament, which had only confirmed their views that politicians behaved like a rabble of rowdy schoolboys. We emphasised again that women were less interested in abstract political debate, and only motivated by policies that affected their lives. We advised dropping the use of statistics, which lacked credibility; a point could be made more effectively by telling one person's story rather than quoting stats.

We came up with a mnemonic device – a trigger to remind campaigners what to do – 'the four Ps':

1. *Pertinent* – make what you say and do relevant to women's lives or they simply won't notice.
2. *Plain* – be as simple and clear as possible, so no jargon, say what you mean, don't obfuscate.
3. *Personal* – bring the story you are telling to life with examples of real people – you, your own family, people you have met – and talk directly to the voter as though the intermediary of the media wasn't there. Human stories, no statistics.
4. *Positive* – women are much more turned off adversarial politics than men are. Let the shortcomings of others speak for themselves, while we focus on our positive story. It's possible to win this election rather than goad them into losing it.

The reaction to our presentation this time was much warmer, and we came away feeling that they really had 'got it', especially after we emphasised, for the benefit of some of the more doggedly macho politicians round the table, 'that on TV, you are not addressing a public meeting, you're talking to a woman, nowadays often in her own bedroom!'

Blair's approach to communications had been to follow some of this advice instinctively. Now he adopted a more systematic approach. . . and, possibly taking their cue from him, rather than accepting our proposals, some male colleagues began to follow suit. Whatever the motive, the change of strategy started to work. Women were coming over to Labour. At that point, though we hardly dared believe it, the polls were consistently giving Labour a lead of 20 per cent or more, often showing its support at above 50 per cent.

DOING POLITICS DIFFERENTLY

One of the most extraordinary aspects of the 1997 landslide was the extent to which women were converted to the Labour cause. Some 44 per cent of women voted Labour, up 10 per cent from 1992. Our voter analysis back in 1989 had shown that the toughest group of female voters for Labour was also the most important, both in terms of likelihood to vote and sheer numbers: older women, over-55s. Post-poll analysis showed that, while voters from all demographic groups had shifted, the single biggest shift was amongst women aged over fifty-five.

This, in the heady days of the new government, was borne out in the focus groups. Men, of course, were positive about New Labour – really positive – but women were ecstatic. For the first time they felt that they had a government that was on their side, embodied by a leader who understood them and cared about them.

Being representative mattered too, and we knew that women voters had appreciated the greater numbers of women MPs, believing that this might make a difference to the government's approach.

> Like I said, women and men are just made differently and women are more likely to think about other people than men.

> They'll get on with it, get things done – they're more down to earth.

At the time, the famous 'Blair's babes' photo was derided by the Westminster Village. The women MPs in the picture had to endure being sneered at by fellow MPs. Claire Curtis Thomas commented, 'I was always being told by Tory men that it was nice to have a better class of totty around.' Even their clothes were part of the joke, with *The Times* asking, 'Who will save the utterly dowdy class of '97 from years of brightly coloured polyester?' But for women floating voters at the time, the cynicism passed them by. Instead it was a wholly positive icon – a vivid image that seemed characteristic of the way that Labour was changing politics.

> I remember that photo – it was everywhere at the time – Tony Blair with all the Labour women. I was really impressed.

> It was one of the things that made me feel optimistic. That this was a real fresh beginning.

> I wondered if politicians would start to do things that I liked more. . . someone like me could be a politician.

WOMEN: CANARY VOTERS

Just as women had been the first to embrace the positive change in Labour, so they were the first to be disappointed. Hope set so high is vulnerable to being dashed. The deeply unpopular Dome would flag up early signs of a government that was not listening. Slow delivery in public services was another problem that women, as the main users of those services, were quick to spot. By summer 2000 many women were starting to feel cheated and were looking out for problems.

Being representative was another area where the government suddenly looked weak after an initially strong performance. Where were all the women? One first time Labour swing voter, Julie, was bemused.

> There don't seem to be as many women MPs as there were – or they're not putting them forward… at least that's the impression I get.

And one very prominent and hugely popular woman was especially missed:

> Why has Mo Mowlam been sacked? She was doing so well – all the credit for Ireland should belong to her. It seems very unfair and you wonder what's gone on behind the scenes

Once again the support of women voters looked fragile. By 2000, women's satisfaction with the government trailed men's by 13 per cent, and their irritation in focus groups was becoming increasingly hard to ignore. Harriet Harman and I urgently revisited the work on women's votes that I had published with Patricia Hewitt in

1998. I ran some focus groups amongst women and men swing voters and Harriet conducted interviews with women MPs. Using this material, together we drafted a new Fabian pamphlet, giving it a title with a subtle twist: rather than *Women : The Key to Winning*, as Labour was in government it was all about how it used that power: *Winning for Women*.

Harriet had free time available because she had recently lost her Cabinet job after just eighteen months –another prominent woman 'disappeared'. She shook her head with a wry smile as she read the comments made by one disillusioned woman swing voter:

> Are women judged on the same basis as men? Men seem to get away with murder but if a woman doesn't absolutely toe the line all the time, she's out!

In the pamphlet we warned that, while New Labour's achievements with women voters were immense, there was a real risk that they were already disaffected at what they felt to be the slow pace of change. We reiterated how women engaged with politics differently from men. It was a 'show me' rather than a 'tell me' imperative that could not be addressed by what was increasingly becoming known as 'spin'. We set out a formula for recovering the situation, and turned this into a presentation for the Labour Party and No. 10.

I had a powerful feeling of déjà vu as we again set out the familiar ground about female friendly politics and how Labour must not lose its focus on clear, jargon-free, voter-friendly communications, seeking out voters where they were, not expecting them to find us. . .

The Fabian pamphlet was published in June 2000, and I received a call from Sally Morgan, Blair's political 'fixer' at No. 10, the day it came out, scolding me for being 'unhelpful'. I protested that that had not in any way been my intention, or Harriet's, and that I genuinely felt concerned that the women's vote was drifting. Sally had once been women's officer at the Labour Party and knew only too well what the issues were. Perhaps, like me, she was just getting bored of repeating the same message. Certainly, Sally had battled away internally, doing what she could to make the message stick. Combined with a lamentable performance from the Conservatives, the women's vote held up in 2001.

LET-DOWN LADIES

The next crisis for the women's vote came in the run-up to 2005, and this time it was much, much more serious. Patricia Hewitt was now Minister for Women (as well as Secretary of State for Trade and Industry). She had worked hard to put what we had learned into practice, introducing new maternity and paternity rights and other family-friendly legislation. However, Tony Blair's focus was now elsewhere. We had had the Iraq War and the damaging exposure of the government's spin operation. Even where things were going well, voters were very mistrustful and down on the government. This was becoming serious.

What we now saw was not a gender gap in voting terms but a gap in other ways: an attitude gap, where women were consistently less satisfied with the government; an activism gap, where women had become less engaged in politics; and a very worrying turnout gap – latest estimates for the forthcoming 2005 election were that turnout could drop as low as 50 per cent. Women were also unhappy with the PM's performance. As journalist Rachel Sylvester, writing for the *Telegraph* at the time, put it: Worcester Woman had become

Let-Down Lady. Women had been so in love with New Labour and its personification in Tony Blair that their disappointment was acute. This felt personal, like being let down by a close personal friend or even a lover.

Harriet Harman, now back in government as Solicitor General, and I drafted a presentation for the party's campaign managers on winning back the 'Let-Down Ladies'. We proposed that the government should take a major shift back to domestic affairs, especially public services. We stressed that economic success was the one thing that women as well as men gave the government credit for and this should be the centrepiece of the campaign. We also proposed policy ideas showing more empathy with women's lives and the challenges they face day to day.

It took us some time to get this presentation in to Alan Milburn, installed by Tony Blair as campaign co-ordinator: it was early 2005 before we finally presented the material to him. We arrived to find he was forty-five minutes late for an hour-long session. He swept in, surrounded by advisors, tossing his hair back, jacket swinging around his shoulders. There was no apology. We had fifteen minutes to present our recommendations and agree action points. We raced through and paused for his response. He said, 'Well, we're doing all this. What's the problem?'

Harriet, by now bristling with indignation, having restrained herself for the past hour or more, snapped, 'Well, if that's so, why were five men and no women on the platform at this morning's press conference?'

He gave her a withering look. 'That's politics, Harriet, that's politics,' he said.

Our presentation did not fall entirely on deaf ears, however: Gordon Brown picked it up and used the pro-economic arguments to make the case for playing a more prominent role in the campaign himself. As Labour's poll lead dwindled from a 6 per cent lead in January to neck and neck by March he replaced Milburn as number two in the campaign, the 'double act' of TB and GB moving centre stage as the economic story gained importance. In the 2005 election, 38 per cent of women voted Labour compared with 34 per cent of men. Labour won by 3 per cent.

WHERE ARE THE WOMEN IN 2010?

Apart from that brief shining moment in 1997, women swing voters have remained generally uninterested in and sceptical about party politics and politicians.

After the 2005 general election, two academics at Birkbeck College published a fascinating study into the different ways that men and women talk about politics. They ran a detailed analysis of the vocabulary used by each gender when guided through the same political conversation. Confirming the more anecdotal evidence of the focus groups, they reported that women were a staggering ten times more likely to refer to people when making their points. Their references were always personal contacts, with any the policy seen through the prism of their kids' lives, their parents, their friends.

In 2010 Harriet Harman asked me to join a small group of advisors that she and Sally Morgan were convening to maximise the potential of the women's vote. This time, polls running up to the election showed a much less clear picture. Just as they were inconsistent about overall electoral outcomes, so they were inconsistent about the women's vote. One pollster, ComRes, in January 2010 gave Labour, generally trailing the Conservatives across the board, a rare if small lead amongst women, while many showed women lagging behind. All could agree that women were more undecided how they were going to vote and that two main groups were 'up for grabs': young mothers (the so-called Mumsnet demographic) and older 'baby boomers'.

We faced the same old familiar problems: women were more gloomy about 'the condition of Britain' and less likely to concede any improvement in public services like health and education. The most noticeable thing that had happened in politics was the expenses scandal of 2009. If women had felt it likely that politicians were 'on the make' before, this had only confirmed the worst. Sally and I developed a plan we called 'independent voices', whereby local, non-political spokespeople would be mobilised in key marginals to talk up what the government had achieved and to express concerns about the Conservatives' likely programme of cuts.

Yet on the eve of the campaign, a row broke out in the Labour camp, with senior women disgruntled that the election line up – headed by Peter Mandelson – was too male to appeal. There were also complaints that the party was ignoring advice that briefing the media about explicitly targeting groups of women would not work as it would be seen as too political, counter to our group's proposed 'softly softly' style (the *Observer* had run a big feature on so-called *Take a Break* Women).

As the ill-fated campaign progressed, many commentators – firstly mostly female, then many male writers too, as the fact became increasingly obvious – noted how few women were featured in any of the party's campaigning. This was not something that our swing voter panel seemed to notice as the debates had led to a more presidential approach that focused almost entirely on the party leaders. However, many of the lessons about how to make language more female friendly had been lost, and this was noticed by swing voters. Cameron and Clegg both followed the 'four Ps' advice (in Cameron's case a little too slavishly as he overused voter anecdotes). Meanwhile, GB spoke the language of a technocrat, failing to make any emotional connection, until the last few days of the campaign, where he found his voice and his passion – by then too late.

In 2010 Labour haemorrhaged support from women voters across all age groups, suffering a 7 per cent decline since 2005. This meant a 10 per cent drop amongst 18–24 women (where Lib Dems achieved the biggest share of vote), 6 per cent amongst 25–34, 8 per cent amongst 35–54 and 4 per cent amongst the critical 55+ women, where the Conservatives enjoyed a massive 14 per cent rise to 44 per cent. In 2005 it was hanging on to the women's vote that enabled Labour to win – had only women voted, Labour's majority would have been in the 100s. In 2010 the gender gap was still there, but much smaller, meaning that Labour's advantage amongst women voters was no longer able to compensate for a poor performance amongst men.

Looking at the very male-biased new Lib–Con Cabinet, and the 80 per cent male line-up in Labour's forthcoming leadership election, it is hard to predict where the women's vote will settle in the future – but its significance cannot be doubted.

5. 'He's in love with Prudence' – winning trust on the economy

Post-'97 it may have got a little easier to persuade people to take an interest in politics, but it remained, I discovered, very hard indeed to get them thinking about the economy.

To start with, many voters knew very little about how the economy worked. There was a clear gender gap. Men talked the talk. This often led to a certain amount of muscle flexing in male focus groups: competitive bandying around of jargon, a defence mechanism masking a lack of confidence about the basics. Women didn't even pretend to 'get it' and it was usually hard work to keep them engaged in the discussion. (This was an area where subterfuge was necessary in focus group recruitment – but merely achieving bums on seats was no guarantee of a successful session. On one occasion a female participant actually volunteered to leave when the economic theme became apparent, so worried was she that her contribution would be insignificant.) Much of the vocabulary was familiar: interest rates, public spending, recession, inflation; but asking a focus group for a definition could induce a collective panic attack, and rarely generated an accurate answer. For example, it was a widely held belief that interest rates were a means of revenue collection for government, like taxation.

At the same time, the subject provoked considerable anxiety. Voters could readily identify the bad times: leaving the ERM, the Winter of Discontent and the recession of the early 1990s. Sometimes these events became conflated in people's minds. In a focus group in 1998, Debbie in Hemel Hempstead recalled:

> I remember the effect of the word 'recession' in any headline. . . made me panic – made me think of the Winter of Discontent.

In 1997 focus groups following the election, during the run-up to GB's first 'mini Budget', the 'word sort' exercises found the most common associations with 'the economy' were:

- Confusing
- Complicated
- Hit and Miss
- Changing
- Complex
- Frightening

Most people's understanding of how the macro economy affected their family's financial wellbeing was slight, which they found scary. Maureen in Heald Green:

> You don't know how it affects you. It just seems to give you a feeling of gloom and doom.

FEELING THE FEAR

This was a particular problem for Labour as management of the economy had long been seen as a weakness: probably the single most important reason for electoral failure from 1983–1992.

There were two reasons for this troublesome legacy. Firstly, entrenched views of incompetence, the feeling that Labour lacked managerial nous. In a policy area where voters felt particularly vulnerable they were looking for reassurance, and that Labour had historically failed to provide.

The second was even more fundamental and lay at the heart of Labour's lack of voter appeal. The electorate, especially swing voters in the Midlands and the south, struggled to believe that Labour politicians had their best interests in mind. They saw Labour first and foremost on the side of the poor, the disadvantaged and the needy. This was all well and good, except that they also presumed that they, ordinary 'Middle England' voters, would pay the price. Again and again, polling in the run-up to 1992 showed three quarters of voters expected that their taxes would go up under a Labour government. Clearly the Conservatives' polling told the same story, resulting in Saatchi's hugely successful tax bombshell advertising campaign, with frightening headlines like 'Labour's Double Whammy', higher taxes and higher prices, and worse: 'The price of Labour: £1,250 a year for every family'.

These views had undermined Labour's entire 1992 electoral strategy. The polls (wrongly) claimed that swing voters were happy for their taxes to rise to fund improvements to public services, but the focus groups, where we could see voters' uncomfortable body language, told a different story. There was real fear in people's eyes. Many had ventured into the property market for the first time and were now feeling out of their depth. More than ever they needed a political party that was on their side through tough times. More than ever they needed a political party that was economically competent. It wasn't Labour.

After the election I conducted a series of focus groups for the Fabian Society. Entitled *Southern Discomfort*, the resulting pamphlet described voters in constituencies like Gravesham, Harlow, Luton, Stevenage, and Slough – seats that Labour had to win in order to achieve an overall majority. Their mood was anxious and insecure and there was no sense that Labour would be there for them.

> They'd help the poor, not the likes of us.

Labour was also thought to be incapable of managing the economy:

> The whole country would go into liquidation.

In short, a vote for Labour was a risk too far. Julie, a typist in Stevenage, was typical:

> I just felt I couldn't do it – things have been bad enough for us as it is.

Giles Radice MP, the pamphlet's author, concluded:

> Despite their fears and insecurities, they voted Conservative because they did not trust the Labour Party. They do not believe that the Party is capable of running the economy. Even more important, they do not consider that it understands, respects, or rewards those

who want to get on. Far from encouraging talent and opportunity, Labour is seen as the party most likely to 'clobber' people.

LEARNING TO LISTEN

The next focus groups I ran on the economy were in 1996. Ed Balls, then Gordon Brown's chief of staff, invited me for a cup of tea at the House of Commons.

Throughout this period, GB had been working tirelessly to address the voter concerns about Labour's economic competence, risking unpopularity within the party as he enforced a new economic discipline, contrasting sharply with previous years, including banning all unaffordable spending commitments and taking tough decisions about work and welfare, driven by GB's own powerful work ethic. These were succeeding in slowly but surely turning around public opinion.

But now, Ed explained, there was a problem. My old business partner, Philip Gould, had been running focus groups for Tony Blair on economic policy and GB was concerned about what was coming out. I did not know it at the time, but the conversation we had was to foretell many we would have in the future. Team GB were locked in a passionate disagreement with Team TB on a crucial policy area. GB and Ed had been keen to explore the introduction a new higher rate of tax at a relatively high salary level, more than £100,000. This, they believed, would be fair and reasonable and not hit the pockets of middle ground voters. It would free up cash for public services or the less well off.

However, Philip was claiming that this would undermine voters' trust in Labour's economic policy. The Shadow Treasury team did not believe this debrief, given how far that sum was from most Middle Englanders' own salaries. They were suspicious that the analysis owed more to Philip's own convictions – or those of his boss – than to the voters' views. Ed asked me to run a series of focus groups independently of Philip's operation to challenge his findings.

I agreed to do this and was genuinely uncertain about what my own work would reveal. I knew how strongly held were perceptions of Labour's tendency to tax to the hilt. I knew that the new leadership had made a lot of headway, but had not yet been able to provide all the reassurance tentative voters required. But then again, £100,000 was a lot of money by anyone's standards. Was Philip being ultra-cautious?

I started the groups with a large display of figures from £20,000 up to £200,000. I asked voters to indicate, using marked up sticky labels, where, if these were annual salaries, subjective thresholds might be reached. These included 'make ends meet', 'comfortable', 'struggling', 'wealthy', 'very well off', 'super rich' and so on. Interestingly, despite having encouraged people to work up the scale by making £100,000 the middle mark, on the whole they did not choose to do this. Most of the action took place lower down the scale, with £50,000 being designated as 'very well off', £35,000 as 'comfortable' and £70,000 plus as 'super rich'.

So £100,000 was indeed a lot of money... would it therefore be safe for Labour to levy higher tax at this level? Here the findings were surprising and somewhat disappointing for GB and the team. I asked the groups to conduct a word sort ascribing certain adjectives to Labour if it introduced particular policies into its next manifesto. Putting taxes up, even at this high level, provoked the strongest response of all. People used the most negative words provided: 'not for me', 'for the poor', 'greedy', 'old fashioned' and avoided words

Team GB might have preferred them to choose, such as 'fair' or 'for ordinary working people'. They also used the blank cards we gave them to scribble some telling ideas of their own: 'punish us all', 'loony left' and 'politics of envy'.

It seemed to me that Philip's caution had been well judged. These groups emphasised the mountain that Labour still had to climb to win back trust. In my debrief note I concluded:

> While none of these voters remotely aspire to a salary at this level, they trust Labour so little that they are worried it could be the thin end of the wedge. They struggle to find rational explanations (brain drain being the most popular) for what is essentially a very emotional response. Putting up income tax will indicate Labour 'reverting to form' at a time when we need to be signalling change.

Any further moves to increase income tax were abandoned, at least for the time being.

BACK IN BUSINESS

As we have seen, by 1997 Blair and Brown's hard work had successfully repositioned Labour as a party that was competent and business-like. Labour now led on economic management for the first time in many years. The worst of the fear factor had been neutralised by Labour's tax pledge, finally agreed after Team GB were persuaded that Team TB were right, and the voter really did need the reassurance. In January, GB announced that Labour would raise neither the basic nor the top rate of tax. A counter attack followed: Labour's poster claiming '22 tax rises under the Conservatives'. By

March Labour's private polling showed the big breakthrough: a lead on tax for Labour for the first time.

However, persuading voters that Labour really was on their side would prove trickier. Success demanded a juggling act: offering optimism in the shape of attractive enough voter benefits while at the same time reassuring those same swing voters that they alone were not footing the bill. This was the point of the Pledge Card: a laminated card that would slip into a wallet with its concrete, costed promises on class sizes, youth employment, fast track punishment and hospital waiting lists. along with an underpinning economic guarantee: 'Labour will set tough rules for government spending and borrowing; ensure low inflation; strengthen the economy so that interest rates are as low as possible'. In focus groups in key marginal seats throughout the campaign, voters could remember each of the five pledges by the end of the first week.

By now the Conservatives' reputation for strong stewardship of the economy lay in tatters. The vivid memory of negative equity as house prices plummeted and interest rates soared in 1994 had a potency that would continue through the '97 campaign and well into the life of the Labour government. Focus groups as late as 2008 still dwelt on it. Adults who were children then remembered the fear that descended on their households and the sense of betrayal. Emma from Slough was close to tears as she told the room:

> My mum felt that they'd been encouraged to borrow and buy their house. Then the mortgage went through the roof and they couldn't afford to pay it. Then house prices went through the floor and it was worth so much less than they'd paid that they couldn't afford to sell it either. . . I was a kid and I'd listen to it all lying in my bedroom feeling scared.

A NEW DAWN

Bill Clinton's advisor James Carville famously had a poster on the office wall of his 1992 campaign HQ stating :'It's the economy, stupid.' Sitting in dozens of focus groups during March and April 1997 had left me convinced that regaining Labour's economic reputation was a critical factor in Labour's win.

Labour's victory party at the appropriately named People's Palace restaurant in London's Festival Hall will always be one of the best nights I can remember. Those of us who recalled previous, less happy election nights were tense to begin with. Gradually though, as the results came in and people gathered around giant screens watching and celebrating, we all began to relax. One of the biggest roars from the crowd came when Tory minister Michael Portillo unexpectedly lost his seat to youthful Labour candidate Stephen Twigg. The biggest cheer of all, though, was reserved for Tony Blair when he arrived just as dawn came up. We all moved outside to hear him speak from a raised platform in front of us.

Moving back in half an hour later, I was suddenly exhausted and thinking of heading home. Across the vast room I saw Ed Miliband, GB's researcher, soon to be special advisor at the Treasury, making his way over. We hugged and swapped notes on the evening. He then surprised me by asking if I was busy the next day.'GB wants a meeting as soon as possible – he wants to set up some focus groups straight away.' A few days later I was conducting my first focus group of the New Labour government in a suburban sitting room in Slough, and, unexpectedly, the conversation buzzed with news of the economy.

Brown had acted swiftly to seize the initiative. The remarkable act of granting independence to the Bank of England less than a week after the election screamed that change was afoot and grabbed the headlines.

The symbolic gesture of placing economic levers in the hands of people who could not use them for political ends hit home and contributed to the honeymoon glow over the new government's early weeks.

A REASSURING MESSAGE

Yet despite the encouraging start, a lingering concern preyed on voters' minds: when the honeymoon glow faded, would it be the 'same old Labour'? It seemed that simply avoiding negative stories was not enough. In early 1998, Team Brown embarked on a programme to strengthen the economic message. This was also about shoring up GB's position in government.

Working with my colleague Mark Bunting, an Oxbridge economics graduate I had recruited recently from MORI, I assembled swing voters in Hemel Hempstead, Heald Green and Stourbridge. The work confirmed that people continued to feel extremely insecure about the economy and uncertain about how it affected their own vulnerable family finances. Paul, a car worker in Stourbridge, asserted: 'You need a government that says: this is what we're doing, this is what we're aiming for, and this is how we're going to get there.' Toni from Hemel Hempstead said: 'You need to trust that they are doing the worrying for you.'

Providing this reassurance was a basic hygiene factor. But building beyond it meant responding to voters' instinctive need to believe in Britain's future. This, after all, was what they had voted for in May 1997. Pam, a housewife from Heald Green, was patriotic: 'I think that we are doing better than the rest of Europe – we should be more proud of being British.'

At a follow up session with swing voters in Totteridge, Morden and Ilford, we tested a variety of expressions of the same reassuring messages – all with stability at their core. The basic formula that emerged was set out in the debrief note:

- We need to explain why we need a stable economy and what the implications of boom–bust instability are.
- We need to set out clearly what the government has done to achieve stability, then how to measure success.
- We need to translate the macro economics into personal implications.
- Most of all we need to be consistent.

Mark Bunting reflected on this period:

> People's overriding emotion with respect to the economy was fear. What they wanted was stability. Phrases like 'no return to boom and bust' spoke directly and powerfully to their pervasive sense that the economy had been out of control. They didn't want promises of growth – they associated those with spiralling house prices and 15 per cent interest rates. The message worked because it matched voters' aspirations.

STICKING TO THE MESSAGE

Having arrived at a message that resonated with voters, the challenge was now to stick to it. The old adage in communications is 'only when you're getting bored with saying it do they start to hear it'. This was even more true in politics. After using the new narrative in a number of speeches and interviews over several months GB began protesting that 'I've already said that' and was clearly itching to move on to a new story.

The Westminster Village conspires to create a barrier between voter and politician in so many ways. While the public, with its lower level of interest in politics, needs multiple exposures to the same line before it will be remembered (ask anyone who works in advertising), the Westminster Village tires quickly and places pressure on politics to offer frequent fresh material. Since most politicians hang out with journalists and other Westminster Villagers rather than ordinary voters, the urge is strong to move on before the message has really reached its target.

Persuading GB and the team to observe occasional focus groups from behind a one-way mirror, as John Smith and his office had done five years before, proved the best way of demonstrating the public's continuing need for the reassurance of a consistent line. It was frustrating to realise that those carefully crafted words had made so little impact on their intended audience, but at least the team understood the importance of saying it, saying it and saying it again. The message began to stick.

A REASSURING MESSENGER

GB's stock was rising in the Westminster Village. As Labour's ratings held steady and its reputation for economic management thrived, he attracted rave media reviews. His first mini Budget was heralded as 'A Budget for the people' (*Independent*) and 'A common sense Budget that deserves support' (*Times*) while his first full Budget the following March garnered even more adulatory notices. Most papers picked up on the new 'Prudence' theme: 'A prudent hand to those in need,' the *Financial Times* asserted.

Yet GB was still not well known to swing voters. Many, especially women, couldn't name anyone but Tony Blair when asked to list key members of the government. Research also showed that when people did know GB they tended to be very favourable towards him, with 64 per cent agreeing that 'he is prepared to take tough decisions' and 52 per cent agreeing that 'he is prudent with public money'. (The 'p' word really caught people's imagination.)

I tested video clips of him in contrasting settings: making the Budget speech, being interviewed on *Newsnight* and on Radio 4's *Today* programme. He possessed a striking ability to cut through the usual voter cynicism and suspicion of politicians' motives.

Roy in Hemel Hempstead offered rare praise: 'Quite genuine for a politician. And Kerry, also in Hemel, agreed: 'He seems honest. You have the gut feeling that you can trust him.'

It seemed that the very traits perceived by Westminster Villagers as shortcomings served to reinforce his reassuring persona. Paul in Stourbridge compared him with his opposite number: 'He's not as relaxed as Ken Clarke, but maybe he's more sincere.' Maria in Heald Green liked his Scottishness. In the job he was doing, this was a real plus point: 'He's cautious, Gordon Brown. He's a real Scotsman looking after the finances.'

THE SQUEEZED MIDDLE

So we had developed a reassuring message about the wider management of the economy and we had a reassuring messenger. But there was still a group of voters who remained to be convinced... We needed to continually reassure middle ground swing voters that this government – given Labour's heritage – really had them in mind.

This critical electoral group were to be known by Team GB as the 'squeezed middle'. They thought of themselves as the group that no government ever really looked out for: too well off to be on the receiving end of Labour hand outs, while too poor to be able to survive a more laissez-faire Conservative approach. We needed to find a symbolic policy that would tell this group that the government understood them, and that they would benefit from its economic policies.

The focus groups explored two areas. The first was Working Family Tax Credit – a way of rewarding 'hard working families' by allowing a tax credit to those earning below a certain level. The key point was where that level would be set. Team GB were eager to explore setting it at a figure that was above the average wage and would include middle ground voters – a bold move that sent a powerful message to Middle England. In focus groups people guessed the cut off would be much, much lower, at a point that would exclude them. As squeezed middle voters they would expect to be left out of any government largesse.

Noreen from Sheffield was surprised:

> This is the first time that the likes of us have ever got anything from government. Normally you work away and pay your taxes and it's all a struggle. Meanwhile hand outs go to the lazy ones who never do a hard day's work. I can't believe that I'm actually getting something from government when we're usually left out!

The second idea appealed to her even more. For years, childcare had been seen as something that families were expected to sort out themselves. With the explosion of working parents over the past decade, the pressure of paying for childcare had become a major burden. Yet most 'squeezed middle' families depended on both incomes to meet their major outgoings such as mortgage payments. Many women found they were working hard to pay *for* the child care and little else besides. Allowing tax credits to help fund childcare was a major symbol that said to working women that the government understood the pressure they were under.

Ten years on, as Labour struggled through the difficult run-up to the 2005 general election, these two policies would prove to be a life saver. People, especially women voters, were angry with Labour. When asked what positive benefits they had gained from the past two terms, the anger would subside as women just like Noreen answered without hesitation, 'Help with childcare and Working Family Tax Credit.'

6. 'We voted for change to get ourselves out of this hole, but where is it?' – how disillusionment crept in

It was ironic that the first rumblings of discontentment with the new government should be triggered by something intended to symbolise its optimism: the Millennium Dome. Just a few months after the election – shockingly soon after all that euphoria – people in focus groups in Nottingham, Chorley and Watford all raised the Dome quite unprompted. They were extremely negative. While their mood as they anticipated the millennium had been cheery, with voters confident that the occasion would be marked appropriately, the Dome itself now cast a long shadow. Reports that the project was running out of money fuelled opposition which grew increasingly vocal. People were bewildered that any government – especially one whose central claim was listening to the electorate – would be willing to go ahead with something so unpopular.

'It's a total waste of money,' protested Paul, a mechanic from Chorley. 'No one wants it so why are they doing it?' asked Sue from Watford, and Andrea agreed: 'You'd think they'd they listen to people more – consult more – they said they'd listen but now they're in power they know best. Of course they do.'

One problem was the sheer scale of the money involved. We had often seen in focus groups that people find it hard to get their heads around the huge budgets – the 'Toytown money' – that governments manage on their behalf. Now news reports day after day were telling them that the Dome was costing £700 million. Clearly this was a large sum of money. However, in voters' minds it assumed a significance way beyond its actual value. They imagined that the money could, for example, completely transform the NHS, building new hospitals, hiring and training new doctors and nurses. They also wondered if it could fix the problems with education, replacing failing schools, hiring new teachers. Maybe it could even do both. In one focus group that I ran in September 1998 voters were furious. Their angry protests tumbled out, and they refused to discuss anything else.

It's a disgrace, spending all that money on a trivial thing that will last for a night.

They know we don't want it, so why are they doing it?

Why not spend the money on building schools and hospitals instead?

They say they want to invest in the NHS – well, why not do so? Spend the Dome money!

In recent years it had suited Labour very well that voters' lack of interest in politics was particularly marked around the area of public finances. Many voters truly believed that the relatively modest sum being spent on the Dome could have had a significant impact on schools and hospitals. Why wouldn't they? Labour had encouraged them to believe that relatively small sums saved, for example from cutting management jobs (a waste argument to be recycled by the Conservatives in 2010), could indeed go a long way.

My report from two focus groups held in June 2000 read:

> The Dome continues to be a weeping sore. Its potential to damage the government is immense. It is a visible sign of wasted resource and undermines key messages about spending priorities. The recent injection of £29 million has generated voter fury about profligacy. It tells them that the government is out of touch with public opinion. Further injection of funds is likely to make this an increasing problem as we approach the general election.

As the siren voices grew louder I knew that No. 10's focus groups must be telling them the same. Asked or unasked this was now a top issue in every focus group, and people were very, very angry. Yet the government's response seemed to be to dig its heels in and carry on. Peter Mandelson, then minister in charge, was apparently carrying the whole project with the force of his personality and his determination to create a 'tonic for the nation' as his grandfather, Herbert Morrison, had done with the hugely successful Festival of Britain exhibition. GB's team despaired that in Cabinet discussions, while the majority opposed continued spending, Peter, unexpectedly joining forces with John Prescott, carried the day. Not for the first time, or the last, Chancellor and Prime Minister traded rival focus groups findings. In the end the Dome was bailed out, more than once, as an incredulous public watched in amazement.

WHERE IS THE CHANGE WE VOTED FOR?

The Dome was not just important in its own right. It was also the first sign of a government disappointingly reluctant to listen to voters. Voters started to give voice to a concern that would grow: why was the government not doing what it had promised to do?

Suddenly, the simple sincerity of the Pledge Card seemed a long way away. Although Labour was still riding high in the polls, this focus group gloom was clearly demonstrating that its support was vulnerable, especially amongst those women voters who had embraced Blair's Labour with such enthusiasm. Men were relatively contented with the status quo:

> They haven't been in long – it took the Tories twenty years to wreck everything. It's early days for them to sort it out.

But women were now impatient for change and indignant at any sign that this government was 'reverting to form'. Lisa, a housewife from Bushey, expressed the exasperation felt by many: 'I thought they were going to be so different – everything seemed so fresh and new but now they look like they might just be the same as all the others.' This was not disastrous, just unsettling. She went on: 'Nothing's gone terribly wrong but I suppose I feel just a bit let down.'

For women, apparent lack of progress in public services was fast becoming a real problem. As we have seen, their focus was their family and their concern was practical. In the main they were the ones who actually used the services: they took the kids to school, took their elderly mum to hospital. No amount of rhetoric would persuade them that improvements had been made if their own experience in the playground or Accident and Emergency unit didn't back it up. Men tended to have a more detached relationship with the receiving end of services, relying on hearsay rather than actual experience. This was why they could be more easily placated; more willing to wait and see.

As early as 1998 a group of mums in Slough were on the warpath:

> In my kids' school there are still classes with up to thirty-five or forty kids. They're nowhere near solving the problem – there are no signs at all of this happening.

> My mum's op was cancelled twice due to bed shortages – I think it's disgusting.

Interestingly, more loyal Labour voters not only shared the swing voters' concern, but if anything felt the disappointment more acutely.

> It's a missed opportunity. So much was promised, so much could have been done but they've been too timid – too afraid of rocking the boat.

Alan, a Labour loyalist from Camden, went on: 'I'm beginning to think they've been dishonourable – all those broken election pledges.'

In late 1998 I was approached to conduct some research to understand what would help the Labour Party to develop a new membership strategy, how Labour supporters could be encouraged to join the party (there had been a short term surge in membership around the election) and also how existing members might be encouraged to be more active.

The research revealed a clear divide between traditional members and the newer joiners who had been prompted to get involved by the appeal of Blair and New Labour. The former, like my old 'comrades' in Battersea, were a deeply committed bunch. Many had been members for years and it was a vital part of their lives, central to their personal philosophy, a raison d'être:

> It's integral to me, makes me feel part of the community.

> There is a moral duty for human beings to think of people who are worse off than themselves. That's what my membership means to me.

These were unusual people, admirable in many ways, often spending more than twenty hours a week on party matters and frequently taking a holiday from work to devote to party business, such as canvassing for local elections. They were the people that the Shadow Communications Agency had interviewed in our survey back in the 1980s.

The newer members were different. They had often joined full of enthusiasm for Blair's New Labour. But with no tradition of political activism, they had been unsure what to expect. Certainly they had expected a more fulsome welcome:

> I got a note through the door telling me about meetings coming up but nobody actually knocked or rang me to introduce themselves.

> I got a welcome letter three or four months after I joined. A week later I received another one.

Those that made it along to meetings complained of feeling excluded. This was especially true of women who often found themselves to be the only females present. Just like me and Jenny more than a decade earlier, they were puzzled by the procedures which no one explained.

It was like a game – I had no idea at all what they were on about.

They were all anoraks – people who were obsessed with big-P politics.

What these diverse members shared was an idealistic commitment to a broad aim of social justice and a desire to personally 'make a difference'. Those who had been around longer focused their energies internally on party structures, while the newer members were more outwardly focused.

What they also shared was a complete rejection of the ideas that I had been asked to test out. In an effort to build both loyalty and fundraising potential, the Labour Party had developed a series of 'packages' that might encourage members to sign up for a longer or larger subscription. A marketing expert with a commercial background was drafted in to develop a range of propositions. His ideas included discounts on gas and electricity bills, or for leading stores like M&S and Boots, days out to tourist attractions such as Alton Towers, even free trips to the Dome.

Party members' first responses to all this was total disbelief. Most were frankly outraged by what they saw as attempts to 'bribe' them. At best, this was a misunderstanding of why people join a political party, and attempts to commercialise the relationship were seen as misplaced. At worst this spoke to a deeper concern about the commercialisation of the party itself and in particular its relationship with the businesses in question. Some just assumed that our researchers were malevolent newspaper reporters having a joke. They expressed their distaste openly:

It's really embarrassing. It undermines any sense of values.

So they say, here's your regular policy briefing – oh and here's your discount on your gas bill.

What a disaster. They're going to shoot themselves in both feet and the head.

Most offensive of all was the Dome offer. To many, especially those living outside London, offering free tickets to Dome added insult to injury – they shared swing voters' views of the ill-fated project.

The one idea that had real potential was the only one that demonstrated real understanding of why people join a political party. 'Community membership' didn't offer the member any tangible personal benefits, but rather asked that they became involved with a range of practical community activities, helping in local schools, old people's homes, volunteering in environmental projects and civic societies. Interestingly, this was also the idea that held most appeal with potential members. It was true to Labour's values, and true to people's views of what an involvement in active politics should be about: giving, rather than receiving.

Our debrief presentation and subsequent report was clear about what worked and what didn't. Thankfully, the 'discount' ideas never saw the light of day, but neither did the more positive 'community membership' proposition. Labour membership continued to decline from its post-1997 high. The lessons about what a different approach to politics might look like, from the grass roots up, were not learned.

TOWARDS THE 2001 ELECTION

There was one area, however, where the government, against the odds perhaps, was starting to build its reputation: the economy. Time spent developing the economic message had paid dividends, and throughout this period, polling showed Labour's performance on economic management steadily rising. The view had settled in that the economy was in good shape, exemplified by low, steady inflation, low interest rates, a strong pound and relatively low levels of unemployment.

Looking towards the Budget for 2001, likely to be a pre-election Budget, voters were very clear that their priority was to find funds for investment in public services. At the same time, a series of family friendly measures were underway: working families tax credits, child tax credits, more nursery places and funding for childcare. These proposals appealed to parents and went some way to offsetting the disappointment of the Dome.

Yet even this relatively strong area for the government was not plain sailing. Achieving positive media was still something of a novelty for Labour, after years in the wilderness feeling beaten down by negative headlines. Gordon Brown had taken on board the voters' desire for investment in public services, but, in his eagerness to make a big gesture, he was tempted by the lure of a congratulatory headline. In his rush towards the Westminster Village media he had ignored advice about people's mistrust of politicians offering large sums of money. The day after the Budget there was great rejoicing about the headlines it generated, trumpeting '£40 billion to spend on health and education'.

However, discussions in focus groups a few days later revealed three problems: firstly people had no idea at all what £40 billion would buy;

secondly, big money talk just reminded people of how cross they were that, so far, Labour seemed to have done very little; and lastly, people were of course aware that this Budget would be close to an election and it all smacked of opportunistic electioneering:

> They have to show where it's going and what they are doing with it.

> That's the election speech then!

> When we see the improvements then fine but we're sick and tired of all the talk!

One of the reasons why Labour failed to heed the worrying messages coming from the focus groups was that, in electoral terms, it didn't need to. The Conservatives, under William Hague's ill-fated leadership, were almost invisible with their ratings bumping along the floor. Asked in focus groups most people couldn't think of anything at all to say about them, and when they did it was usually unflattering to Hague, whose performance, especially around the death of Diana, contrasted unfavourably with Blair's:

> How can you take them seriously with William Hague in charge?

In the run-up to the 2001 general election I conducted a series of on-air focus groups with swing voters in Luton for BBC's *Newsnight*. In the final session before Election Day, I used so called 'projective techniques', explained in detail in Chapter 7, to get under the skin of what people felt about the party leaders.

We asked of each one: if the leader were a car, what kind of car would he be? And if he were a drink?

For William Hague it was a dispiriting set of descriptions. As a drink he was:

Water. Forgettable.

A glass of water. No substance there, just weak.

Horlicks. He sends me to sleep.

Lager. Trying to be one of the boys.

Or as a car:

Like an old fashioned car, rusty, splutters a lot.

A Crusader. Just not stopping to think of the little people really.

But the same exercise offered warning signals to Tony Blair also. As a drink:

Lucozade. When you first open it it's fizzy and they promise it's going to make you feel better, but if you don't drink it in it soon goes flat.

As a car, he was a BMW – and this was not meant to be a compliment:

Flash, heavy and you've got to pay for all the extras.

Nandy, an engineer, put his finger on it: 'A couple of years ago, the Vectra was in the top three of car sales, and now it's started dropping. That's how I see Labour now. It's lost its shine.'

7. What is a focus group?

DRAGGING THEM ALONG

This week – or any week you care to choose – hundreds of men and women will take part in focus groups up and down the country. It could be you. You could be stopped in the street, the playground, or the pub and invited along to one at any time. The person who approaches you will look vaguely familiar: that's because they are a specialist recruiter, hired to be rather like the people they are finding. He or she will ask you to answer a short questionnaire, check if you meet the spec and are free on the date required. You'll also be told what the session will be about and probably be offered a payment to attend, generally around £25.

Attending a group usually means turning up to a nearby house or flat in the early evening. You will be joined by seven or so other men or women, with whom you will spend an hour and a half chatting about whatever topic the market researcher running the session has been briefed to take you through. What brand of coffee or shampoo do you buy? How often do you use analgesics for pain relief? Where do you go on holiday? Do you have a child at university? What mobile phone do you use? Or, of course, how will you vote in the next general election?

Focus groups (or group discussions, as they were originally known in the UK) were first developed by psychologists in the 1950s as one of a number of qualitative research approaches to complement the statistical data gleaned from quantitative polling: the more familiar large scale survey work that you might see published in the media. Small scale, informal and discursive, they provided deeper diagnostic information that was quickly adopted by business, especially for marketing and communications. The benefit was the ability of the focus group to provide insight into consumer behaviour.

Advertising agencies were amongst the first to recognise the practical application of the focus group in enabling them to write better briefs for their creative teams, briefs that gave them a vivid picture of the people that the advertising was trying to reach. Enthusiastic embracing of the focus groups was one of the factors that led to the UK being established as a world leader and innovator in advertising and communications in the 1970s and 1980s. Focus groups remain the most popular qualitative research method today, extensively used by business around the world and representing a market worth millions of dollars.

Their use in politics began in the US, as did the name 'focus groups', describing their distinctive ability to focus in depth on a topic. Mrs Thatcher's advisor, Tim Bell, pioneered their application to UK politics – which had been using large scale quantitative polling since the 1960s – in 1978 while developing Saatchi's highly effective 'Labour isn't working' campaign. Tim Bell, now a Conservative peer, observes: 'We did not set out to do anything radical. We simply used the tools that we would have used for any client to help us to refine the message that we were sending to our key target audience – disaffected Labour voters. It worked because it spoke an obvious truth.'

Labour's first focus groups took place almost a decade later, during the 1985 Labour Party conference and were conducted by adman Leslie Butterfield and a qualitative researcher specialising in focus group methods, Roddy Glen. As we saw in Chapter 1, their first outing was either side of Neil Kinnock's brave and memorable speech made against the backdrop of an increasingly explosive fight with the Militant Tendency. With Liverpool Council leader Derek Hatton and prominent Militants jeering volubly at the back of the hall Kinnock ad-libbed with passion:

> I'll tell you what happens with impossible promises. You start with
> far fetched resolutions. They are then pickled into a rigid dogma code,
> and you go through the years sticking to that, outdated, misplaced,
> irrelevant to the real needs, and you end with the grotesque chaos of
> a Labour council – *a Labour council* – hiring taxis to scuttle round
> a city handing out redundancy notices to its own workers . . . I'll
> tell you this – I'm telling you and you should listen – you can't play
> politics with people's jobs and people's services.

Leslie and Roddy ran focus groups the day before, the day of the speech and the day after and reflected later that they had never before seen a target audience change their opinions so fast. Voters who had written off Neil Kinnock and the Labour Party were suddenly willing to take another look as they saw the Labour leader apparently listening to their concerns and acting upon them. Labour politicians were amazed at the vivid nature of the feedback provided from the work. The Labour Party politicians did not like everything that they heard but it rang true. They were hooked.

From that point on, focus groups became a regular feature of campaign activity. One of my first jobs, working as a co-ordinator for the Shadow Communications Agency, was to pull together a team of focus group moderators who, like almost everyone involved in the SCA, were prepared to give their time as volunteers. By the 1987 campaign we had gathered a team of a dozen or so senior practitioners.

Initially, although I was a trained focus group researcher myself, I recruited and managed this team and reviewed their findings, acting as a liaison between them and the party and politicians. Increasingly, though, I began to feel that there was no substitute for being in the room myself, seeing people's non verbal reactions first hand, and I began to conduct fieldwork personally on a regular basis.

Typically, at about seven o'clock in the evening eight swing voters would gather in ordinary suburban front rooms up and down the country. Each would come along, shyly at first, clutching a glass of wine or diet Coke, perching gingerly on the edge of their chair. To accommodate the numbers, kitchen chairs or plastic garden furniture would be arranged around the edge of the room alongside the three-piece suite. As people did not know one another there would be a slight scramble to get to the more comfortable-looking armchairs and to avoid having to squeeze up next to a stranger on the sofa. Bowls of crisps and plates of biscuits would be passed around as the group of men or women would introduce themselves, self conscious at first, but growing in confidence as the discussion wore on.

Getting people to come along to political focus groups, given how uninterested most people are, has always proved problematic. When we mention 'politics' as the group discussion theme to potential recruits, we often find it very hard indeed to persuade anyone to sign up. In the early days, back in the 1980s, Frances, the recruitment team leader who managed our freelance network of recruiters situated all around the UK, came back wringing her hands: 'My girls just aren't interested in politics and can't find anyone else who is either – they're used to inviting people to groups on things they want to talk about – like TV adverts – specially the ladies.'

It became such a problem that, in order to avoid a half empty room, we had to use subterfuge, pretending that the session was about something else – local schools, family finances, health – anything but the dreaded 'p' word. Distressing for me personally, the team leader was right on the gender difference too. I'd argued at the time, not wanting to accept her judgement and willing women to be more politically engaged and active, but yes, women were even less keen to come along than men. One reluctant attendee commented, after it became clear that a focus group about 'local schools' was also set on exploring wider issues, 'If I'd known this was going to be about politics I'd have sent my husband – he likes all that, likes talking about it – he's got much more to say than I have.'

A related problem is the need to avoid, or manage the expert. With any focus group topic there will always be a minority who think they know more than anyone else – and they may well be right. This is more common when the theme is politics. In many groups of typically shy, diffident voters there will lurk the self appointed expert. The expert will have some knowledge, strongly held opinions and the very unusual desire to talk about politics. To the dismay of the focus group researcher, and the relief of other group members reluctant to contribute, the expert will hold forth. He – and it usually is a he – will correct anyone else who ventures a point of view. Managing the expert and encouraging the whole group to articulate their views requires specialist techniques and, over the years, we have adapted many from commercial market research.

ANIMAL, CAR OR DRINK?

A room full of people who are not very interested in the subject can lead to predictable problems with group dynamics, especially with an expert in their midst. Confidence can be a problem too, particularly, as we have seen, when talking about a more 'technical' subject like the economy. Most people's instinct is to remain reticent or to go with the flow. Why challenge the expert if doing so risks exposing you to ridicule? Too often I would hear comments like:

> I agree with her – she sounds as if she knows what she is talking about.

> When they talk about politics at work or in the pub I just switch off. My eyes glaze over!

Of course the views of those who are naturally cautious in coming forward are no less interesting than the views of those who are eager to be group spokespeople. And they are arguably more useful because their reticence is more typical. The challenge is to elicit those opinions ensuring that they are the individual's own and not steered by the expert sitting next to them.

For this reason I often start a focus group with a written 'trigger' session. The voter will be asked to write down the first word that comes into their head following a written or verbal prompt. The prompt may be the name of a political party, of a politician or of a policy area.

So, on 8 March 2010, I asked members of the Harlow panel set up especially for this book to tell me the first thoughts that came into their heads when they heard the words 'Labour Party'. This is what they wrote:

- Working class
- Red
- Welfare state
- Compassion

- Working men
- Failed
- Dishonest
- Changeable
- Traditional
- Let Down
- Working

While 'Conservative Party' produced this:

- New
- Snobbish
- Changing
- Trying
- Hopeful
- Future
- Cuts
- Rich
- Privilege
- Thatcher
- Higher class

This technique works because each person, regardless of how much or little they *think* they know, is obliged to commit to their own viewpoint. They gain confidence from the fact that their thoughts are often quite like others and will be encouraged in a well-run group to feel good about what they have written. This is particularly useful in a controversial area and worked well in the Barking constituency prior to the 2010 election, where Labour MP Margaret Hodge was being challenged by Nick Griffin, leader of the BNP, giving shy

BNP-leaning voters the licence to say what they felt, so we could understand their underlying motivations and develop the successful campaign strategy that pushed the BNP into third place and led to all twelve BNP councillors losing their seats.

Focus groups are perhaps best known for their use of so called 'projective techniques', where the group is encouraged to reveal private feelings comfortably by 'projecting' their own views onto another person or an object. At its most basic it might mean answering a question like 'Why do so many people enjoy watching *The X Factor*' – so that the group can tell us what they like about *The X Factor* without admitting to watching it themselves. Very often we will use similes to enable the group to express themselves, particularly helping them to get beyond their rational responses to a more emotional reaction.

Steve Bell, the *Guardian* cartoonist, ran a series poking fun at these methods after the 1997 election. He drew voters floating in a 'sensory deprivation tank' being asked, 'If Tony Blair were a vegetable, what sort of vegetable would be he?' 'Porridge,' replies one of the 'floaters', 'A really strong turnip,' says another. I'm often asked if these techniques are just a gimmick or if they really can add value. I reply by explaining how big companies use them to get under the skin of consumers. If I ask a BMW owner why he chose that brand, he will provide a very rational response, talking about roadholding or petrol consumption. Common sense dictates, however, that he could have bought a car with these features for much less money. An advertising campaign or product development programme based on this information will miss the point very badly indeed. If, however, I ask what animal the BMW is, he'll tell us that it is a mighty eagle, soaring in the sky, or a deft leopard. We begin to understand why he chose the car.

I also use 'picture sorts', where voters are given piles of magazines, sheets of paper, scissors and glue sticks. Their *Blue Peter*-style task is to make up collages representing their views on a particular topic, perhaps working collaboratively in pairs. I also use word sorts, where voters sift through adjectives choosing the most appropriate and adding in their own. Or I may give them photographs of politicians with thought bubbles or speech marks – what is David Cameron thinking today? What would Gordon Brown say now?

Another technique demands some creativity: drafting birth announcements, for example to welcome the arrival of New Labour in 1997, or obituaries. In March 2010 I asked our panel of swing voters in Harlow to imagine that politicians no longer existed and to write obituaries for them. They wrote:

Here lies a good man,
Strong and true.
He gave his all to his country and fellow men.
He also took as much as he could get
In the name of his constituency.
Shame he didn't spread it around.

Tried to change the world,
Tried to be popular,
Tried to be green,
Tried to be the face that fitted,
Tried to be honest,
Tried and tried and tried.
Your entertainment will be sorely missed.

On this day we are not sad to report
The demise of our politicians.
It comes as no surprise that today

We will miss the media attention and scandals.

We are also saddened

That many jobs in Savile Row are lost today.

Good and bad in everyone

But not that many good.

We are pleased to announce that all MPs

No longer exist.

We can all join as one

To celebrate no more Prime Minister's Question Time,

No more lies.

They have really gone.

Who cares?

STEPPING INTO THE POLITICIANS' SHOES

Another useful technique demands that voters step into politicians' shoes and look at life from their perspective. I used role playing like this in August 2008 at a very difficult time for GB. Dividing each group into two teams, I asked one team to represent the voter and the other to represent, in turn, David Cameron and Gordon Brown. Each team then nominated one spokesperson and the chosen two sat facing each other on chairs in the middle of the room. The voter asked the 'politician' questions prompted by his team. The 'politician's' team collaborated to devise his answers too.

The questions revealed the central issue for each man. Team GB was asked:

- Why did things go so badly wrong for you?

- Why are you a poor PM when you were a good Chancellor?
- Do you need a style overhaul?
- Do you enjoy your job?
- Are you more comfortable out of the public eye?
- Do you have the backing of your party?

It is another striking example of the gap between the Westminster Village and the voter that the questions chosen were mostly not ones that the politician would ever be likely to be asked on the *Today* programme or *Newsnight*. Yet these questions went to the heart of the voters' concerns. Along with the answers given and the discussion that followed they revealed fundamental truths. Voters believed that GB was a good and able man struggling with the pressures of office and confronted by a smooth talking opponent who highlights his own awkwardness. Voters saw his problem as an inability to put his case – they assumed that his case was strong.

By contrast, DC's central issue was all about integrity and authenticity. He was asked:

- You look the part – but are you?
- Are you really your own man?
- How can you appeal to everyone as you set out to do?
- Do you have the backing of your party?

Again, the discussion unearthed how the voter saw DC. They decided he had been selected by the Conservative Party because of his looks: modern and youthful, an ordinary guy. However, they had serious doubts about just how ordinary he really was. The discussion touched on both men's recent holiday photos, where GB's stiff and formal attempt at 'smart casual' seemed to sum up his problems and contrast with DC's relaxed beach wear. The media had applauded DC for his ease and normality: 'The rise of Boden man'. Yet voters found his photo opportunity on an apparently deserted Dorset beach staged and false. It reinforced both his telegenic suitability and the cynicism of his approach.

The upshot of using these techniques is to create a level playing field where the 'expert' voter who is better read and more assured no longer has any natural advantage. Everyone else rapidly gains confidence and surprises themselves as they do so:

It's incredible what you actually know, isn't it?

You'll have to chuck us out now – you'll never shut us up!

I would often find myself making the same joke as the discussion grew ever more lively at the end of the group: could they please leave now and finish up in the pub as I'd had enough and wanted to go home.

WHEN FOCUS GROUPS WORK

I believe passionately that focus groups can play a unique role in engendering better understanding between voter and politician. You need to use focus groups alongside quantitative polling, of course. They are not a substitute for each other. But often the focus groups can tell you something that the polling cannot. If an opinion poll where hundreds of people have been interviewed can tell you that, say, 75 per cent think one thing or another, focus groups can help you understand why. Because they use semi structured 'discussion guides' rather than a more formal questionnaire, they give the voter a chance to set the agenda rather than be led by preconceptions of the Westminster Village – all too often the voter's agenda will be very different, as we have seen.

If well recruited, focus groups give a startlingly accurate view of how people see politics and where it fits in their lives. Graeme Trayner, who worked with me on Labour research projects from 2002 until 2008, observed:

> People often ask me how eight people can be representative . . . but focus groups use such similar reference points, and such similar language to describe those reference points. There's remarkable homogeneity. Those moments that symbolise how they feel become seared in the national memory: Cameron with his bike, Blair after Diana's death, their hatred of the Dome, 15 per cent interest rates. Those symbols are how people connect to politics.

This insight cannot be gained in any other way.

Sometimes focus groups have proved to be a more reliable barometer of public opinion than large scale polling. In 1992 the polls famously got it wrong, predicting a hung parliament or even a small Labour majority, when the reality was a comfortable Tory win. They also got the underlying attitudes wrong. Both the published surveys and our own private work suggested that people would be willing to pay more in taxes provided the cash generated was spent on education or the NHS. Yet, in focus groups, looking into the whites of people's eyes we knew that they would never ever be happy about paying more without very clear reassurances about the economic competency of the government taking their money. They felt no such comfort about Labour. Rational argument told us to trust the polls. But the polls were wrong and the focus groups were right.

MEETING RESISTANCE

Yet focus groups have, over the years, attracted criticism, controversy and even ridicule. Peter Mandelson often introduced me to journalists in the run-up to the '87 election as Labour's 'secret weapon', and certainly the extent to which Labour was using modern campaigning techniques, including focus groups, did not become apparent until after the policy review process that followed that defeat. The review kicked off with a joint meeting of the Shadow Cabinet and the National Executive Committee at which the SCA presented a research study entitled 'Labour and Britain in the 1990s'. As we rose to present the data, left wing MP Dennis Skinner muttered 'Another load of bloody rubbish' in a stage whisper.

This comment, half in earnest, half in jest, was nothing compared with the criticisms that the focus group work undertaken for the policy review itself provoked, as every single policy within every theme was rigorously tested amongst swing voters, leading ultimately to the elimination of unpopular policies like unilateral nuclear disarmament. Roy Hattersley, Neil Kinnock's deputy, commented that it was strange that 'Neil Kinnock, who is, I should think, the great evangelical politician of this half century, presided over a Labour Party that was less interested in evangelism than it was in graphs, diagrams and figures'.

When focus groups are commissioned for companies and brands the client will often attend some sessions to get a first-hand sense of what the consumer looks like: to see the body language, and hear the vocabulary and intonation. Many politicians will argue that they don't need to do this, that the people they meet out and about in their surgeries and public meetings connect them to ordinary voters. They do not realise that the self selected or even cherry picked citizens that they are exposed to may not be typical at all, and when they do see a focus group in action it can be a shock.

After the 1992 election I received a call from Hilary Coffman in John Smith's office. To my surprise she explained that John, known to be a sceptic, had expressed an interest in setting up some focus groups and would I be willing to organise this? More than that, he actually wanted to observe the groups to see the results for himself.

A couple of weeks later found his team settling into a 'viewing facility' – a space designed to look like a suburban front room with sofas and coffee table, connected via a one-way mirror to an adjacent room, set out cinema style, where clients, unobserved, could watch the proceedings. We were in Billericay in Essex and the participants were typical Middle England swing voters. They had all voted Tory in 1992, and were the voters that Labour had to win back to win. They were anxious, insecure and reluctant to believe that we could be on their side. The first group were all middle-aged mums preoccupied with paying their mortgages, keeping their jobs, finding the right schools for their kids while caring for elderly relatives.

There was a short gap between the end of the first group and the second, who were the same demographic as the women, but male. I popped next door to where John Smith and his team were watching to check if they had anything to add to the next discussion. The team looked worried and John Smith was purse lipped, sitting back in his chair with his arms folded high across his chest.

When I opened the door he swung round to face me. 'Who were those people?' he demanded'

'They were recruited as C1C2 swing voters to our usual spec—' I began.

He cut across me. 'They were awful!' Spluttering with rage he could hardly bring himself to voice the ultimate insult: 'They were all Tories!'

It seemed that the progress that we had made in recent years was ebbing away. I didn't see John again as he did not stay until the end of the session. I was not asked to do any more work while he remained leader of the party, and nor, to the best of my knowledge, was anyone else.

GB also occasionally attended focus groups, especially in his early days as Chancellor. We would book a 'viewing facility' in central London and bus voters in from suburban marginal seats. GB would arrive early surrounded by a protective circle of aides. There would be much nervous jollity as we prepared for the participants to arrive. "So, they're going to all say how much they hate me, are they?" GB would joke. This banter would continue throughout the groups with loud peals of laughter sometimes audible to the voters. I would always feel incredibly nervous, too, and my anxiety was the same as that of the observers – I lived in fear that a voter would say something rude and personal about GB as he sat there listening. Luckily, although this happened often enough over the years, it never happened when the man himself was behind the screen. Oh the relief!

POWER BROKERS OR IMAGINARY FRIENDS?

The use of focus groups is now standard. In some ways it seems an old fashioned method compared with the new ways of interacting with people, especially using on line technology. More recently I have been involved in developing new ways of running focus groups on line. They certainly have their advantages – they are cost effective and very useful for bringing together geographically dispersed people. However, for me, there is still no real substitute for recruiting eight people who would not usually choose to come together and sitting down with them, watching their reactions and listening to their views.

Tony Blair once echoed Bill Clinton's observation that 'there is no one more powerful today than the member of a focus group, if you really want to change things and you want to get listened to, that's the place to be'. But to achieve this level of power, voters are dependent on the moderator asking the right questions, and then passing the findings on. The voters' views can be silenced if they clash with a vested interest or party line. An unpopular project like the Dome – or even an unpopular leader – may be propped up as the voters' feelings are misrepresented or ignored. Tony Blair himself dismissed Philip Gould's protestations that John Prescott was not popular as deputy leader, telling him to 'go away and refocus your focus groups'.

I am in no doubt at all that politicians are better at what they do when they are in touch with the public and guided by public opinion. Taking Labour from 'beyond the pale' in the 1980s to being the people's politicians in 1997 could not have been achieved without insight and advice from members of the public. But it cannot be a substitute for really being in touch. One SCA researcher angrily described giving a research debrief only to hear a politician using the very words she had used in an interview as she drove home an hour or so later: 'It was as if he had no time or inclination to create his own normal life so he had to use the research instead.' In the 2010 campaign Cameron was laughed at for his use of 'ordinary voter' anecdotes in the first leader debate. They were clearly sprung from focus groups and lacked authenticity. While they may not always be power brokers, focus group members should never be used to provide workaholic politicians with imaginary friends.

8. At risk: the jewel in Britain's crown

What makes people most proud to be British? The answer may be surprising. It is not the Royal family, nor Shakespeare nor the Mini, not David Beckham or any of our top football players or clubs. It is the National Health Service. More British than a cup of tea, the NHS seems embody the best of our national characteristics more than almost anything else. It is about fairness, tolerance, responsibility and even inventiveness. This reputation has burnt bright for many years. We Brits believe it to be the envy of the world and in a survey in 2007 nine out of ten Britons *still* agreed that 'the NHS is as important as ever in portraying a positive Britain abroad'.

> The NHS is fantastic – just brilliant – because it's fair and for everyone. If you get sick in America they want a credit card just to say hello to you.

It is an intimate emotional bond, a bond that grows stronger with voters as the NHS plays host to the most poignant and moving events in their own lives and those of their families: having a baby, coping with serious illness, the trauma of an accident, even the death of a loved one. These voters were typical, talking about the importance of the NHS in their lives after the election in 1997.

I can't walk past the cottage hospital without my eyes filling with tears because my dad passed away there.

Everyone was so wonderful when I had my daughter – she was a bit early and things were difficult at first. But they were so efficient and so kind.

When my mother-in-law was ill she was first in the hospital then she was moved to a care home. She spent her last seven months there and although it was hard I have very happy memories.

You know it'll always be there for you.

BROKEN PROMISES

During a campaign that was mainly notably for its moderate and costed claims, the NHS was one area where rhetoric was allowed to run free in 1997. With two weeks to go in the campaign, Labour could not resist the claim 'fourteen days to save the NHS' then again on eve of poll 'twenty-four hours to save the NHS'. In his Budgets during New Labour's first term, Gordon Brown, understanding the importance of the NHS, but without much wiggle room to spend money on it, had talked about allocating large sums of cash, and huge figures had been splashed all over the newspapers: 'A Budget for the people' with an 'unexpected £3.5 billion for health and education'.

Initially this did the trick, with Westminster Village acclaim translating into voter gratitude. I watched GB's first Budget live with a focus group in Roehampton. When the announcement was made about contingency funds being reallocated to the NHS the group broke out into spontaneous applause. Expectations were high and the government satisfaction ratings in the polls reflected that.

However, the latter years of Labour's first term saw a sharp drop in poll ratings with just four out of ten people claiming to be satisfied. In the focus groups we could see that this was emerging as a significant area of vulnerability for the government's. The *Daily Mail* began to complain about Britain's 'third world health service'. GB's initial reaction was to play the numbers game again, claiming he had increased funding for health and education to the tune of £40 billion. Focus groups in Slough in 1999 were all aware of the much trumpeted injections of funds. Most were able to quote the £40 billion figure, but this time there was no enthusiastic round of applause.

They're pumping funds into the NHS.

They may say that they've spent more. . . they would do. But we're not seeing any of it. They all play with figures to fool you.

Well, it's got worse, not better. My mother-in-law has just had a big op cancelled. It's disgraceful.

I really thought that they'd sort this out.

Things got worse. At first GB ignored the warnings from the focus groups, since the media still seemed to reward his announcements with the desired headlines. In January 2000, needled by newspaper reports (much discussed in focus groups at the time) about the plight of Mavis Skeet, a cancer patient whose treatment delay had been life-threatening, TB, in a TV interview, promised funding increases of 5 per cent each year until 2006. GB now pledged still more cash, promising £20 billion over the next four years. Now seen as posturing, rather than solving the problem, this served to compound it.

Once again, focus group voters saved their deepest scepticism for politicians bandying large sums of money around. Big spending talk was quickly dismissed as 'politician's speak'. Looking back on this period, it seems obvious now that the voters were right and that the spending talk was just that – talk, with a certain amount of sleight of hand and double counting going on. At the time this was not so obvious, but what I did know was that this was building up into a major source of discontent. Only one thing mattered now: delivery – delivery that voters could see.

A STATE OF CRISIS

The subject had taken on a massive importance as voters saw it as symptomatic of a more general decline in modern Britain and as a symbol of the government's potential to disappoint. The NHS was always seen as one of Labour's core strengths – integral to the Labour brand. Failure to sort it out would be reneging on one of the election pledges – which, perhaps surprisingly, many respondents could still trot out from memory. Women voters felt the let down most acutely. The electorate's conclusion as we drew towards the end of the first term was that Labour had not, as they had hoped and expected, brought about any visible improvement.

After the 2001 general election it became clear that the NHS, whose history was intertwined with that of the party, was emerging as a powerful barometer issue. People were judging the success of the government on its management of the NHS, and it was found to be wanting. Both GB and TB understood this, but now their solutions were somewhat different: TB was increasingly eager to develop a reforming programme, while GB now understood that a real injection of funds had to be part of any solution. He briefed me in late 2001 to conduct a major qualitative and quantitative study to explore how voters saw the NHS, and, specifically, whether they would tolerate raising taxes to fund it.

I quickly learned that, for voters, this impending crisis was not an abstract concern but one that they felt might impact on them and their nearest and dearest. What if the NHS was no longer there for them when the need arose? People felt that this deterioration had been rapid and was getting worse: could the NHS ever be strong and effective again? Voters began to articulate their worst fear: that the NHS might not survive, a nightmare they thought had receded after the Tories were voted out in 1997:

> You wonder if that's it for the NHS – it would be a tragedy, but is it so run down now that it can never be revived?

We started the focus groups with a verbal word association game which produced the following words – unremittingly negative – when voters were asked, 'What is the first thing that enters your head when you think about the National Health Service?'

- Waiting lists
- Closures

- Cuts
- Waste
- Bureaucracy
- Dirty
- Bring back matron
- Run for immigrants, not us
- Run down
- On its knees
- Overpaid management
- Underpaid nurses and doctors
- Variable

Specifically, voters complained about long and growing waiting lists, overworked staff, and general lack of funding resulting in patients' lives being placed risk. They had seen the newspaper reports that under-funding was compromising the overall levels of care, and that hospitals' purchasing power had become so diminished that patients were being fobbed off with cheaper drugs rather than the most effective or suitable ones.

Every single focus group member would illustrate their point of view with anecdotes drawn from their own experience. They were increasingly angry:

I took my daughter to casualty last week because she cut her finger. We were waiting four hours. It was chaos. There wasn't even anywhere to sit and someone was sick just by us but no one came and cleared it up. I felt like getting a mop and doing it myself – it was disgusting.

My neighbour has breast cancer and she's read that there's a new treatment that you can get so she goes to her GP to ask for it and she's told it's not on the NHS – it's too expensive.

The one area where people still kept faith was in the event of a 'real emergency' like a car accident or a health trauma such as a heart attack. In that event they still believed that the NHS was 'second to none', but in all other cases it was now looking like a poor relation.

WHAT WOULD SUCCESS LOOK LIKE AND HOW WOULD IT BE PAID FOR?

Part of the brief for this project, which occupied much of winter 2001/2, was to understand what success would look like, what signals voters would have to see to be convinced that the NHS was on the mend. GB was finally persuaded that politicians' talk about money spent was not going to be enough. He now knew that unless people saw clear evidence of change as they used the services themselves, the Westminster Village was wasting its collective breath. We were now living in a 'show me' rather than a 'tell me' world.

The most urgent problems were waiting times in A&E and operation cancellations. The shabby look of the NHS infrastructure – run-down buildings, old fashioned equipment, tatty decor – seemed to symbolise the decay. Another issue, predicting the scandal that would emerge around hospital transmitted infections like MRSA, was poor hygiene. Voters told grim stories about being treated in visibly grubby environments:

It was so filthy where my husband was that I had to bring in rubber gloves and a scourer and clean up the loo myself before he could use it – disgusting!

When I had my second baby I had to stay in overnight and the shower was so dirty that I just waited until I got home. It made me feel really depressed.

Bringing back Matron was top of many voters' wish-lists, to impose old fashioned cleanliness, discipline and order. They also believed that medical staff – nurses and doctors – were forced to exist on unsustainably low wages.

I conducted these groups amongst voters of different ages and found a difference in the attitudes of younger ones, who, unlike the older generation, did not feel unconditional gratitude towards NHS staff for their dedication in difficult circumstances. They were unforgiving when things went wrong, seeking the same positive consumer experience that they were used to getting in other, non public sector, environments. They were indignant that this should be achievable in the NHS too:

You get better customer service in Tesco's than you do in your average casualty.

The staff treat you as if you were a problem to them.

The early voter research confirmed that this was not a 'quick fix'; in fact the only 'fix' that would work required a significant investment of cash – the kind that could only be funded by increasing taxes. Inevitably and rightly there were concerns that making this move would break one of the cardinal rules of New Labour's success: not putting taxes up, as voters might have expected 'Old Labour' to do. The central challenge was how to raise taxes without risking that hard won reputation. This was the source of much anxiety in No. 11, and even more in No. 10 as Alan Milburn was pressing ahead with plans to introduce foundation hospitals and making the case that reform would be more effective than spending.

I began by testing a number of scripts that set the problems of the NHS into a wider context. I was keen to see what voters believed had caused the decline that they identified. Was it just politicians' incompetence? We looked at a range of arguments including:

- People are living longer nowadays, placing greater stress on the NHS
- NHS is a victim of its own success as we can now cure illnesses that people died from years ago.
- NHS needs modern management to be more efficient.
- NHS has been underfunded for twenty years and that is what we are paying the price for now.
- We pay less for the NHS than other countries do for their healthcare.

We found that, despite people's general readiness to blame politicians for most things, there was some willingness to accept that the NHS's problems were not just their fault. People tended to believe – partly because this was a strong Labour narrative during the 1997 campaign – that NHS managers were not effective and were overpaid so talk of 'modern management' met with a raised eyebrow. But people did agree that this was a long term problem, not one that had suddenly appeared. They also agreed with the argument that there was more strain on resources as patients were surviving more illnesses and people were generally living longer. There was also broad acceptance that other countries may spend more than we did.

The single most important finding, however, was that these swing voters almost entirely rejected any proposals for introducing private or part private funding of the kind that the Tories were suggesting at the time. Voters immediately made the comparison with the US system which they universally believed to be inferior to ours, so much so that describing anything as American or US was a shorthand insult:

> I'd hate us to move towards the American way, where if you can't afford it, you die.

Paying for certain services such as visits to the GP also met with a thumbs down:

> It's like eye tests – it just means that lots of people who need to go won't go and that stores up bigger problems for the future.

Despite this, the knee jerk response to funding the NHS by raising taxes met initial resistance. Voters were concerned that the money would be wasted, and that it would disappear into a bottomless pit of government funds, never to be seen again and certainly never seen by the NHS. There was also resentment that the 'squeezed middle' – people like them – would pay the price for undeserving 'scroungers' who do not pay up but still benefit. Scroungers included asylum seekers or people on benefits. Some also suggested that the NHS might instead be funded by releasing cash from the voters' pet wastes of money, particularly the Dome – a bone of contention still talked about several years on.

However, this was the NHS – almost nothing mattered more to most of them. The scripts that we used that talked about how demands on the NHS were greater than ever, and comparing UK spend unfavourably with other countries worked well. The most persuasive argument, though, was a promise to ring fence funds exclusively for the NHS, then put in place some guarantees about how the money would be spent, countering cynical accusations of waste.

Some of the euphoria from 1997 had worn off, but, in the early years of the second term, Labour was still regarded as fundamentally competent and well meaning, especially when it came to the NHS. People could still feel optimistic that services would improve in time. Thus my focus groups concluded that voters would find a small tax rise acceptable provided a number of important caveats were in place:

1. It would be important to see that this route was recommended by 'independent' experts, not just government ministers. Some made the case spontaneously for some kind of Royal Commission to review the future of the NHS.

> You need to know that it's not just the government trying it on – doing anything to get more of our cash to throw around.

> If the experts say that's the only way then so be but I'd need to know that it was all properly thought through.

2. The money would be ring fenced and not spent on anything but the NHS.

> I genuinely wouldn't mind a bit more going on the NHS – but it must be the NHS – nothing else.

3. There would be some accountability measures built in, with reassurances that the money would be well spent.

> I don't really trust the government not to waste money – there's terrific waste in government departments.

A PLAN TO PERSUADE

So, in early spring 2002, a plan began to emerge that might be able to persuade the voter that New Labour still was *New* Labour, even as it did something very Old Labour indeed – put up taxes.

Firstly, we had to set the scene effectively This meant clearly explaining how long-term under-funding, along with improved longevity and improved ability to fight previously incurable disease, had resulted in the pressures that the NHS was now experiencing. It involved demonstrating how quality healthcare in other countries was achieved by comparatively higher levels of investment. It would also be important that this case was supported by an independent expert. We had explored in focus groups the idea of using Derek Wanless, the ex CEO of the NatWest bank, for this. He was not a high profile figure amongst ordinary voters but his CV implied the right credentials for the job.

> He is clearly a money man who understands management and finance – and not obviously a Labour supporter. Yes, an independent voice.

One other important point was that, given how run down the NHS was felt to be, Labour needed to make the case that the NHS really was worth saving. Voters needed clear reassurance that a new injection of funds would not be 'throwing good money after bad'.

Secondly, we knew that success would be contingent on two guarantees, the most important being that the money was ring fenced. There would have to be cast iron guarantees, with voters in no doubt at all that the funds would find their way to the right place. This then needed to be followed by a fully accountable action plan.

Given people's impatience for change it would also be critical that there were some 'quick wins' to restore faith: bring back Matron, clean up wards, speed up A&E, a lick of paint, and stop cancellations where possible.

I also stressed in a note that I wrote in the run-up to the Budget:

> We must avoid using numbers and statistics to discuss the NHS. They are rejected unanimously as people neither understand nor believe the data. Indeed the more we throw figures at them the more they think we are 'on the fiddle'. The only proof that they will believe is proof that they see with their own eyes.

Despite the reassuring focus groups, there was enormous anxiety about the tax proposal, with TB even wondering if this might cost him the election. I ran a large scale poll to get confirmation of the focus group feedback. It gave the Treasury team the proof they needed to take the plunge. We saw huge levels of support at 83 per cent for the NHS being 'available, free when you need it', and a clear lead for financing healthcare 'as it currently is, through taxation and National Insurance' (76 per cent) rather than 'through a system based on private insurance like the US' (14 per cent) or 'through a system based on charging people for services' (just 7 per cent).

We found that 83 per cent were willing to pay a 1 per cent increase in National Insurance to fund the NHS, and 78 per cent would be willing to pay a 2 per cent increase. A number of guarantees improved the likelihood of people supporting this rise, the most important of which was the money being ring fenced for use only in the NHS.

So it happened that in GB's 2002 Budget he announced what was to become the most popular tax rise ever. Reflecting on this now in 2010, it makes a marked contrast with the lack of preparation and testing that went into the 2009 Budget, raising the top level of tax to 50 per cent for people earning £150, 000 or more, or into the proposed National Insurance rise in the Budget approaching the 2010 campaign. Much of the painstaking planning of the early New Labour days had been abandoned by then. However, in 2002, armed with extensive voter feedback, using language carefully tested to press the right buttons and with surrounding publicity of TB and GB visiting Chelsea and Westminster Hospital GB argued, 'What we did was look at what the healthcare needs in this country are. The tax is done in a fair way. I would not have asked for a tax rise unless it was absolutely necessary'.

Published polling the following weekend confirmed the success of this audacious move. The Conservative vote share dropped 5 per cent while the Labour share rose 2 per cent, giving a 16-point lead. Seventy-two per cent – and even 54 per cent of Conservative voters – approved of the tax rise. All we had to do now was to wait for people to see the changes that the money brought about.

'I'VE BEEN LUCKY' SYNDROME

I spoke at a private, off the record lunch for *Guardian* journalists organised by leader writer Martin Kettle in early 2004. There I reported a strange phenomenon we were seeing again and again in focus groups around the country. The government had successfully raised taxes and then injected substantial funds into the ailing NHS. Heeding the advice about 'quick wins' there had been a massive focus on improving the those services at the top of the voters' wish lists: cleaning up wards, speeding up A&E and ensuring that appointments, especially for critical treatments like cancer surgery, were kept.

People were seeing the change with their own eyes as I had insisted that they needed to. They were reporting them back to me as clear improvements. Yet they were not extrapolating this experience out to draw a wider conclusion about improvements in the services they used. On the contrary, drawing on continuously negative news reports, they believed their experience to be, not part of a bigger picture, but an isolated lucky fluke. We could not have predicted this. We called it 'I've been lucky syndrome'.

This was borne out in the published polling too. Increasingly MORI were reporting a gap between perceptions of public services in a general sense and 'my' public services, so for the NHS, satisfaction based on personal experience was 10 per cent ahead of satisfaction based on wider perceptions. Schools and transport produced similarly unhelpful gaps. All of this contributed to a decline in levels of optimism about the government's performance. In June 2001, as we had embarked on that NHS review, 54 per cent agreed that 'in the long run, this government's policies will improve the state of Britain's public services. It was this optimism that had given us the licence to raise the taxes in the first place. By December 2003 this figure had dropped more than 20 points to 30 per cent.

This was now feeding into a deep dissatisfaction with Labour. By

2004 the mood in marginal constituencies like Hemel Hempstead was gloomy:

> It's the likes of us that seem to suffer. Ordinary working people. Things are going terribly wrong.

> It's hard to think of one good thing they've done that's benefited everyone.

The media, once so favourable to New Labour, had turned against them. Negative headlines dominated the news coverage. Voters were so convinced that Labour was letting them down that they no longer even trusted their own positive experience as a gauge of the government's success.

9. They call them spin doctors in the States

I was chatting to Barry Delaney, a senior adman who had been helping out as part of the SCA. We were waiting to see Peter Mandelson at Labour HQ, with a new script for a party political broadcast. It was early 1987. We perched on a desk under the watchful eye of Phyllis, Peter's secretary, just outside his office. Peter could see us through the glass window in the door and waved, holding up his hand, fingers spread: five minutes. He was on the phone to a journalist, talking rapidly, laughing, talking some more, making a few notes with the Montblanc pen he carried from meeting to meeting in its box. He winked at us with a grin. 'They call them spin doctors in the States, you know,' said Barry. I had never heard the expression before but, as Labour drew towards the 2005 general election, even the most uninterested voter in Britain knew what spin was, and most would have heard of Peter, too.

One of the many problems that Labour had faced back in 1987 was its inability to control an often hostile media. This was what Peter, a TV executive, had been hired to fix. He, then Alastair Campbell, and ultimately an army of special advisors working for senior ministers or as press officers for the Labour Party, changed all that. The iron grip that New Labour had over the media served it well in opposition as it sought to convey a positive, single-minded message. It worked too in the heady early days of government, when a promise expressed in a headline was more than enough. Yet by 2005 spin, the ability to manipulate the news agenda regardless of the facts, came to symbolise the gap between politicians and people perhaps more than anything else for a disillusioned electorate.

In the last chapter I looked at how the 'I've been lucky' syndrome' began. The government had talked up cash spent on public services so successfully that the Westminster Village began to believe that the headlines created meant 'job done'. Yet, focus groups told us again and again that voters, especially those all important women voters, who were out there using the services day in day out, were increasingly indignant that not a lot had changed. When eventually real money followed the headlines it was just too late. By then the media, following the public mood, took up the complaining role, with the result that, even if an individual's own experience was positive, the assumption was that this was an isolated lucky fluke, not part of a systemic improvement. Labour's most alluring promise to 'do politics' differently remained unfulfilled.

IRAQ WAR

Then the Iraq War happened. More than a million people marched against it. Inside Westminster the atmosphere was highly charged. While a small number, mainly based in or near No. 10, were passionate supporters of the war, most were not. In fact, privately, it was hard to find a Labour politician who could or would justify it. There was whispered talk of insurrection amongst ministers and advisors, but in the main it remained just whispers. In the end the few who did make a stand from within government failed to make a difference. Team Brown was in a strange place, neither strongly supporting nor opposing military action.

Less than a third of voters supported going to war in early 2003, and although this figure fluctuated and even improved a little as the year went on, the war never stopped being seen as Tony Blair dogmatically following his own agenda regardless of the country's opinion. In focus groups up and down the country voters found a multitude of reasons to be irate about Iraq: the government not listening, the government being arrogant, the government focusing on foreign rather than domestic issues, the government making Britain unpopular with the world, the government being the US's poodle, the government placing people in Britain at risk from terrorism. It was a vicious circle as Iraq confirmed some of the anger that people now felt about the government:

> Tony Blair couldn't care less about the likes of us. He just wants to prove himself abroad – at any cost.

> I'm no fan of Europe. . . but if we ever need them they won't be there for us – we're outcasts now.

> The US just has to say 'Jump' and Tony Blair asks 'How high?'

Even voters who agreed that Saddam was a tyrant and supported going to war shared many of these concerns. It was about the way things had been done as much as about what had been done. These angry feelings spilled out in focus groups, contaminating everything so that it was almost impossible to get people to talk about anything else. In desperation, I sometimes forbade people from talking about it at all in order to be able to get through the questions that I had convened the group to cover, thus again, I regret, implicitly conspiring with the Westminster Village and silencing the voter's voice.

Worse than this was happening at No. 10. US pollster Stan Greenberg outlines in his book *Dispatches from the War Room* how he was sacked from the Labour campaign because he would not stop passing on the electorate's fury about Iraq and urging Blair to apologise. He was told on the eve of the election that he was to be replaced by Mark Penn, a rival US advisor sympathetic to the war. No. 10 had already started using Penn behind Greenberg's back. Greenberg observed:

> Penn supported the war and his polling was on Iraq. While I did not know when Penn began, as early as May, Philip [Gould] was deleting all the Iraq message batteries that we tested for our surveys. After one such exchange I responded testily in an email: 'We should talk about Iraq and more. Won't go away.' Apparently Penn was not so sympathetic to the idea of Blair acknowledging disappointments, frustrations and mistakes on the war . . . it isn't something leaders love to do.

By summer 2003, the situation had deteriorated. Voters, now angry, watched as events unfolded around the evidence used for going to war. There was the death of Dr David Kelly, the civil servant who had challenged that evidence, and the subsequent Hutton inquiry. In voters' minds it was no longer about whether you supported the war or not, it was now about being duped – and the settled view was that we had all been duped.

By September, however, while Westminster remained fixated, still playing the blame game, voters had moved on. Focus groups in Hertfordshire were impatient with the continued media and government focus on Iraq and Hutton – they wanted to get back to domestic issues: NHS, education, crime and the economy. My colleague Graeme Trayner wrote a debrief note: 'There is a disconnect between the preoccupation of the Westminster Village and the concerns of ordinary voters. While politicians and the media focus on the Hutton enquiry and the resignation of Alastair Campbell, voters are more concerned with public services, crime and tax.'

However, the events of the year had contributed to the breakdown of trust in the government, and especially in Tony Blair himself. Voters felt that they had deliberately been given the 'wrong information' over the reasons for war in Iraq. They believed that Britain went to war because of the US influence and were flabbergasted at the inability to find WMDs. Jason, an engineer, said: 'It's the United States of Europe, isn't it?' Reeta, a school meals assistant, put it simply: 'They lied to us. It was plain lies.'

SPIN

While Iraq was important this strong sense of disillusionment stemmed more directly from perceived failure to deliver on public services and a sense that Labour, once admired for 'doing politics differently' was obsessed with spin over reality. Blair, as the personification of Labour, was believed to be preoccupied with image over action, and 'in thrall' to spin doctors and PR men who treated him like a puppet or front man – an actor spouting their lines. Terry, a fitter, said, 'Spin, we're all sick to death of the spin.' Cheryl, a shop assistant, agreed: 'They say one thing one day and another day it's something else.'

Their examples of the government's damaged credibility were almost exclusively domestic. Jason again (on statistics): 'They move things into different categories, so "unemployed person" becomes "job seeker".' Morris, a bank worker, added, 'For me, it's the immigration figures. As this gentleman says, it's just recategorised.'

In June 2004, I ran a series of focus groups in the south east and the Midlands for Neil Lawson's new, left-leaning think tank, Compass. The intention was to capture the public mood. I wrote:

> People feel deeply downbeat and disappointed. Swing voters have serious doubts about the accountability of the government. Trust has broken down completely. They believe that New Labour has failed to deliver the different style of government that it originally promised: as such it has turned out to be no different from other political parties in government. Ministers have retreated behind closed Whitehall doors, reverting to a top down style of government, talking only to their own advisors and 'on side' journalists.
>
> New Labour's apparently open, responsive and in touch style in the lead up to the '97 election is perceived to have faded rapidly over the last seven years. Voters see the Dome as a key turning point. This was the first time they questioned whether the government was listening. For most, Iraq has become another, much more sinister, symbol of a government not listening to its people.

The quotes from voters who participated in the study were vivid and negative:

> With this government it's all lies and passing the buck – nobody

in government lost their job over Kelly. Absolutely disgraceful!
They're just all talk.

They don't listen to us. They just tell us what they want us to hear
and we get suckered in and vote for it. Most of us didn't want the
war, but do they listen? No!

You don't believe them any more. They're a bunch of liars but you
get wise to it.

Much of this hostility was focused on Blair himself, once the
embodiment of New Labour's success, now the embodiment of its
failure. Asked what animal TB would be, voters' suggestions were all
deeply unflattering: 'weasel' or 'rat', explained thus:

He's in the pocket of the US.

He's a yes man.

He's scared of the US and Europe. He's a puppet of the US and a
cheat and a liar.

If a drink, TB would be:

The dregs at the bottom.

The slops in the tray.

I've absolutely no faith at all in Tony Blair.

UNPERSUADED AND UNDECIDED

Labour moved towards Election 2005 in a precarious state. The extreme unhappiness with PM and government should have offered an enormous opportunity for the Conservatives as the country moved into the final months before a likely election. However, despite Labour's difficulties, the Conservatives, now led by Michael Howard, were failing to capitalise. Very little was known about Howard himself, despite being selected as an experienced hand by his party. And the party itself was felt to have lost its way – voters had no idea what the Conservatives now stood for, and when asked to describe it, usually resorted to talking about Mrs Thatcher, although it was a decade and a half since she had been leader. People felt resentful about this, deriding both Howard and his party for being invisible at a time when they may have chosen to notice them:

He's wallpaper.

They need to bring themselves more forward to the public.

I couldn't name one of his policies.

Many voters' reaction was to switch off, disengaging from politics almost in an active way. Voters told me that they talked about politics even less with friends and family, deliberately turning their back, expecting that they may not vote at all:

The whole country is in a dilemma. There is a general feeling that we're not sure what to do and that we won't vote.

Half my friends won't be voting. They've got no interest at all – fed
up with the lot of them.

As the election grew closer, the Conservatives moved into a small
lead in the opinion polls, although more than four out of ten were
still claiming that they might change their mind, compared with a
third in 2001 and just a quarter in 1997. The election was up for
grabs. Despite its reputational crisis, in the polls Labour still had
the edge on a number of vote winning attributes: best team of
leaders to deal with the country's problems (+17), most clear and
united about what its policies should be (+10). Blair polarised
people's views: his satisfaction ratings were actually a little ahead of
the unfortunate Howard's, but his negative ratings were very much
higher (+18) and his trust ratings tipped the scales with almost 60
per cent claiming to find him untrustworthy. Nevertheless, Labour
led on 'best policies' for many key issues: health, education, and,
critically, unemployment and management of the economy.

ECONOMY GOES CENTRE STAGE

This came as no surprise. The Conservatives had historically been
seen as the party of economic competence (hence Labour's inability
to capitalise on the recession of 1992). Yet, post-'97 the failures of
Hague and Duncan Smith had resulted in a crisis of competency.
We found again that people's memories were long when it came to
remembering the negative impact of high interest rates leading to
negative equity and people losing their homes. Howard did and said
nothing to suggest his credentials in this area might be better than
those of his predecessors. When I had tested reactions to the very

popular pre-election Budget a couple of months before voters had laughed when I had shown them a tape of Oliver Letwin's post-Budget broadcast. They could not believe that he really was the Shadow Chancellor, so ill qualified for the job did he appear to be.

The economy was the government's only outstanding achievement given the aching disappointment they felt with public service delivery and bitter disillusionment with foreign policy. When asked what the government had achieved the focus groups, once the outpouring of dismay had finished, started spontaneously talking about low interest rates and low unemployment. Tax credits, childcare help and nursery provision had all helped people to feel better off. Despite their anger with the government over Iraq, their own wellbeing had improved.

I have to say that I'm personally doing well.

Gordon Brown, as a result of this, was emerging as the most popular character in the government. His personal style was also popular: an un- spun persona that contrasted very favourably with TB's. He was increasingly seen as the government's greatest asset:

He's more of a real person.

An honest character – and you don't get many of those in politics.

He does exactly what he says he'll do.

At this time the relationship between GB and TB was at an all time low. GB was exiled from the forthcoming campaign. Alan Milburn – frankly a hate figure in Team GB – had been appointed into GB's traditional role of election strategist. Yet what had been clear in No. 11 for some time was becoming increasingly clear at No. 10 too: Labour could not win unless the economy moved centre stage. And the economy could not move centre stage without GB back on board. Negotiations started and GB demanded a list of concessions to re-enter the fray. One was to take over Milburn's role. Blair agreed. The first that Alan Milburn knew was when GB's team appeared unannounced to take charge of the 8.30 strategy meeting that Monday.

THE ELEPHANT IN THE ROOM

So, the economy was the linchpin of Labour's campaign. But another issue loomed and it wasn't Iraq, which, although still toxic amongst some core Labour voters, had broadly subsided as an issue with middle ground voters. I had set up a panel of women swing voters for the *Today* programme in Watford, a tight three-way marginal. To track the campaign I interviewed them regularly over the weeks. On the first meeting, Ian Watson, the BBC journalist, commented:

> So what issues would sway voters at the next election? Initially, most women talked about public services – health and education in particular. But then it turned out there had been an elephant in the room. As soon as one person was brave enough to admit spotting it, suddenly most of the others could see it too:

> 'I'll be honest, I was too frightened to mention immigration because I thought maybe it wouldn't be politically correct.'

'I mean it might sound awfully, you know, but you look at Australia! They don't have the problem we have.'

Then you've got the case of all the asylum seekers that can come in and we can fund them finding houses and they're saying we can't have pensions for our own people later on.'

This was not a new issue. Anyone watching or conducting political focus groups for the first time would often come back shocked at the voters' vehemence about immigration. This issue topped the poll of 'issues that matter to me' year in year out. Eight out of ten said that 'immigration laws should be far tougher or stopped altogether'. In focus groups people often needed a licence to talk about it and would fear group censure. They would start the issue up very apologetically: 'I'm not being funny or anything. . .' That expression was so well used by voters to preface a complaint about immigration that it became shorthand for voter vernacular amongst Team GB.

Immigration, perhaps more than any other issue, illustrates the disconnect between the voter and the Westminster Village. Whenever training a new focus group moderator to do political work, I would prepare myself for his or her reaction after the first exposure to swing voters. Unrestrained this would be a topic that would dominate everything. We described it as a 'vortex' issue, one which sucked all other issues in – the NHS is struggling? That's because it's crowded with immigrants. Schools aren't teaching our kids well enough? That's because teachers have to cope with immigrants' kids who can't speak English. Can't get a job? That's because immigrants have undercut your rates, working for less. Can't get a house? That's because the government have given priority to immigrants.

Fuelled by the tabloid media, especially the influential *Daily Mail*, voters would explode with fury once they felt comfortable to discuss this issue without censure from the rest of the group. It is hard to know to what extent the media influenced views and to what extent it simply fed feelings that were already there. Voters would use anecdotes from their own personal experience and stories from the press interchangeably. The consistency between the two was so strong that both felt equally real to them, and both would produce identical outbursts of outrage.

I think it is important to be clear here that the strength of feeling I witnessed night after night in front rooms around the country does not mean that most people are racist. This is one of the gravest misunderstandings between the voter and the political classes. Quite simply it is that middle ground voters feel the economic security of their own families to be permanently under threat. That threat is felt to be worsened by the burden of newcomers to Britain, competing for jobs, housing and public services.

It became an issue that, in the focus groups, we always shut down and moved on from and the voters knew it. I fed back their feelings as faithfully as I could, as often as I could, but it was never top of anyone's agenda, there was never much of an appetite to listen or act. Politicians seemed in paralysis: unwilling either to make the positive case for immigration or to do anything about it. The voters' voice was not just ignored, they believed it was being actively silenced. This was another source of intense frustration: 'political correctness' became a shorthand for Westminster Village immunity to their concerns. Up until now, as the polls narrowed, and action had to be taken.

A week or so into the campaign and all the parties had launched their manifestos. All made some mention of immigration; Labour had hastily added an extra pledge on border controls and combating asylum abuse, while the Conservatives had run a full page newspaper ad in the form of a letter from Michael Howard promising an annual limit on immigration. While the content of this message was well received, it exposed increasing concerns about Michael Howard himself:

> I think it's very good [the ad]; I mean, it summarises how I feel. It's just a pity that you've got Michael Howard's name at the bottom. He just comes across as such a wally, he really does.

> Oh, Howard was on television, wasn't he, for an hour. It was a programme all designed to make him look more appealing, but he made himself look a complete and absolute prat apparently.

The unfortunate truth for the Conservatives was that their campaign was perceived as a one-man show, and the more that voters saw of Howard the less they liked him. Their view shifted as the campaign wore on, from indifference to active dislike. Howard was seen as remote, vain and slippery. When asked what animal he was, voters would say 'vulture', 'hyena' or simply 'an old one'.

> The Tory campaign was definitely the most visible, but it backfired, to be honest, because people had quite a negative response to it.

> Michael Howard just came across incredibly badly.

At his hand even the potentially popular immigration message unravelled:

> They were just trying to frighten people in this country and turn people against immigrants. I agree with some of the things being said, I do worry about the amount of people coming into the country and I don't want it to pick on them.

Ironically, even the so-called PC accusation that voters themselves so resented was levelled at Howard:

> I thought Michael Howard was blatantly racist.

In this context Howard's attacks on Labour felt hollow, especially as he tried to refocus the campaign on Blair and Iraq. Iraq became an issue that polarised the electorate. Lib Dem leaning, more affluent, middle class voters were still turned off Labour and the Lib Dems would go on to win many more seats because of this. However, less well-off, 'squeezed middle' Labour/Tory swing voters were now focused more on the economy, leaving the Conservatives derided for being negative and personal, seemingly having a knee-jerk response to anything that Labour did:

> I don't agree with backstabbing.

> All that backbiting – I'm sick of it.

In Watford the Conservatives slipped back through the campaign from second to third place as the Lib Dems mopped up any anti-Iraq protest. It wasn't enough to win, though, and Labour prevailed in Watford, albeit with a greatly reduced majority.

THE BORING ELECTION

The overwhelming emotion that voters felt about the 2005 general election was boredom. The campaign lacked the energy and excitement of previous contests. Despite the closer start, many voters felt that there was not much choice on offer, especially as antipathy to Howard grew and the Labour campaign recovered as the Blair/Brown 'double act' found its feet. They compared it with 1997 and found it wanting:

When Labour got in the first time the campaign really got people going. It was exciting. This time it's nothing.

It's really boring.

Little of the campaign impinged on people's consciousness. Very few read or saw the manifestos (unless we asked them to in focus groups!) Few had come across a canvasser although a few in marginal seats had encountered a pre-recorded phone call from the Tories. They found this as unnerving as a real life encounter with the Conservatives' leader might have been: 'a bit creepy'.

Echoing the Watford result, Labour won, on a low turnout and with a reduced share of the vote. Focus groups after polling day did not reveal huge enthusiasm for the vote – it had been a begrudging gesture, and definitely a vote for 'the devil you know':

I feel safer with what they done so far.

The Conservatives haven't got a better policy and Labour are already there. Whether you like it or not they are doing certain things OK.

The voter mood was spookily echoed in the Labour Party too. Despite winning an unprecedented third term, there was no celebration. Labour had endured significant losses, especially in the South of England, where Labour core vote protesting about Iraq had allowed the Lib Dems in. In a way nobody had got what they wanted: Blair was weakened, Brown was frustrated, and everybody was exhausted. Newspaper headlines over the next few days reflected this gloom' Labour edged painfully into a third term', the Guardian proclaimed. The election was 'a warning, not a triumph'. Everyone trudged back to work.

10. Project 3D – preparing to be leader (1)

PROJECT 3D

It was early 2004 and Gordon Brown was sitting on the GMTV sofa. He sat like a small boy, hands underneath his thighs, leaning forward slightly, smiling bashfully. The interview was about the new pensioners' winter weather fuel allowance. The presenter fed GB a gentle question about why he felt that the allowance was 'so important to pensioners.' GB answered earnestly, 'Well, some elderly people have told me that they are worried about putting the heating on.' The questioning then became more personal, about John, GB's baby son. GB laughed and leaned forward again, now freeing up his hands to gesticulate as he talked, for the first time in the national media, about Postman Pat.

GB did not often do interviews like this. Testing this clip later with focus groups was a revelation. I had shown videos of him in a variety of media settings: his formal Chancellor post Budget broadcast, *Newsnight* and *News at Ten*. In these he seemed authoritative if a bit keen on jargon-spouting. Male groups – as ever, more tolerant of abstract language – were warmer than women. Both, however, responded with amazement when they saw him for the first time in this more relaxed setting. The friendly questioning used layman's language and avoided Westminster Village vocabulary, so GB instinctively avoided it too. He joked and laughed and answered questions directly, relaxed and unafraid of being 'caught out' by a wily political journalist's trick question. He even flirted shyly with the effusive presenter.

'I can't believe it's the same guy!' said Mark, a builder who had watched the more Chancellor-like performance respectfully but now sat up and took notice. 'You warm to him as a person – he's really nice – I've never seen that before!' said Annette. Everyone was similarly surprised:

> I saw this at the time and said to my husband that he came over really different.

In my debrief note a few days later I concluded that GB should show voters the man behind the authoritative Chancellor's persona. Project 3D was so called because its purpose was to develop a more three-dimensional image for GB. Having seen the positive voter reaction I believed that GB's personal positioning could and should embrace a broader scope, introducing the private man to a wider audience. Project 3D became my primary focus. It was clearly intended to play a part in developing GB's future prime ministerial positioning, a crucial piece in the overall jigsaw. The first stage of research, conducted between March and April 2004 included a section where we tested 'possible lines on GB as PM'.

GB had spent years positioning himself as the quintessential 'politicians' politician'. He had barely left Westminster since becoming an MP in 1983. His entire life was his work and in his rare moments of leisure he chose to hang out with Westminster Village insider buddies like Charlie Whelan and Ed Balls. On one occasion he had been sent tickets to watch England play football and it was agreed that, in the spirit of the Project 3D objective of widening his horizons, he should go along and be seen there with a 'normal' friend, unconnected with politics. He loved football and readily agreed to this. 'I'll go with Ed Balls,' he said, and was bewildered by amused protests that Ed was hardly non-political. . . In the end the lucky guest was one of his brothers.

His diligence impressed the media and many fellow politicians. Voters respected him too, but their knowledge was sketchy. They knew he was Scottish. They thought him 'strong' and 'honest'. They might envisage him giving the Budget speech in the House of Commons. He was associated with a rare Labour success: the thriving economy. He was thought to 'know his stuff', to be 'steady' and 'consistent'. Voters felt respect without any real affection. Seeing the daytime TV interview gave him a different dimension: not just a Chancellor but a human being sitting on the red sofa. They looked at him again and actually liked what they saw.

Project 3D really started in earnest in early 2004. The government was looking tired. It was tainted by perceptions of lack of delivery on public service and the feeling that Blair was focused abroad, especially with Iraq, and not interested in ordinary people here in the UK. Overall, there was a sense that this government, after promising to be so different, was turning out to be just like any other – the Dome remained a constant reminder of this. More recently there had been the MMR crisis, where, amidst attempts by the government to give its approval to the controversial vaccine, Blair had refused to say whether his young son, Leo, had been given it. Voters saw this as just another example of 'say one thing, do another'. In a survey that I ran for Opinion Leader Research we found that people were three times more likely to trust Richard and Judy to give them truthful information on MMR than the then Health Secretary, Alan Milburn.

Early in 2004 we conducted a series of focus groups in Radlett, Edgware and Sale amongst both usual switcher audience and also amongst loyal Labour voters. They confirmed the disillusionment with the government. I wrote in my debrief notes, 'The dream 1997 has been replaced with the nightmare of 2004.' And that 'the feeling of hope and belief has turned to anger and betrayal'. Much of this antipathy was directly squarely at Tony Blair, who was losing support. Women felt almost personally affronted, as if let down by a good friend. Projective exercises revealed that the animal he was most like was a fox, a snake or a cheetah. As a drink he might be cava:

> Lots of bubbles but it's fake, not the real thing.

Partly with an eye to the competition, I also explored the reputations of other Labour politicians in the research. Most were failing to cut through beyond Westminster. Charles Clarke, then the Education Secretary, was the best known of the 'others', but known for an unpopular policy: tuition fees. He was seen as tough and no-nonsense but aggressive and remote. We also checked out John Reid and Alan Milburn. These last two were scarcely known at all, even on prompting with a photograph. Just one voter triumphantly claimed to recognise John Reid. 'I know him,' she said, delighted to at last see a familiar face. 'That's John Prescott, isn't it?'

I tried to dig beneath GB's 'money man' image. On extensive prompting, men, a little more interested in Westminster Village machinations than their female counterparts, offered occasional mentions of him falling out with TB (over Iraq and tuition fees) and some had heard that he had ambitions for the job of leader. Both of these largely enhanced his reputation rather than diminished it.

The projective work was the most interesting, revealing distinctive personal qualities: GB was seen as an ox, a bear or a bull – strong and trustworthy, with personal integrity born partly out of his unspun and unflashy image. He was solid and reliable, tenacious and determined. Women, who knew less about him, liked him more, admiring his intensity.

Further examination also revealed significant weaknesses. Politically, men were most likely to blame him for 'stealth taxes' which, for some, implied a personal weakness – is he sly? He was also thought to lack charisma and people skills, to be dour and grumpy, glowering, even aggressive. Looking at Budget broadcasts reinforced this view. His powerful, strident House of Commons performances, with bellowed speeches accompanied by podium thumping, said he was strong but also belligerent. Political set piece interviews portraying him as uncomfortable and ill at ease were not serving him well either as he struggled to present a more three-dimensional character.

NAILING THE NARRATIVE

Later in 2004, we used a series of focus groups to develop some 'scripts' that we would go on to review in a second round of work, aiming to nail a narrative that would reveal 'Gordon Brown' – the whole man. With 'wave two' of the focus groups we spent some time discussing what makes a good leader. We generated a list of personal qualities: honesty, listening, open-minded, firm, good communicator, 'people person' as well as an approach to the job: focused on Britain (not abroad), keeps promises, accountable.

We used a 'written trigger session' where voters were asked to scribble down their first thoughts on both GB and Conservative leader, Michael Howard. For Michael Howard they wrote:

- Steely
- Stuffy
- Pompous
- Lawyer
- Older generation
- Suit and tie
- Bank manager
- Starchy
- Unapproachable
- Creepy
- Old guard
- Clever
- No new ideas
- Cuts
- Smarmy
  and of course
- Something of the night

And for Gordon Brown:

- Solid
- Trustworthy
- Down to earth
- Competent

- Not media friendly
- Miserable
- Dour
- Numbers man
- Family man
- Grumpy
- Clever
- Working class
- Taxes
- Gave back pay rise
- Pensioners (poor deal)

We also explored aspects of GB's back story. Little was known so we prompted using statements handwritten on cards:

> GB was a very bright student – he was accelerated at school and became Rector of Edinburgh University at twenty-one.

> GB is a keen sports fan who supports Raith Rovers.

> GB was a keen sportsman until he lost the sight of his eye in a rugby accident.

> GB does not use the Chancellor's grace and favour accommodation.

> GB is married to Sarah and has a baby son, John.

Voters responded to this information with interest. The academic information confirmed their belief that GB was clever, but was not very engaging beyond that. The personal sports story, the loss of an eye, was real news; no one knew about this, and all were interested. It spoke to GB's courage and resilience. Eschewing Dorneywood, the Chancellor's grace and favour country home, won a big thumbs-up and underpinned GB's contrast with TB, who was increasingly looking 'on the make'. Most marked was the reaction to GB's family situation. Some, but by no means all, already knew about the sad loss of his baby daughter Jennifer in 2002, which we had not prompted on; GB was insistent that he could not and would not discuss this. Understandably it evoked deep sympathy, especially amongst women voters, and was a rare glimpse at the man who was the politician.

SEARCHING FOR THE RIGHT WORDS

GB loved slogans and believed them to be imbued with a mystical power capable of persuading the most intransigent voter. No matter how many times he was told that words must be matched by actions if they were to persuade, still he searched tirelessly for the perfect summation of his position. 'So, which of the themes works best?'

It was probably the question he asked me most often over the years, and, despite my own protests, I had been sent out to test 'themes' or 'slogans' more often than I could count, especially in the run-up to major announcements or Budget speeches. 'So,' he would ask, 'which do they like best? Is it "Investing in Britain's Potential" or "Investing in Opportunity for All"?'

In meetings I would will inspiration to leap from my pages of notes. It was in vain. The truth was that the voters really didn't give a damn whether it was potential or opportunity. They weren't hostile to either thought, but they were pretty indifferent. I made this point as clearly as I could but too often failed to stall a lengthy debate about the relative merits of a dozen or so slogans that had been agonised over for several weeks. And in the end, the theme usually went unnoticed because the things that made a difference to people's lives, help with childcare, tax credits, new school buildings, shorter waits at A&E, mattered more.

By 2004, as disappointment had set in and people had become so much more cynical about politicians, this focus on presentation rather than substance really went against the grain and ran counter to GB's own greatest strength: the unspun politician who contrasted so sharply with TB's tarnished reputation.

I have in the cupboard of my office at home more than a dozen bulging folders labelled 'GB materials'. These mainly consist of slogans blown up to A3 size for testing in groups. Some of the folders are yellowed and dog eared and date back to those very early days in government. Some take us right up to just a few months ago. The astonishing thing about them is how similar they all are. GB had developed a positioning for himself in his early career and stuck to it doggedly, changing little as the years passed by.

Lines we tested most often were:

- Aspiration for all
- Opportunity for all
- Future opportunity for all
- Fairness for all
- For the many not the few
- Rights and responsibilities for all

The campaign slogan for Election 2010, the first to be chosen solely by GB, was an amalgamation of many of his favourite words: A Future

Fair for All. We had tested different 'fairness' approaches for years and had explored the very same line just about eighteen months before, then as a possible conference theme. Voters misunderstood, thinking that this might refer to some sort of futuristic theme park – a 'future fair'. Certainly their reaction to a sci-fi Disneyland was a lot more enthusiastic than when the line was explained as a political theme. I was not surprised to see that the election theme settled on was a recycled one, but I was surprised that it was flamboyantly launched in a way that reflected GB's faith in the ability of a slogan alone to change public opinion. Interestingly, the Conservatives followed suit a week or so later launching their own election theme: Ready for Change.

DEVELOPING GB'S FUTURE OFFER

One of the main challenges was to find the right expression of GB's beliefs and vision. This was going to be partly about developing GB's character: where he had come from, what had made his the man he was. It was partly about where he was going, his philosophy, and this was where the obsession with 'theme' came in. It was also going to be about how all this led to what he actually wanted to do: his offer to the British people. This had to provide tangible outcomes for the voter and relate both to what had been achieved so far and to GB's future aims. Starting to scope out GB's future offer, we explored a range of new policy ideas.

During his time in the Treasury GB had steadily built his team. The Council of Economic Advisors included policy experts drawn from a range of backgrounds: Shriti Vadera was a City specialist, Michael Jacobs an environmental expert. This team had grown and was informally supplemented by external advisors, like Wilf

Stevenson, who ran the think tank the Smith Institute, and co-ordinated by GB's own team of political special advisors: Sue Nye, GB's loyal and longstanding assistant; Spencer Livermore; and the two Eds, Balls and Miliband. This group was charged with coming up with policy ideas that developed GB's offer beyond his current Treasury brief.

Some related to reforming politics: an elected House of Lords, working with talented people from outside the Labour Party, and cleaning up politics, including banning MPs from outside work. As a contrast with Blair's approach, we also tested 'a less presidential approach to being PM'. We also explored ideas for education and skills: bringing back 'old-fashioned apprenticeships', scrapping tuition fees, and one-to-one tuition for every child. Some ideas we tested were about health, including a guaranteed maximum of three months on the NHS waiting lists. We also looked at mandatory National Service (community based, not military) for all teenagers.

Like the Pledge Card policies, these ideas were all tested in focus groups in different ways and refined. Some worked because they promised the change that people sought, while others made a specific and desirable policy promise. Some were attractive but lacked credibility – cutting NHS waiting times to a maximum of three months and one-to-one tuition for all seemed too good to be true. As we had discovered so often before less was more if you wanted your pledges to be believable.

A note that I drafted at the time set out the challenge as I saw it from the polling:

> There is now higher awareness of GB and a positive aura of strength and integrity dominates. However, he still needs to develop a fuller, more 3D image or his negative attributes come too easily to the fore.

> There is a need to differentiate and to address the jaded view of politicians. There is a yearning for a more value-based leadership than TB is thought to have provided, illustrated by a clear vision, rooted in visible change and expressed by an empathetic leader in touch with the things that matter to people.

The last package of materials that I tested for GB in this Project 3D phase was in June 2004. We had drafted a written statement that set out GB's background, beliefs and policies. It set out what was different and what he would change. It acknowledged the 'breakdown in trust between people and government' and pledged to 'make government more accountable and in touch by reviewing the role of the MP, ensuring that they spend more time in their constituencies by banning paid work outside Parliament'.

It said that 'we made a mistake by introducing tuition fees, and that this would be ended, replaced by a new graduate tax'. It observed that 'we need to give young people the discipline and responsibility gained after the Second World War by taking part in National Service' and that 'I will introduce a new community National Service – a gap year where all young people, not just the well off – can become involved in community projects at home ... learning new skills and a new sense of purpose'. I handed it to a focus group in St Albans. They read it in silence, then one women asked me: 'Is this real? Would he really do this?'

I said that I didn't know but this was the sort of thing that he'd been talking about.

'Then bring on Gordon Brown!' she exclaimed.

NO ROOM AT THE TOP

I was, of course, never party to the various conversations that took place between GB and TB. The work that I was conducting was contained within Team GB and strictly confidential; my guess would be that the people who knew about the rationale behind Project 3D would not run to double figures. However, by spring 2004, rumours were swirling around Westminster that TB's family had had enough and that TB himself was losing his appetite for the job. Although many in his camp were determined to boost his spirits, the media and voter reaction, especially to Iraq and its continuing problems, was grinding him down. Voters noticed how TB had aged, how physically exhausted he looked as the stress of the job took its toll. 'It's hard to believe that he's the same sparky young guy we voted for back at the beginning – he looks about a hundred years old,' Chris from Slough commented, adding uncharitably, 'not that I feel sorry for him – he sold us a pup.'

It was clear that talks were moving ahead fast. I was asked to accelerate my work on Project 3D – this was real now, we were preparing for leadership. Out of the blue Philip Gould, my old business partner, called up. Philip had steered a fairly wide berth from me for some time, knowing that my polling was often pitched against his in increasingly bitter internal battles between Chancellor and PM. I had dropped off Philip's party invitation list some years before and had heard nothing from him beyond a quick wave across the hall at Conference.

But suddenly Philip was on the phone or emailing me all the time. He took me for lunch in a smart Soho restaurant and proudly showed me his coat of arms (he had just received a peerage). As we ate, he explained how important it was that we all worked together now, that the next election would not be easy and that we needed the best of both teams to collaborate. He invited me to a series of regular meetings on polling and strategy held at Labour Party HQ and my PA and his spent hours scheduling these in. I was also invited to his summer party. He seemed genuinely disappointed when I told him I'd be away: 'You have to be there! Everyone has to be there! It's where everything will come together and start the healing process.'

Then, just as suddenly as they had started up, the calls stopped. I finally knew that our short-lived reconciliation was over when Greg Cook, the Labour Party's internal polling expert, emailed my office to say that the meetings in the run-up to the summer break had all been cancelled. At the end of the summer Greg emailed again to say that 'those meetings were no longer happening'. The invitations ceased completely.

Voters were all fired up and ready to go. Team GB was fired up and ready to go. However, TB had changed his mind, and decided to stay on to fight the 2005 general election. One of GB's team, six years later, reviewing what had passed and what went wrong, blames this period for burning GB out, sapping his energy and using up all his ideas: 'When the time finally came three years later, the locker was empty. He had nothing left to say. The problem was that he'd used everything up as heir apparent, especially in 2004. After that he had nothing left to give.'

11. Project Volvo – preparing to be leader (2)

I was feeling more nervous than usual about presenting focus group feedback to GB. It was a bright, sunny morning in January 2006 and we were in the usual Treasury meeting room, overlooking Horse Guards Parade and St James's Park. It was chosen because it housed a giant screen so that GB, with his poor eyesight, could easily see the power point presentation. Spencer Livermore was already there, helping me to set up. Sue Nye joined the meeting, escorting GB into the room.

I was particularly nervous because Sue and Spencer had urged me to be blunt and honest, especially about some of the more personal things. They were both concerned about GB's appearance. They urged me to tell him he should lose weight. Certainly it was true that the focus groups did identify his scruffy, tired-looking, out-of-condition appearance as a barrier to the top job. Maybe these things shouldn't matter but, it seemed, they did. I fell short of spelling this out overtly but did include some focus group quotes that referred to GB's appearance. The 'Action Plan' that I presented after the debrief talked about the need for a fitness programme and a wardrobe/hair makeover.

GB laughed nervously – who could blame him? 'Well, I do run, you know. . . it's just fitting it all in. Very difficult. . .' He knew very well that he needed to listen all this but, entirely understandably, that knowledge didn't make it any easier to do so. He sat mainly in silence, scribbling away, scarcely looking up. As the meeting had unfolded, and I had talked him though some of the more personal voter judgements, he had turned his body from the meeting room table so that, slightly awkwardly, he faced away from me and towards the window. I tried pausing as I spoke to make him look at me but he would just glance up and wave his hand impatiently for me to continue, then back down to his notes. I raised my eyebrows in a query to Spencer. He nodded to continue. I tried not to race to the end, and to take it calmly but, in truth, I was longing to get out of the room. So was GB who left without a word or a backward glance as I concluded.

WHAT KIND OF LEADER?

Soon after the 2005 election, things had started to move forward again. Our new work was code named Project Volvo. This name was chosen because in projective work in focus groups the car that GB was most like was a Volvo: solid, reliable, does what it says on the tin. It was not the most exciting of images, but as a contrast to voters' continuing irritation with TB it worked well enough. By early 2006 Project Volvo took off in earnest. We agreed a work plan which was presented to GB on 24 January. During that session I explained that the context we were working with was dominated by three things.

The first was the strong anti-political sentiment that had built relentlessly through the 2005 election, in which Labour had won with a similarly reduced turnout to 2001. The election had emphasised voters' boredom and disconnection from politics. The outcome had generated no enthusiasm whatsoever. Meanwhile, the view that all politicians were 'the same', and 'in it for themselves', as well as ineffectual, tainted everything.

Second was a more specific disillusionment with Labour. People had voted Labour begrudgingly as the lesser of two evils. As Sue from Birmingham had put it, 'OK, I put my cross there – I did it. But I don't feel good about it – I feel almost resentful, like I had no choice.'

Blair continued to personify all that was wrong both with Labour and with politicians in general. Women felt especially let down. To them he had promised so much and achieved so little. Even the 'family man' tag was wearing thin, as Cherie Blair's personal unpopularity had grown. The lavish holidays abroad, usually paid for by a political contact, became a metaphor for TB's out-of-touch behaviour and convinced people that he and his whole family were using office of Prime Minister for their own ends.

Thirdly, the Conservatives had found a new leader in David Cameron, who contrasted favourably with Michael Howard. He seemed different, certainly unusual for a Tory, and in fact not a typical politician at all. It was a fresh taste for the voters' jaded palates.

Project Volvo refreshed our knowledge of what voters sought in a leader. Consistent with the national mood, top of the list was now a leader who embraced 'a change of direction', a leader uncontaminated by the Westminster bug. Other ideals included connecting with people, being in touch with how we live our lives and understanding modern Britain. As always, being 'strong' was a necessity; he must have the courage of his convictions. Being 'trustworthy' had ridden to the top of the list too; voters talked about it now with a wistful longing.

He has to do what he says he'll do.

He needs to have balls.

I want someone who's down to earth – who knows what it's like.

They need to listen to what the people want.

Given voters' thirst for a fresh approach, Cameron's appeal was straightforward. His youth, energy and conversation about normal non-political issues made voters look twice. But, at this early stage in their acquaintance with him, they still had many questions to ask. Was he really different, and if so could he take the party with him? Was he really different or just pretending to be? The alcoholic drink he resembled was an alcopop: the nice taste masks the damage it can do. Was he too slick – was he insincere? People had noticed that he talked about liking the band the Killers and wore trendy Converse trainers – was this trying too hard for someone aspiring to be PM? Was he too posh – a classic Tory, born to wealth so that he didn't even think about it? The car he was like was a BMW: easy, effortless luxury. They also worried that he lacked substance. Cathy observed: 'His policy announcements say "what" but not "how". Is he just telling us what we want to hear?'

GB's image was the polar opposite. On the plus side he was strong and experienced, a serious father figure contrasting positively with both Blair and Cameron. He was reliable and steady – hence the Volvo car. Voters rightly believed him to be uninterested in the trappings of power; he would never go on holiday in Cliff Richard's villa in Barbados, as Tony Blair had done several times. His alcoholic drink was a simple pint of beer (or, given his Scottishness, a whisky). He was determined and driven and credited with having stood up to and tempered the very worst of Blair. Most of all, he was thought to have made a pretty good fist of being Chancellor, and without doubt had turned a Labour anxiety – a poor record of managing the economy – into a strength, as had been clearly demonstrated through the 2005 election campaign.

His perceived shortcomings stemmed from and were intimately connected to his strengths. Voters still saw him as a rather one-dimensional numbers man. His determination could tip over into being obsessive and his tendency to overload on jargon suggested he lacked the common communications touch that appeared to come so easily to both Blair and Cameron. Voters felt that he that he had few interests outside work – could he really be in touch with them and their lives if he never left Westminster?

And his untidy appearance was off-putting. Would he really be able to represent Britain abroad? Years of high pressure living in the Treasury hothouse had taken its toll and the once sporty GB now looked distinctly jowly and tired. This added to the sense that he was both old and old fashioned. Given that number one on the voters' wish-list was 'embrace change' there were serious worries that he would be looking backwards not forwards.

Project Volvo went on to set three objectives:

1. Address the '3D' problem
2. Build GB's strengths
3. Show GB to be connected and listening.

The first was about demonstrating GB's 'hinterland'. It was a Westminster Village cliché that people who knew Gordon well found him to be warm and witty. This was the personality that we had seen showcased so effectively on daytime TV. Those interviews had always been an exception – now they needed to become the priority, as did the personal 'tie off' visits that GB had rarely done up till now. I also suggested that it might be very effective to try to think himself into daytime TV mode even if the interviewer was Jeremy Paxman or John Humphrys. This, I felt, was what Blair and Cameron both succeeded in doing instinctively. It meant using everyday language, examples of real people not statistics, cutting out jargon and tub thumping. It proved easier said than done.

We also needed to continue the work started by Project Volvo on GB's 'back story'. GB, admirably in my view, was very reluctant to talk about his children. At that point Sarah preferred to stay out of the limelight. I actually tested a very effective explanation of this, which contrasted well with DC's photo opportunity approach. Voters were very sympathetic and this would later become a line in a conference speech – 'my children are people, not props'. He was, however, prepared to talk about his parents: he had grown up with a Presbyterian minister for a father and a family commitment to public service that had shaped him. While Westminster knew all this, voters didn't, and it gave them a valuable insight into his values.

Perceptions of GB's strength was his major advantage. Again, knowing more about his back story helped to reinforce this, in particular that formative experience from his youth, already explored with voters in Project 3D: a rugby accident that cost him the sight in one eye. This incident helped to explain what had made GB the man he was: it spoke to his courage and resilience. Our task would be to tell these stories through a new media strategy.

We also discussed finding new ways to connect with voters. GB was determined to find his own 'trademarked' approach to this. He had been impressed by TB's 'masochism strategy' in 2005, where, to vent the voters' spleen, TB was exposed to a series of unscripted 'meet the audience Q and A sessions' so people could challenge him however they chose.

I devised a tailor-made approach which grew out of the Citizens' Jury model that my business, Opinion Leader Research, had pioneered. This involved bringing together citizens and politicians for open collaborative sessions. Citizens would be given information, have the chance to quiz policy makers and deliberate in small groups, not unlike a focus group. GB took to this like a duck to water. We ran sessions on family policy, health and budget priorities, with voters discussing the issues in round-table discussions, while GB moved from table to table hearing people's views. He would later sum up what he had heard, delighting participants by namechecking them and pledging to respond to what he had heard. We took to posting someone behind him to scribble notes of the conversations so he could use the anecdotes in his summing up. GB loved the process we had created – it was a way of managing those personal interactions that he often found difficult.

CONDITION OF BRITAIN

Most important of all, though, was the challenge of 'newness'. I characterised this as the need to find New, New Labour. Speaking at a Fabian Society conference around the same time I reiterated Chris Powell's mantra that the only two election slogans were 'Steady as we go' or 'Time for a change'. The whole country felt it was time for a change – to succeed, Labour had to be that change.

That change had to be the one that people wanted to see, however. To find that out, we felt that we needed to get a really in-depth view of voters' thoughts on 'the condition of Britain'.

So during summer 2006 I took advantage of the long break to conduct a series of focus groups in Gillingham, Leamington Spa, the Wirral and Wolverhampton. By now, James Morris, a bright young researcher who had worked at the ad agency TBWA conducting dozens of focus groups through the 2005 general election, had joined me. We listened to voters with a range of different voting backgrounds: some who had voted Labour in '97 and '01; some who had abandoned us either for the Conservatives or the Lib Dems in 2005 (we defined these as 'quitters'); and some who we described as 'stickers', who had continued to vote Labour.

It was just over a month since the 7 July terror plot had shaken London with bombings on the Underground and a bus, killing fifty-two people and injuring more than 700. People felt that we were a nation under threat. At the same time, national pride was given a boost by London winning the 2012 Olympic bid.

It was against this febrile background that we asked voters to tell us about 'Britain today'. We began each session by breaking each group up into pairs and giving each pair a folder of magazines and newspapers, glue sticks and pens. Everyone was asked to make collages representing the best and worst of Britain today. Voters presented back to us a striking and depressing litany of negatives: they had chosen pictures of mosques, armed police, dawn raids etc. We were struck yet again how important immigration was to the voter – yet, as outlined in Chapter 7, often ignored by politicians.

The terrorists had heightened the anger, but were essentially feeding an already ingrained concern. This was now framing voter reaction to almost everything. It was not going to go away.

RESPONDING TO THE MOOD

Working with these groups of voters we developed some overarching themes that would respond to the hostile national mood and which GB could also consider for his personal positioning. We developed statements to explore these themes to further focus groups:

- *Responsibility.* We need to take responsibility for our lives and our country. We must all take responsibility for the kind of country that we want to live in and the sorts of lives that we want to lead. We can't have rights without responsibilities.
- *Fairness.* Government should be about fairness. Britain remains an unfair country and we need to change. Too often the balance is tipped in favour of a privileged few and against people who lack the wealth or influence to make their voice heard.
- *Community.* People feel isolated from each other, we need to bring them back together. People do not want to live their lives as isolated individuals. We are at home in families, in neighbourhoods and communities. Britain needs to regain this sense of society.
- *British pride.* Britain has a history to be proud of and a future to look forward to. Working together, we can make sure that Britain's economy remains strong, that our streets are safe and that our schools and hospitals become the envy of the world.
- *Responsiveness/accountability.* Government only works if it works with the people. Government has to recognise its limitations and your strengths. Government needs to direct less and empower more, working with people more to solve the problems we all face.

This was an iterative process. We would develop ideas with one group then test them in the next. The themes above evolved over a period of time and all worked relatively well. Most successful were 'responsiveness/accountability', being seen as distinctive, although needing to move beyond process to outline some clear benefits for voters 'Community' was also highly resonant, if a bit nostalgic. 'Responsibility' did well too as it obliquely addressed voters' concern about free riders. 'Fairness' was true to Labour's roots but lacking in distinctiveness. 'British pride' had them cheering in the aisles although it needed strong support to have credibility.

We concluded that the appetite for change was stronger than ever: change both in terms of moving on from TB's now tired premiership as well as change for the whole country. Cameron, after a good start, was now struggling to connect with Middle England, who were bemused by his attempts to reposition the party by taking on the environment and softening the Conservatives' approach to crime, after his 'hug a hoodie' speech in July 2006. It seemed that there was openness towards GB but still no real enthusiasm. The vision statements worked well but lacked a binding connection to his personal motivations, and this needed to be addressed. The vision then needed to be married together with policies that reflected it.

This work was debriefed to Team GB in September '06, stressing that we now needed to urgently tackle GB's personal programme, refining the vision and policy offer and keeping the voter connection open with our Citizens' Jury programme and with new quantitative polling. Following that, GB sent me his latest draft speech for Conference 2006, encapsulating his ideas on how to incorporate this thinking. He had developed a new theme about 'the British way of life' and was also experimenting with an idea that Ed Miliband had come up with: 'the good society'.

I replied in an email, explaining that the 'British Way of Life' theme was working really well and the phrase tested positively as it connected to something that people felt passionate about and addressed the main areas of fairness, duty to contribute, respect for others and wanting children to get on. I pointed out that it might perhaps say more about discipline and the need for greater respect for the law, for teachers and for parents. I also felt that he should say more about pride in being British (this always worked well), British inventiveness and creativity, and the British spirit of adventure.

Most importantly, I felt that the speech dwelt too much on process, rather than on the benefit – what that change will deliver to people – so we needed to set out more clearly what the desired outcome was: for example streets you can walk down at night, schools where teachers are free to teach, communities that work together and help each other and so on. The speech also needed some practical examples of the kind of good society that GB was referring to: for instance a community group that turned a disused building into a youth centre.

I pointed out that, stylistically, the speech read very dryly with lots of stats. I reminded him that these were a big turn-off and suggested that he redraft it with more personal examples, talking more about things that people will recognise, such as kids who used to join the Cubs or Scouts now joining MySpace communities. This would have the effect of making it less abstract. I also reminded him of the campaign's emphasis on listening and suggested that the speech should reflect this more strongly.

In conclusion I stated the need to connect to the consensus view, that most people want to try to play by the rules. GB needed to show that he understood what the public felt was right and wrong about Britain today, and that he shared their views and would do something about it.

The plan was agreed but Team GB were already distracted as the TB/GB saga was about to take a new turn.

A PARTY AT WAR AGAIN

As everyone else returned to the routine of their lives after their summer breaks – kids back to school, mums and dads back to work – MPs, as usual, had time on their hands in the run-up to the party season. The House of Commons would not reopen for weeks. The political season kicked off in earnest when an article from Alan Milburn proclaiming TB's right to go 'on and on' tipped the Brown team over the edge. A few days later, following a furtive curry dinner and plotting meetings disguised as social calls, a couple of junior ministers resigned and group of GB-sympathising MPs finally bit the bullet and sent a letter demanding that TB should quit. All hell broke out in the Westminster Village. The media wrote about nothing else and the entire political community was transfixed by Labour's internal squabbling.

If this was not what the voters wanted to read about or watch on their TVs then it was too bad, for they had little choice. Against the backdrop of extreme voter discontentment it was potentially toxic. Focus groups conducted in the middle of September certainly picked up some frustration with Labour for looking inwards and bickering amongst themselves rather than following through on the voters' issues. They had picked up more of the soap opera than usual (unsurprising as the story had dominated the media for days). However, Labour's share had held up, and even improved a little. Most had not changed their views of TB. They wanted him to go and go soon – although there was some discomfort at a forced exit of the kind endured by Mrs Thatcher.

It was a mixed picture for GB. Over the previous weeks there had been more positive signs that people felt they knew him better and that he was the front runner for the job because of his track record and stature. In voters' minds, however, he was clearly implicated in the plotting, and published polling at the time showed his favourability falling; the plotting threatened to undermine the progress that we had made. Crucially, what the public would be least inclined to forgive was focusing inwards at a time when they felt the country was in crisis and politicians should be addressing that. We had taken our eye off the ball, but the crisis had brought the TB/GB confrontation to a head. While he did not confirm a date, to the fury of the Brownites, TB announced his departure, saying that the Conference speech he would make on 26 September 2006 was to be his last.

12. Transition to PM

I WILL TRY MY UTMOST

'I am convinced that there is no weakness in Britain today that cannot be overcome by the strength of the British people...' Gordon Brown paused, looking around at the army of photographers and TV cameras. There was a momentary hesitation. Sarah looked on. He continued: 'On this day I remember words that have stayed with me since my childhood and which matter a great deal to me today. My school motto: I will try my utmost. This is my promise to all the people of Britain. And now let the work of change begin.'

And with that, he took Sarah's hand, turned around and walked into No. 10. Watching at home I began to cry.

In December 2006, just six months earlier, James Morris and I had conducted a review of the mountain of polling data which had been assembled over the years with a sole objective in mind: GB taking over from TB as Prime Minister. Team GB always referred to this phase as 'the Transition'. The core team remained constant throughout the period: Spencer, the two Eds, Douglas Alexander and Sue Nye at its heart. I was meeting with GB and different combinations of this team several times a week by now. The review that James and I prepared was to become a blueprint to help develop strategy and set goals for the coming months. We planned to judge all activity against agreed targets and, having established a benchmark, work to improve on it as the months took us closer to a possible contest and ultimately towards the Transition ...

Working closely with Spencer, now GB's chief of strategy, we commissioned fresh quantitative polling evidence and conducted new focus groups to identify GB's scores on 'leader' qualities with the public and understand how these differentiated him from David Cameron. GB beat Cameron hands down on 'substance and strength' issues. His positive attributes were his experience, his competent management of the economy and being a strong politician. These were powerful advantages, the more so because they mirrored David Cameron's weakest traits. GB was 'competent' and 'tough' while Cameron was 'lightweight' and 'will say anything to get votes'.

However, our most recent polling also told us that GB's poorest scores were 'listening to voters', 'understanding what ordinary life is like' and, most worrying, meeting a broader desire for change: 'setting the country in a better direction'. Despite the best efforts of Projects 3D and Volvo, he remained a somewhat aloof figure; this was something that Team GB needed to address. He needed to step out of the constraints of being Chancellor.

Working flat out on this now were the office-based team: primarily Sue and Spencer, with whom I interacted on a daily basis, then the extended family of the two Eds and Douglas all attending regular meetings, fitting them in with their own political and ministerial commitments. Ed B. chaired a weekly meeting which all attended. We brainstormed ideas to get GB out and about more, connecting with the people he met. Sue masterminded a programme of public meetings around the country, which dovetailed with the listening programme that I had been working on. We all worked hard to make GB's language more conversational. Scripts for events would be emailed between us several times a day.

GB had always been hungry for voter feedback; now he was ravenous. He would quiz me for more detail: When they say this, what exactly do they mean? Would this or that be the right way to address that concern? What would they do if we suggested this? He worked even more intensely, making ever greater demands on the team; emails and phone calls would arrive at all times of the day or night. The competition for the strangest location to take a call from GB was heating up: I talked to him in the corridor leading to the loos in a Chinese restaurant, shouting over the bustle at a school parents' evening, even in the pet food section of my local Sainsbury's. I once explained, without divulging my whereabouts (Topshop on a Saturday morning waiting as my daughter tried on jeans), that I hadn't seen his latest email as I wouldn't have internet access for the next hour or so. Undeterred he replied, 'So what's your fax number then?'

The most difficult challenge we faced was the voters' appetite for change. The price GB paid for his experience was to be closely associated with the past decade, even if in the public eye he owned the greatest successes of that period. We had tested a number of ways of refreshing the Labour Party: *new* New Labour. While this was an excellent shorthand for the Westminster Village, voters had been very clear indeed: they were looking for a change that they could see. It had to be about them not about us. This meant acknowledging what they felt had gone wrong. It also meant taking it on the chin for mistakes made.

I tested various formulations for this. One, written by GB himself, was slightly clumsy but had enough contrition to work: 'where we have gone wrong – and I will not hesitate to accept that – we need a new direction', as did 'we must learn from what we got wrong as well as what we got right'. But one of the dilemmas here was that GB was receiving conflicting advice. The inner circle, the Eds, Douglas, Spencer and I, were strongly of the view that he should distance himself from some aspects of New Labour; meanwhile he was also receiving advice from TB and his inner circle that warned against this. It was a tension that GB struggled to resolve.

I explored a number of 'vision' statements in focus groups. These had been developed with voters' views from our work during summer '06 and discussed with Team GB and GB himself. Many of the inputs were hammered out on GB's own PC and circulated during his dawn email round. The strongest was about 'defending the British way of life', reflecting people's antagonism towards immigration and the threat they believed it posed to their lives and livelihoods.

Weary of 'warm words', voters tended to reject all political utterances as empty promises unless they were supported by a tangible policy pledge. The 'British way of life' statement was supported by a proposal that everybody who wanted to live in the UK should have an obligation to learn English. Statements underpinning GB's commitment to the NHS also worked well, as did a promise to 'reclaim the streets with police spending less time on paper work and more time on the streets'. Returning to 'old fashioned' apprenticeships was a winner, too.

As 2007 dawned the pressure grew. Most voters were vociferous that the country's direction was wrong and blamed the government for failing to sort out anti-social behaviour, immigration and problems with the NHS. The economy continued to be the only real positive – women talked as enthusiastically as ever about child tax credits and financial help with childcare. This all pointed to the opportunity that the forthcoming Budget might present for GB to showcase his own achievements.

JUST MORE OF THE SAME

It seemed that the more that Team GB were determined to make the 2007 Budget a springboard for his leadership bid, the more the public were determined to presume that it would be 'more of the same'.

Putting a toe in the water with focus groups in February, I started by asking people what they thought about Budgets in general. Despite their respect for GB, they were cynical and knowing.

They're all the same!

Give with one hand, take with the other.

They make some big announcement then when you get the small print you realise that they've pulled the wool over your eyes.

It was very hard to get voters to take seriously that this Budget might be different. I tried another tack: what would they most like to see in the Budget? The answer was unequivocal: sort out inheritance tax.

Over the years I had seen that people become more and more sceptical about talk of tax cuts. It would be dismissed out of hand as 'politicians' speak'. Somehow, whatever happened, they did not expect to see the money themselves, whatever the headline promised. They were also aware that tax cuts come with a price, and, as our previous work on the NI rise for the NHS had showed, were not averse to paying provided they felt they were seeing a benefit.

Inheritance tax was different, though. Over the past few years its mentions in focus groups were becoming more frequent and more intense. Thanks in part to a sustained campaign in the media, with the *Daily Mail* calling it a 'death tax' which would 'hit ten million families', middle ground voters now felt truly aggrieved. I believe that the reason why this particular tax took on such extraordinary prominence was closely related to the symbolic importance of the home. I first saw this with the success of Mrs Thatcher's council house sales policy, and now, many first-generation property owners were set to make their children first-generation wealth inheritors. They and their (now adult) children were outraged that this opportunity might be diminished by what they saw as a punitive and unfair tax on their family's achievement. This was not 'well-to-do greed' but outraged indignation from people who felt that 'bettering themselves' in this way had been a struggle.

> My mum's paid taxes all her life. She's worked hard for that house. Why should we pay again? Inheritance tax means paying again for something you've already paid for!

Over the weeks the Budget package was refined. It was branded as 'the Family Budget' and the key measures I tested included:

- Raise child benefit and child tax credit by £30 per week
- Double the point at which inheritance tax is paid so that married couples could pass on up to £600, 000
- Cut income tax by 2p in the pound
- Take 400,000 pensioners out of tax.

This might be paid for by a mix of:

- Increasing duties on petrol, alcohol and air passenger tax
- Changes to corporation tax
- Removing the 10p rate of tax on the first £2,090, which at the time ensured that the least well off had some income at a lower rate of tax.

The message from the focus groups was straightforward. The stand-out policies were inheritance tax, child tax credit and pensioners out of tax, with inheritance tax as the most motivating by a long way. If GB had been able to do only one thing it should have been inheritance tax, as this suggested a government on the side of the 'squeezed middle', listening to them in a way that no other policy did.

My presentation on 8 March said, 'The inheritance tax measure is the high point, and the policy that differentiates this Budget'. The sum spared had to be big enough to cover property prices for people living in London and the south east. £600,000 achieved that.

By contrast, the proposed 2p income tax drop was met with a sneer. It seemed too good to be true and the starting point was 'where's the catch?'. People found it hard to see what a 2p reduction might mean to their weekly budget. They suspected not very much. Meanwhile they did not have to look very hard for the catch. Removing the 10p tax rate immediately set off warning bells. It felt like penalising the least well off, and some better-off voters also questioned whether it would remove an incentive to work, thus actually costing more.

All this was fed back to team GB. Spencer attended many of the groups, and I or my colleague James Morris would write a note the next day, then come in and present findings to GB once or twice a week. The Budget took shape and we reviewed drafts for the speech, press releases and Budget broadcast.

On Budget day I sat in my office with James and watched the speech on the TV. As GB sat down we turned to each other open mouthed. 'What happened? Where was inheritance tax? Had all our advice been ignored? Why?'

I sent a text message to Spencer. It was some hours before his reply came through. 'We lost the argument, I'm afraid.' When I talked to him almost three years later he identified this as one of his biggest regrets. It was a rare example from that period of GB ignoring focus group feedback. 'He was persuaded by others. . .' Spencer shrugged sadly.

The Budget received an ecstatic reception in the Westminster Village. Will Hutton described the income tax cut as a 'master stroke' and went on effusively, 'This allows Prime Minister Brown to be the tax-cutting Prime Minister as well as prudent, investor in public services, generator of jobs, supporter of wealth generation, scourge of poverty and friend of science', while the *Guardian*'s Larry Elliot raved, 'It was a good way for Gordon Brown to hang up his boots. . .like Alan Shearer thundering home a last minute goal in his final match at St James' sPark.'

The reaction from voters, however, told a very different story. I went to Ruislip six days later on 27 March. The most encouraging news I could report back was 'The Budget has had a fairly neutral effect on floating voters'. Most felt that they would not be any worse off, but would also be no better. . . it was a grudging 'could have been worse' feeling:

In the end it was a non-event from my point of view.

The difference is only pennies when you add it all up.

Much more worrying, however, was that voters felt they could see the method. There was a strong sense that the Budget had been presented dishonestly, being positioned as one thing then revealed to be another when you read the small print:

All spin.

He dressed it up then minute by minute it unravelled.

As I reported in the note I prepared the following day, 'this referred mostly to the 2p/10p switch, and the concerns that people had expressed in pre-Budget groups, especially for lower-paid workers, were confirmed'. I went on to point out two other problems that voters inferred from what they had seen:

Firstly that GB does not have any fresh ideas and so has to resort to sleight of hand to create a story, and worse, that GB, who is universally thought to be very clever, thinks the electorate are stupid. 'He's a cute customer, very shrewd and canny – and if you were dumb enough just to believe the headlines he'd have fooled you.'

This was the tenth Budget that I had worked on for GB. It was the most important, but, unfortunately, the least effective. It produced GB's first ever negative rating in the job of Chancellor: more people thought he was doing badly than well. The problem was that the electorate were not that dumb.

CHANGE – OF A SORT

In tandem with the final Budget, again working with Spencer, we had begun what we called 'Project Firth', working with an ad agency to develop materials for GB's leadership contest. We developed a website, lines and a 'corporate look' which was styled mimicking the 'grown up' image of Hillary Clinton's campaign website.

We also began testing more detailed messages looking at vocabulary and GB's beloved 'slogans', supported by policy initiatives. The feedback on him remained consistent: strength was his major asset, while his negatives included being dour and one dimensional, not listening enough and, on the back of the Budget, there were now worries about sleight of hand with taxes.

> Giving it with a big fanfare, then taking more through the back door.

Most of all, though, voters were concerned that he was too associated with the past and would not bring about the change that they craved. GB understood the need for change but was very anxious about blatantly distancing himself from TB. This was partly because he was somewhat persuaded by TB and others telling him that rehabilitating the New Labour legacy was the only way forward. It was also partly because he feared a spin backlash from TB's colleagues if he appeared to be critical.

The slightly ham-fisted compromise was to construct a change story that drew on external reasons for change: we showed groups a statement that talked about 'changing to meet the new challenges that are different from the challenges of ten years ago', citing examples of new external threats that demanded change, such as terrorism, global economics and climate change. Although the concepts were abstract, this was all broadly acknowledged in focus groups.

We then went on to offer a solution with a statement that said 'We will change where we need to'. It read:

Where we have kept to the principles of 1997 things have worked:

- For the many not the few
- Opportunity and security for all
- Long-termism
- On people's side

Where we have gone wrong – and I will not hesitate to accept that – we need a new direction.

The first part of the statement was the least successful – voters were mystified by what the '97 principles might be, the coded allusion to New Labour totally lost on them. In any event they were very clear that they wanted to move forward and had little sentimental affection for 1997. However, the idea of GB apologising was well received, but as it stood the statement as tested begged more questions than it answered. Voters wanted the apology to get specific: about Iraq, about immigration, about slow public service delivery, about broken politics. The fudge was unlikely to hold up for very long.

The most powerful statements we tested were headed 'judge me by results' then listed some very specific pledges, all time limited, for example 'within two months I will bring forward my proposals for affordable housing'. This format held a powerful appeal as long as the pledges were attractive. One pledge – to bring about an inquiry on Iraq – was liked by GB as it was something the Westminster

Village were campaigning for, yet voters rejected it as 'a waste of time and money' and assumed that any inquiry would be a whitewash however it was established.

Another popular statement was headed 'Action not image' and sought to reinforce GB's 'unspun' reputation. It read: 'I offer myself as a candidate not because I seek fame or celebrity or headlines but because I can make a difference.' This was really well received and gave GB the opportunity to make a broader point about politics of substance.

At the beginning of April David Miliband, widely predicted to be the main contender to GB, announced that he would not stand. On 11 May GB announced his own candidature, setting out his positioning: 'I have never believed that presentation should be a substitute for policy.' This was just as well, as the presentation that day looked terrifyingly amateurish, with GB's face obscured by an autocue screen.

One week later, in a triumph of backroom politics, Team GB were able to announce that he had reached 313 nominations – the figure that meant no other candidate could beat him. Six weeks later, on 27 June, GB stood outside No. 10 promising to 'try my utmost'.

THE HONEYMOON

Many of GB's carefully made plans for the first 100 days of his premiership went awry. First terrorist bombs in London and Glasgow, then flooding in the south east and the Midlands, followed by a new outbreak of foot-and-mouth, consumed all the time and energy he had, and more. Yet the series of crises played to his strengths as 'a serious man for serious times', and Labour got the 'Brown bounce' poll boost that it had been hoping for.

A sunny morning in July found me driving up to Chequers to attend a special meeting of the new Cabinet. It was the first time that most of us had been there and the grand house buzzed with excited chatter. Sarah had already slipped into her new role as first lady and showed small groups of us around before the meeting began, pointing out Oliver Cromwell's sword over the fireplace as well as the tiny room where her small sons John and Fraser sat watching cartoon DVDs. I had prepared an extensive presentation using the most recent polling data. Apart from catching the heel of my shoe on the rug as I walked in to present and almost flying headfirst at the grand oak table where the Cabinet sat expectantly, all went smoothly.

In his successful book *The End of the Party*, journalist Andrew Rawnsley tells how one minister later described my briefing as 'saccharine'. This made me smile because I can honestly say that, on that occasion, I held back on the positives, partly at GB's own insistence. Briefly he was enjoying the euphoric voter reaction that TB had enjoyed for months. Although 'enjoy' was not quite the right description. He watched the presentation, even in this toned-down state, grimacing with embarrassment. Afterwards each Cabinet minister commented in turn. Their response could not have been warmer.

The private polling was showing an 8 per cent lead, and the 'poll of polls', calculated by taking an average of all published polls over the period, gave Labour its highest score since Cameron took over. Labour had pulled ahead on every policy area except immigration, and the poll lead increased still more if GB's name was mentioned in the question as well as the party name. GB's personal scores were high on all positive attributes, especially on 'experienced and strong', and ahead of Cameron on every attribute except 'likeable', where Cameron still enjoyed a small lead. Crucially, the main message driving the shift of opinion was 'change'. This was quite an achievement and exactly the message that the voters had craved.

I had spared the Cabinet (at GB's pleading) information from a recent analysis that James and I, now joined by Ben Shimshon (a bright think tank researcher who had recently become part of the team), had put together, contrasting views of GB and DC over many focus groups. We had added up all the comments that people had made about the two men over the past few weeks and could see that while GB led on leadership qualities, DC led on 'style and appearance'. Both were 'family men', but DC was 'posh' while GB could be bland or boring. Most tellingly, GB was strong, serious, a safe pair of hands, principled and intelligent, while DC was inexperienced, unimpressive and weak.

Using our 'animal' projective tests, GB was a bear, dog, lion or dolphin while DC was a cat, an antelope, a spider or a shark. We also asked 'If DC/GB were not a politician, what career could you imagine him pursuing?' GB was seen as a headmaster, accountant, or barrister. DC was seen as a salesman, estate agent, or working for Daddy's business.

On 19 July Labour faced a by-election in Ealing Southall, London. The Conservatives fancied their chances and put a lot of energy into the campaign. This was with good reason: governments don't tend to win by-elections mid term, especially mid term of a third term. David Cameron visited the constituency to support Tony Lit, his hand-picked candidate, no fewer than five times. He even put his name on the ballot paper: this was not just the Conservative Party, it was 'David Cameron's Conservative Party'. Not only did he fail to dislodge Labour, he even failed to dislodge the Lib Dems from second place. Reviewing the campaign in the *Sunday Times* the following weekend I wrote:

What went wrong? The Tories' Ealing campaign lost out because it misjudged the mood. It offered showbiz and razzmatazz when Britain is feeling sober and reflective. It was style without substance and the style set the wrong tone . . . slick communications skills may have been enough to put Cameron on the map a year ago but the electorate has moved on and such slickness is simply not enough now.

NOT THE ELECTION

Spencer called me the evening that I returned from my family holiday at the end of August. 'I've been thinking more about the idea of an early election,' he said. 'What do you think?'

'How early? This autumn rather than next year?'

'That's what I'm thinking,' he confirmed.

I had also thought about this over the summer. Labour's, and GB's, poll ratings had continued to rise. But I was worried by some analysis that Ben Shimshon had worked on, looking at the fate of other 'transitional' Prime Ministers. It seemed that all enjoyed a poll bounce of varying proportions. It also seemed that three months into the job tended to be as good as it got.

Two weeks later, mid-September 2007, found me on a business trip to Washington DC for Chime, the company who owned the group of six businesses that I was responsible for in my 'day job'. I had agreed that I would meet with possible US advisors for Labour while there. I met with several top pollsters and strategists, some recommended by Philip Gould, some through other contacts. My preferred partner was Pete Brodnitz, introduced through a Chime colleague, whose business was the Benenson Strategy Group, and whose colleague Joel Benenson was polling for a little-known Democrat hopeful, Barack Obama. Very early one morning, I received a call from Spencer. Things were moving fast back in London. Pragmatically, Stan Greenberg would be the best option. He already knew the UK scene well, as he had been TB's pollster before being replaced by Mark Penn. I hastily made an appointment with Stan's office and briefed him the following morning.

Stan came over to the UK the next week, and it was really helpful to have his experience to draw upon. As well as being plunged into preparing GB's conference speech – his first as leader and therefore even more important than usual – we began a round of polling in those key marginals that Labour would have to retain in order to win a fourth term.

Published polling continued to look positive as we made our way to Bournemouth for GB's first conference. The press were speculating about an autumn election. I boarded the crowded train on the Sunday morning and everywhere I went it was the same question: 'Are we on for October?' I was non-committal, of course, but it was hard to resist being swept along by the febrile mood.

The results from the private polling that Stan, James and I had worked on came in halfway through Conference and the day after GB's speech, which had been well received, with the *Mail*'s Benedict Brogan headlining his announcement of a 'return to British values'. That night pollsters Yougov had a poll for *Channel 4 News* showing Labour to have a 11 per cent lead and expectations were high.

We assembled in the early evening in the office in GB's hotel suite. Bob Shrum, the US advisor, Sue Nye, Ed Miliband, Douglas Alexander and Spencer were there. GB looked exhausted and was short tempered with Stan's slightly hesitant delivery of the findings. The atmosphere was highly charged. The tension in the room was only relieved when John, GB's young son, padded through the room in his pyjamas bringing his dad a bowl of chocolate ice-cream.

The poll did not predict the landslide that GB had hoped for. The marginal seats that we had sampled were not reporting a uniform swing. Labour had made some headway in Scotland, and in clusters of Lab/Lib Dem seats lost in 2005 due to voter reaction to Iraq. But the real disappointment was a group of critical marginal seats that Stan called the 'South East Middle Class'. There the Conservatives boasted a worrying lead of 5 per cent. GB quizzed Stan about this group: did the expression 'middle class' mean that these were 'upmarket' people who would never vote Labour anyway?

It did not. In fact this group were swing voters in the most important southern marginal seats. 'Middle class' meant middle ground. They were the seats that had featured in the 'Southern Discomfort' research back in '92. They were seats we needed to win for overall electoral success. GB, growing more irritable by the minute, repeatedly requested clarification, as if this would magically change the findings. Stan and I agreed to go away and run further polling and to conduct some intensive focus group work amongst this critical voter group to see what was going on. As Team GB dispersed at the end of Conference the early excitement had been replaced by anxiety.

The following week was the Conservative Party conference. On the Monday George Osborne made his speech pledging to raise the inheritance tax threshold to £1 million. David Cameron made his 'no notes' conference speech two days later. James, Ben and I were in the field every evening, in a variety of 'South East Middle Class' locations (now renamed 'Frontline Marginals': these after all were people whose views mattered most). The shift that we saw in voter attitude reminded me of the shift I had witnessed during my very first Labour focus groups all those years ago before and after Neil Kinnock's 'expulsion of the Militants' conference speech. Suddenly the Conservatives had momentum and it was Labour left looking tired and old. A written trigger word exercise for the Conservatives revealed:

- Got good ideas
- New policies
- New direction
- New blood
- Ambitious
- More interesting
- Hopeful
- On the up
- Aiming for Middle England
- Go-getting
- Modern

The inheritance tax promise was at the heart of this transformation. With powerful symbolism it had spoken to these voters, saying that the Conservatives really listened and understood, just as it had promised to do for Labour, and for GB's Budget, back in March.

Spencer was not able to come along to the last set of groups on the Thursday evening. I caught up with James to ensure that his findings were consistent with mine. They were. They were grim. I then called Spencer who listened in silence. A few minutes later my phone rang again. This time it was Ed Balls. I ran through the same notes. Finally, some twenty minutes afterwards, GB called. Did they go for the inheritance tax promise? Was I sure they were not too 'middle class' to vote Labour? Were they really our target voters? How would they vote? I ran through the voting intention question I always asked at the end of every group: 'If there were an election tomorrow how would you vote?' Of eight women six were Conservative, one Labour, one undecided. The men were five Conservative, two Labour, one undecided. I stressed the usual health warning attached to focus groups: this is a small sample, attitudes are volatile. But I also said that if Stan's findings, due in overnight, reflected this then the situation had deteriorated since the week before in Bournemouth.

I met Stan at his flat in Shepherd Market at eight the following morning. Stan's fantastic team in the US had worked into the night to process the data as it came in. Stan was purse lipped as he typed in the final numbers to his presentation. I added the toplines for the focus groups. We were all pale faced and nervy. Although within the margin of error, it was psychologically important that the front line marginals had shifted from a small deficit to a small lead. Certainly based on this date we could predict a Labour win – but the indications were for a win with a smaller majority than Labour currently held – we would lose seats in significant numbers. And the focus groups, so often ahead of the curve as views changed, suggested the momentum was against us.

We hailed a cab to Downing Street and assembled in a small room at the front of the building. Team GB seemed to attend the meeting in shifts, and Stan and I kept starting the presentation again or recapping on the earlier points as new audience members arrived. No one chaired or owned the meeting. GB himself arrived late, tired and monosyllabic. Impatiently, he waved Stan on to the conclusions. There was a repeat of the discussion that we had had in Bournemouth the week before, although by this time those in favour of the early poll were quieter than those arguing against.

Bob Shrum told GB that he'd spoken the night before to 'Teddy' (Kennedy): his message to GB was 'What would I have given to get three years in office? What could I have done?' This inspiring thought did not seem to fill GB with hope. He pushed his chair away from the table, roughly grabbed his papers and left to attend a meeting with an overseas visitor. The discussion continued, the tone gloomy now. I left and returned to my office.

The following day I awaited news from Spencer. Late morning I received a text message: 'Complete carnage'.

13. The honeymoon is over

A LONG TIME IN POLITICS

I usually challenge the premise that a week is a long time in politics. Voters, unlike some journalists, tend not to flip-flop and change their minds very quickly. They are measured and thoughtful and make their judgements after weighing up what they see over a period of time. But back in autumn 2007 in the roller-coaster ride of the election that never was, it really did seem as though attitudes had shifted in the space of a week. By 4 October ICM showed Labour's lead fall away, with the parties neck and neck on 38 per cent each. A week later the Tories had moved into a 7 per cent lead at 43 per cent, compared with Labour's 36 per cent. 'Gordon Brown hit by Tory poll surge,' bayed the *Telegraph*.

Swing voters in Middlesex were in very gloomy mode in focus groups on 1 November. They were worried about their own family finances, and pessimistic about the economy: rising prices, debt, interest rates and taxation. They were worried about the country as a whole, too. There was fresh anger about immigration and the knock-on effect on crime and public services. Suddenly this was a government that looked as though it had run out of steam, with nothing new to say, and which seemed to be defined by its past again (Iraq, failed public services and spin) rather than its future.

GB's own standing had taken a hefty blow, although his reputation continued to run ahead of the government as a whole. His longstanding positive attributes were enduring: strength, experience, cleverness and determination. However, now he always seemed to wear a hang-dog expression, which was being noticed, and although voters still sounded impressed by his crisis management skills as witnessed in his first three months as PM, they began to question his commitment and staying power:

> He looks knackered.

> His body language gives away how he feels – I thought he was a toughie but now it all looks too much for him.

> He was a great Chancellor but even though he started well, I'm not sure that he's up to the top job.

I wrote up my notes the day after the groups:

> There is an urgent need to channel GB's qualities in a positive new direction for the government. This will require a small number of eye-catching policies in each area, to symbolise how this government is different from what has gone before. Remember how strong the appetite for change was. We need a clear communications strategy that will make this change explicit, then some quick wins with rapid implementation that people can see.

Two weeks later, more voters – this time in Winchmore Hill – and the situation had deteriorated further. Talk was of 'drift' and 'lack of direction'. GB cut a solitary figure. The post-'non-election' media onslaught with its bitter briefings and counter-briefings had been vicious, with members of Team GB under personal attack, not just from the media but also from each other: 'Brown's young Turks who got it all wrong,' screamed the *Daily Mail*. Once again, though, this was an example of the Westminster Village and the electorate being on different pages.

The day after Andrew Marr's interview with GB was screened, focus groups had nothing to say about it or the non-election, even on prompting. However, what voters had noticed was GB's own reaction to events. The action man image he cut in the first three months was over. Suddenly he seemed tired, isolated and old fashioned. Once focused and determined, he now seemed paralysed, contrasting with David Cameron's more confident, energetic and modern presentation. His only activity in the public eye was a series of stilted and formal presentations where he seemed to be a lone figure hiding behind a lectern.

> You never see him with anyone else… who else is there? He's always on his own, giving a lecture.

By the end of November, we had seen the desperate mini Budget, imitating the Conservatives' inheritance tax policy, missing Inland Revenue data disks, Northern Rock's failure and the Labour Party donation scandal. All government energy was spent on reactive fire-fighting rather than getting a positive story across. I had sent so many notes in to No. 10 that I lost count, but had not seen GB since the meeting the Friday before he cancelled the election. Ed Balls called me, worried. I emailed over my thoughts to him, stressing the urgent need to regain momentum, and pointing out that people 'do not have a feel for the character of GB and the new government …

our initiatives are not joining up to create a bigger picture and so are not being noticed.' I proposed that we should establish a uniting theme and that 'in communicating this we need to bring back some of the discipline we had at the Treasury with single minded and repetitive messages'.

I felt strongly that we had forgotten those all-important middle ground voters – who had been so impressed with the Conservatives' inheritance tax policy – and suggested policy areas that would connect: council tax, immigration, apprenticeships, NHS, discipline in schools, police on the beat and our top-scoring policy, 'Youth Community National Service'.

I added that we needed a stronger sense of team. More ministers around GB all singing to the same tune, younger ones to signify energy and enthusiasm and older ones to signify experience and competence.

Most of all though, I wrote, this is all about GB himself. He is the personification of the government. At the moment he looks angry and beleaguered. He needs to be out and about with people, and with his team, active and engaged. Voters want change. He must to convey that sense of dynamism.

And I added a PS: 'Oh, and we need a concerted attack on DC and the Conservatives. This just doesn't seem to be happening, while they are landing real hits on us.'

THEMES

Returning from the Christmas break, Spencer asked me to come in for a chat. He had handed his resignation in to GB the day before. He had initially considered leaving immediately after the transition, but, believing that there would be an early election, had decided to stay on and work though that. Spencer was one of the people that GB now blamed for the debacle, and, ultimately, for the turning point in his personal fortunes. This was ironic since Spencer had called it right at every turn, recommending a very different Budget earlier in the year, and urging decisiveness on the early election, in particular that GB should either announce it or call it off during Labour conference week. He now felt that his job was impossible. Certainly it was not much fun. It was time to go.

At the same time, GB had, rightly, decided to hire someone to run No. 10. Stephen Carter was joining in a few weeks time, from Brunswick, the PR firm. His much-negotiated job title was chief of strategy and principal advisor, and his brief was to get the Prime Minister and office back on track.

Carter initiated a flurry of activity and worked hard to get the old team on side. He sought to streamline the No. 10 activity and in particular the way that it supported GB himself. He found that GB talked to so many advisors, formal and informal, through the day, making it hard for him to focus on a clear and consistent line. Much of the earlier part of every week was spent in lengthy sessions with scores of advisors coming in and out as GB planned his Prime Minister's Questions approach. This took so long because the advisors often did not agree. One Carter innovation was to convene the advisors first and force agreement. Only then would GB be briefed, this time with a single-minded line to use.

Another initiative was an awayday involving GB, the two Eds, Douglas, Sue and key No. 10 staff. This was hard to set up as Ed B. had organised a rare weekend away with his wife, fellow minister Yvette Cooper, in the Basque country for the chosen weekend. It was essential that he was there so the session ended up being in two parts – first on Thursday evening and the second on Sunday afternoon. During the Thursday session several external experts gave the group their thoughts on the problem and its solutions: Robert Senior and Kate Stanners from Saatchi and Saatchi, Roy Langmaid, a top researcher and strategist from a firm called Promise, and Alice Cartner Morley, who had worked with Philip Gould.

I prepared an update drawn from published polling and recent focus groups to kick-start Sunday's discussion. By now the 'poll of polls' had Labour trailing by 5 points. A slight lead amongst 18–24s was outweighed by a deficit that grew with voters' ages, leaving Labour 15 per cent behind with over-55s. I talked about the negative mood of the electorate, and how powerfully the disgruntled 'squeezed middle' felt. Immigration and crime continued to be top concerns but the economy was now rising as an issue.

I reiterated how GB's strengths were still recognised, but that these qualities were in danger of being eclipsed by his negative personal demeanour. DC meanwhile was seen as enthusiastic and fresh but DC also had powerful weaknesses, mostly that he was 'all talk and no action'. Back in April 2006, DC had staged a photo opportunity of himself cycling to work. Closer inspection revealed that his briefcase and change of clothes were being transported in a chauffeur-driven car travelling a discreet few yards behind him. This strange entourage is still mentioned in focus groups three years later as it symbolised people's worries that Cameron 'says one thing and does another'. I also showed the group that his poll ratings were very much worse than Tony Blair's over the equivalent period after being Leader of the Opposition and no better than Neil Kinnock had done in his first months.

We sat in the Cabinet room and discussed the findings and the work that had been presented in the same room a few nights before.

The debate that followed was interesting if inconclusive. GB went round the table asking everyone to pitch their ideas for recovery. The discussion ranged from positioning of the government to the Labour Party and GB himself. There was agreement that we needed to be more disciplined and single minded. GB listened attentively, as always scribbling notes with his thick felt tip pen. One of those present sighed afterwards that 'GB is often criticised for not listening enough. That's not the problem, he listens too much. He listens to everyone he speaks to then he top-slices 5 per cent from all their advice and mixes it up to create a solution.'

Following this session, Saatchi and Saatchi developed a number of campaign themes which I was to test in focus groups. These included 'We're backing the talents of all our people' and 'We're working hard for hard working Britain'. There was a problem with almost all of them because they presumed a positive relationship between voter and politician that simply was not recognised by the voter. To succeed, they needed to recognise and address the negative mood of most voters, but instead they trumpeted the government's achievements. Where voters were looking for change they tended to be congratulatory about the status quo.

Paradoxically, the theme that provoked the loudest peals of derisory laughter in the focus groups – 'Your government' – also had the greatest potential. Its sentiment was a million miles from where voters felt that government currently was, and provoked sarcastic responses like:

'My government'? Are they kidding?

It's not 'My government' – it's their government – they're all just in it for themselves.

However, it did speak to a desire for a different role for government and a different relationship between voter and representative. In an ideal world this theme might signify: less talk, more action; listening to us; more grassroots activity; politicians out of the House of Commons, less on TV and more on the street – but doing something useful, not campaigning. I wrote at the time: 'In short, there is something potentially very exciting here, which is about redefining the role of politicians: in purpose and process – and making them more open to public scrutiny and accountability.'

Unfortunately, this theme never saw the light of day. It morphed into a crucially different variation: Your Labour. But linking the theme to the political party only served to heighten voters' cynicism. As they had told us during the transition period, it needed to be about them, not us. Many more themes were developed and refined, only to be discarded. . . or used half-heartedly and then discarded. Stephen Carter's frustration grew. He left No. 10 that autumn to take up a peerage and a ministerial job.

WE NEED A JOLT

Meanwhile, GB's reputation continued to plummet. The Tories had moved into a consistent double-digit lead, regularly polling near to 50 per cent that summer. This was landslide territory. We began to move towards the usual frantic party conference speech testing phase. I ran some focus groups in August and drafted a presentation outlining the task ahead for when everyone returned from their summer breaks.

I concluded that the voters' negative view of GB was in danger of becoming settled and that it was vital to provide a 'jolt' that would force a reappraisal of him and the government. The reappraisal should present GB in a different light, and reaffirm his enduring strengths. Once again, I pointed out the disconnect between Westminster and the public, adding that 'voters are bemused by how badly his leadership had gone – according to the press – because they don't actually think he's that bad'. I stressed that the stumbling block was 'GB's personal style of leadership, not his policy offer' and that 'a raft of new policy announcements would not provide the jolt that was needed' because 'voters are not listening to him any more'. I also pointed out that 'his personal style is the elephant in the room if we don't talk about it – because everyone else is. . .'

I believed that 'GB urgently needs to have an unmediated conversation with the British people, perhaps through a documentary or interview but ideally interactive. Tone of voice is all: not apologetic, confident, even defiant, building on his longstanding strengths, strong, powerful, purposeful'. I drafted some script lines that might be included in the speech:

- I'll tell you what I care about.
- And I'll tell you what I don't really care about.
- I am what I am.
- I'll always do the right thing – even if it isn't the popular thing.
- I won't lie to you.

A draft speech was prepared for the crucial forthcoming leader's speech at the party conference. It had become a favourite media cliché for this speech to be 'the speech of that politician's life'. This time it really mattered. GB would be under unprecedented scrutiny from the media and from his Labour colleagues. There were rumours of leadership challenges. A strong performance was essential to survival.

GB was persuaded, for the first time, to perform excerpts that we could film to test. Much of the speech content was good but, tested in this format, exposed GB in a way that a researcher simply reading out the words did not. It was like the famous presidential debate between Kennedy and Nixon, where Kennedy won on TV but Nixon won on the radio: voters were judging the man more than the words. Once they could see him perform they could see his awkwardness and discomfort. He seemed too nervous, rushing at the script as though the speech was an ordeal:

The words say one thing, his body language says another.

He seems faltering and uncertain.

He gabbles his way through it – it's hard to understand him.

The biggest problem was that GB's delivery of the speech seemed weirdly unrelated to the audience at home. It was as though he was speaking his lines in a vacuum, not as a piece of communication.

Where is he looking in the room? You want him to look straight at you – it's like he's avoiding contact.

It's as if he's been told to explain himself but he doesn't really want to.

Watching the groups with me was David Muir, who had joined No. 10 from an advertising background in spring 2008, and, as Stephen Carter's departure grew imminent, had moved into a more prominent role, spending most of the summer break reviewing conference speech drafts with GB. He sat at the back of the Epping sitting room with his head in his hands. He emailed me the next day confessing that he had been awake since 3 a.m. 'fretting'. I sent an addendum to my earlier note, stressing:

> Most important of all, delivery matters more than words. You must rehearse with GB a slower, more contemplative style that really connects with the viewer and draws them in. It needs to be more conversational and interactive: 'ask yourself', 'you all know how it feels when. . .', 'how many times have you. . .' etc.

Being up in Manchester for Conference that year was a very different experience than the year before. Gone was the excited atmosphere, replaced by an anti-GB whispering campaign that occasionally broke cover when disgruntled backbenchers, including Fiona Mactaggart and Siobhain McDonagh, spoke out against his leadership.

In the end, the Conference speech, complete with the wow factor of GB being introduced by his wife, Sarah, was not bad at all. GB also completed a post-conference reshuffle that won rave reviews in the press as it heralded the return of Peter Mandelson, once again darling of the Westminster Village. By October the Tory lead had narrowed again to 8–15 points.

FINANCIAL CRISIS

The jolt GB needed to get noticed again did not come from either of these events. Instead the world was stopped in its tracks by a financial crisis that had started in September following the failure of

Fannie Mae and Freddie Mac, the two giant US mortgage businesses, the Stock Exchange crash and then the collapse of investment bank Lehman Brothers. As the UK's Royal Bank of Scotland began to look precarious, here was a opportunity for GB to showcase his crisis management skills again.

By the end of the year, voters could talk about little in current affairs beyond the financial crisis. I ran an extensive series of focus groups though the late autumn to understand voter reaction to this situation and to the government response. The closures of furniture retailer MFI and of the much-loved family store Woolworths were seen as weather vanes, indicating how grim things had become. Focus groups in Wolverhampton were really feeling the impact of rising food and fuel prices. Given the time of year, voters were very worried about not being able to afford Christmas presents for their kids. The mood was extremely pessimistic, with people convinced that what they were seeing was just the beginning – that worse was to come. They feared for their jobs and their homes.

The crisis had given GB the licence to be listened to again. His experience, especially at the Treasury, meant that voters felt he was the most reassuring leader to deal with the crisis. However there were two problems: firstly, if people agreed that this was a crisis that started in the US, then they also were likely to think that there would be little that the UK government could do to solve the problem. Secondly, their understanding of what the government had done so far was limited to the bank bailout, which tended to be understood as borrowing billions to save the banks rather than safeguarding people's savings.

Voters were seeing little to translate this initiative into something to reduce the impact on their own daily lives. There was a general feeling that the government was focused on the 'big boys' and not ordinary people. The VAT cut introduced to ease consumer pain was seen as too little to make a difference and the mortgage deferral scheme introduced to ensure that few people would lose their homes if they lost their jobs was almost unknown. We were not getting our message across. Although the financial crisis had resulted in a wobble in the Tories' opinion poll lead we now seemed to be treading water. At the same time, the Tories' attack – that Labour was not blameless – was beginning to get some traction.

I could paper my sitting room with notes written for No. 10 around this time. I was still conducting focus groups very regularly for Labour, although increasingly having to fund them personally, as donations to Labour Party funds had now dried up. The old adage, often in mind when doing pro bono work for charities, that 'you don't value what you don't pay for', again seemed all too relevant. Team GB had changed beyond recognition and my relationship with GB and team had changed beyond recognition, too. I ploughed on, hoping I could make a difference.

Many of the notes I sent, to No. 10, to Alistair Darling and his team, and to anyone else who might listen, reviewed the economic plan and suggested that it was vital that it be presented as – well, an economic plan, one that had voters in its sights and was clear about what it was setting out to do, so that the government could be held to account. It was also vital to clarify that we had saved the banks for the people, rather than for wealthy bankers, and to say this again and again.

I urged that there should be an umbrella theme for all government activities and that we should pick out the most appealing new policies and publicise them. Possible winners included kick-starting small businesses and protecting them through the crisis and a 'Special Benefit Support Plan' for people who had never been on benefits before and were shocked by what they had to endure after working hard all their lives.

I also suggested that we needed to look beyond the economy, repeatedly making the 'Winston Churchill' point: that voters would not necessarily vote gratefully for a government that had helped them through this period after the event (just as they did not vote for Winston Churchill gratefully after the war). Labour needed to 'own the future' and, as well as concentrating on the economic crisis, should project forward. To that end, I proposed emphasising 'future-ness' by commissioning a 2020 Vision project that would look forward at how life for individual voters, families, streets and communities might look in ten years time and positioning the government to meet the challenge.

I noted that Labour was failing to land an effective attack on the Conservatives. Accusing them of not supporting the government and of being a 'do nothing' opposition when the nation was in crisis was hitting home when tested in focus groups but not being fully and consistently deployed. One of the ironies of this period was that while Labour was not performing well, the Conservatives, too, were consistently underperforming, and, following their brilliantly successful conference in 2007 now seemed to rest on their laurels waiting for GB to lose.

Finally, I also suggested that the Positive Politics project much debated in No. 10 in 2007/8 should be revived with a 'radical and far-reaching review of the role of the MP, complete with job description setting clear goals, rooting the MP more in his/her constituency, voting and debating online rather in person, one job only, no lobbying, no perks and a root and branch review of expenses'. I was talking to myself, but even if anyone had been listening it was unfortunately too late.

EXPENSES AND BEYOND

The government had known that all MPs' expenses would have to be published later in the year, but, in April 2009 they became aware that this information had leaked and was in the hands of the media. The news broke slowly at first, with one or two MPs singled out: Jacqui Smith for designating her sister's home her main residence to allow second home funds to be allocated to the family home in the constituency; Tony McNulty for making a claim on his parents' home. The drip-drip effect became a torrent as the *Daily Telegraph* began to publish the whole gory story.

Voters were, of course, outraged. Yet, despite the press positioning this as a once in a lifetime event, my judgement is that the *Daily Telegraph* revelations and surrounding media furore only served to confirm emphatically what the electorate already thought rather than tell them something new. In focus groups in Essex on 19 May voters felt vindicated: of course politicians were greedy and self-serving. While much of the detail was lost, a wide sweep of misdemeanours had been noted. Generally there was little differentiation – all were felt to be 'as bad as each other'. The only difference was that DC was seen to have acted more promptly in addressing his own party and urging them to get their side of the House in order, while GB appeared to prevaricate, seeming once again horribly out of his depth.

As Labour slumped in the polls to its worse showing since the 1980s, once again it started to look divided as ministers' energies were focused on chatter about how to bring about a political coup. Local elections in June looked bad and, as the polls closed, a bombshell hit the Westminster Village as James Purnell, one of Blair's favoured sons, announced his resignation. Although the

Westminster Village could talk of little else, voters scarcely noticed as Peter Mandelson stepped up to the plate, and, behind the scenes, began to reconstruct the Cabinet in a reshuffle designed to save Brown's skin. It worked and the Brown government set off for the summer break heaving a sigh of relief.

There were anti-GB whispers at the highest level throughout this period. One of the accusations was that, quite simply, the Conservatives were not that good, and given that, if only Labour could get its own act together it would be possible to win. Labour pulled off a holding operation through autumn 2009. The Tory lead shrank back a little bit, although, just as the previous widening was not about enthusiasm for the Conservatives, but rather disappointment with Labour, so the narrowing of the gap seemed to be more about disappointment with the Conservatives than satisfaction with Labour.

The Westminster Village narrative was that it was over for the government. The Tories were odds on to win the next election, every newspaper except the *Mirror* ran pages and pages of negative analysis. Public affairs firms stopped hiring Labour people to help them advise clients in the future, anticipating the need for people who would know the workings of a Conservative government instead. Andrew Rawnsley's book *The End of the Party* painstakingly chronicled the demise of the Brown government. And yet by March 2010, despite continued economic gloom, negative stories about GB's 'bullying character' and ongoing expenses revelations, the polls moved closer and many pundits began to predict a hung Parliament.

14. Labour, me and GB

'I feel very honoured to be the only man allowed in here tonight. . . but Sarah's given me clear instructions – she's told me that I must say a few words, then leave you all to it, so I'll be off now. Have a good night,' and with that, GB, at the Labour Party Women's Fundraising Dinner on 9 December 2009, stepped down from the platform.

He worked the room as he left, greeting people and moving briskly from table to table. Guests included a smattering of celebrities: Tracey Ullman, Jo Brand, Lesley Garrett, Nancy Dell'Olio and an assortment of women Labour MPs, peers, journalists and other members of the Westminster Village female Labour aristocracy, all of whom had paid more than £100 to be there. A handshake here and hug there: 'Hello there, how're you doing?' 'Thanks for all your help.'

My table was in the middle of the room and he was bound to come past it. He shook hands with two or three of my neighbours. When he reached my seat he paused, momentarily flustered. There was a slight hesitation, then the repartee kicked back in: 'Hello there, how're you doing? Er. . .' A slightly clumsy hug and he was off, straight out of the room, missing the tables en route to the door altogether. Although still dubbed 'Gordon Brown's personal pollster', it was the first time I had seen him in months.

ONE TO WATCH

Back in the mid-1980s, I had been working with the Labour Party for some time before becoming aware of either TB or GB. A Labour Party staffer had referred to the rising of the 'trio of bright young Scots'. I asked who she meant and she described Robin Cook, Gordon Brown and, by virtue of his Scottish schooling, Tony Blair. A few weeks later, over a glass of wine in the Soho offices that I shared with Philip Gould, by now my business partner, Peter Mandelson told us both about a speech that he had heard a talented MP of the new generation give at a party rally that weekend. It was GB, who had urged Labour activists to sign up, get involved, stand up and be counted. 'It was extraordinary – inspirational – he's one to watch,' Peter enthused.

The first time I talked to GB one to one was during the Labour Party conference in 1988, in Blackpool. A group of us went out for a fish and chip supper and I ended up sitting next to him. He quizzed me about public opinion and the forthcoming Policy Review. He was particularly keen to hear what people thought about the business brief that he had recently taken on. It was hard work responding to his interrogation and I remember looking enviously at the other end of the table, where I could see people laughing and joking. GB lit my cigarette for me (I was a smoker in those days) and told me how he had given up himself with great difficulty. He showed me the very badly bitten finger nails that he now chewed instead. We then returned to the polling.

At that point GB was still little known, though just months later he was to become the darling of the Westminster Village when, following John Smith's first heart attack, he stepped in to his Shadow Chancellor's shoes as caretaker in his absence. As the SCA began its work for the Policy Review, GB was one of the team most eager to hear what the public thought. It was a little unnerving as he placed high store by what we had to say. In debrief meetings he would listen intently, noting every word, scarcely looking up, writing rapidly, pausing only to sweep back that messy black fringe with an impatient hand.

One SCA researcher found himself briefing GB on the public's attitudes to the economy. He describes a terrifying experience, still vivid twenty-five years later:

> It's honestly my worst memory. It didn't go well at all. He gave me no signals to read as I was talking things through. He was this very intense man sitting there making copious notes, not saying anything. It felt like I was being signed into prison – you know, where they take your particulars down without looking up at you.

After the '92 election, the SCA was cast into political Siberia by John Smith, and my involvement with Labour became only occasional. I had two small children, and my third was born just a few days before John Smith's death in 1994. I also had my own new business start-up to concentrate on. I worked on a number of political projects, semi detached from Labour: the Southern Discomfort series for the Fabian Society, looking at why Labour lost in key marginal constituencies in southern England; and a study on turnout and the youth vote. After Blair became leader, and the communications and research work that the SCA had undertaken was rehabilitated, I ran the 'Winning Words' survey of women voters. During the '97 campaign, I managed an extensive qualitative monitor of 'battleground marginal seats', amalgamating findings which I presented to the Campaign Strategy Meeting, every week, usually chaired by GB. Each week he would ask the same question: 'So, are we going to win?' I would take a deep breath, try to put memories of 1992 polling out of my head, and reply that yes, I believed we were.

PART OF THE TEAM

By Election 1997 my relationship with Team GB was already established. As I set out in Chapter 5, it had started over a cup of tea in the House of Commons canteen with Ed Balls a year earlier. Ed did not like the advice that Philip Gould was giving and, bluntly, didn't trust it. He asked me to carry out a clandestine operation challenging Philip's findings.

I was later to discover that this was not the only check on Philip's advice to be briefed. Senior members of Blair's own team, head of office Jonathan Powell and Sally Morgan, later to become director of government relations, complained that Philip was 'too frenetic, too frenzied' and asked a small group of ex-SCA researchers to provide a 'quiet feed of information'. I never saw what they did feed in, but my research on the proposed tax hike told me that Philip's instincts judged the electoral mood correctly, and his conclusions were not, as Team GB had suspected, coloured by his own political position.

Despite confirming research findings that were unpopular with Team GB, this was to be the beginning of a close working relationship that would last for thirteen years. During this time I must have conducted literally thousands of focus groups, analysed hundreds of opinion polls, and sat in dozens of meetings with both Team GB and GB himself, providing a frequent injection of voters' views and analysis to help develop strategy. I explored attitudes to Bank of England independence and the first mini-Budget in 1997, and then advised throughout the year, every year that GB was in the Treasury, on pre-Budget Reports, Budget and conference speeches, as well as running some bigger set piece projects, especially advising on the development of the economic message.

Spencer Livermore was a special advisor throughout that time. He said:

> The polling and focus group work in the Treasury was central. It took us to our core theme of 'no return to boom and bust' and cemented GB's reputation. It gave us a narrative to take us through the down turn. It showed us the importance of the stability message. I think our message work in 1998 was very sophisticated for the time and very effective.

In parallel with this activity, my business partner Viki Cooke and I continued to develop our own research and strategy business, Opinion Leader Research. It had grown considerably since its launch in 1992, and by 1998 employed a team of more than twenty, carrying out research for a wide range of organisations including BT, Esso, NatWest Bank and the NSPCC, as well as several local authorities and government departments. That year we sold the business to the Chime Communications Group, chaired by Mrs Thatcher's old advisor, Tim Bell. Viki and I continued to head up Opinion Leader and Chime gave us a brief to build a group of research agencies through founding more start ups and looking out for businesses to acquire.

The Team GB demands ebbed and flowed through this period, but, after the 2001 general election, the volume of work increased substantially for a time. Top priority was research to feed into the development of a strategy for funding the NHS. Spencer again:

> I think the NHS tax rise was in many ways GB's finest hour. We really understood how people thought. We were in the field twice a week every week. It's hard to have that much contact with where people are at, to really listen to them, and not get it right.

The emerging pattern of working was that I or a colleague would conduct the focus groups. They would often be attended by Ed Miliband or Spencer. I would then draft a note the next day that would be emailed – faxed before the internet era arrived – over to the Treasury. I would talk through the findings in meetings most weeks; I became so frequent a visitor that all the reception and security staff knew me by name. As Spencer recalls, GB was 'incredibly receptive' to the information.'He was utterly engaged. . . enthralled by it, totally captivated. He invested a lot of trust in the findings. I don't recall him ever challenging findings even when he didn't like them.'

TAKING IT PERSONALLY

Receiving research was harder for GB when we looked at views of him personally, especially as we moved into Project 3D, developing his leadership positioning. GB was uncomfortable. Spencer again:

> If it was bad news about him personally, he would be mortified. I remember watching some of those NHS groups from the other side of the mirror with him. It was one of the most tense experiences of

my life. He was incredibly impatient. The thing was a bit delayed because one of the swing voters arrived late. You were running though the background with the group and everyone was in the back: the Eds, Douglas, Sue, me. They were like, 'Why won't she hurry up?' When you asked questions about GB everyone laughed to ease the stress but he just had his head down, he found it very hard. All very Gordonesque.

As we grew closer to the point of transition to PM, research told us that one of GB's greatest areas of vulnerability was not appearing to 'listen' enough. The focus groups were helpful but they did not give him the direct voter contact that he needed. At Opinion Leader Research, I had been working on citizen engagement and participative democracy projects like Citizens' Juries. The idea of these programmes was to give ordinary citizens the opportunity to have their say on public policy. OLR had worked successfully with several local authorities and health authorities, looking at how to involve the public in complex decision making on issues such as health rationing and trade-offs on local planning problems.

The effect was to help members of the public and their representatives understand each other's perspectives better: politicians would get a detailed view of what the public thought and why they thought it, unmediated, straight from the horse's mouth. The public would get an insight into the dilemmas that politicians and policy makers faced.

From 2006, drawing on this experience, I set about creating a listening programme for GB where he would work at first hand with members of the public, debating future challenges that may involve difficult trade-offs: funding elder care, motivating smokers to give up, childcare policy and redefining British values. Sometimes the sessions were small and intimate, sometimes larger. What they all had in common was that GB would listen to what people felt on a wide range of subjects, and respond. He consistently exceeded expectations with his ability to focus carefully on what they had to say, taking in detailed evidence from experts and responding decisively. For people who thought he was just a one-dimensional money man this was a revelation.

By now the work that I was doing in citizen engagement was getting noticed. I had become an industry spokesperson for so called 'deliberative techniques' like Citizens' Juries. Opinion Leader had been responsible for managing several very large scale projects including the Department of Health's Citizens White Paper on out-of-hospital care, and the National Pensions Debate which DWP Secretary of State John Hutton commissioned to involve citizens in the challenge of how we fund our ageing population. These were high profile projects, and were getting noticed.

The work I was doing for GB was getting noticed too. As he drew closer to the big job, Team GB came under ever greater scrutiny. Although still based outside the office, I was spending more and more time on GB's project. The Westminster Village media ran more and more stories profiling the team, often featuring me and using the same old photograph of my younger self plucked from Chime's website.

One of Opinion Leader's areas of expertise (as its name suggests) was work amongst opinion leaders from business, government, media and academia. We ran a panel of such 'movers and shakers' whom we interviewed every month on behalf of commercial clients and to provide a database for our own marketing. In 2006, we published a poll that gave GB a strong lead amongst this important audience, and a furore developed with Conservative Party complaining to the Market Research Society that the poll broke its rules. After several weeks' deliberation the MRS ruled that the methodology was sound. Of course the apology received considerably less media coverage than the original (wrong) accusation. This was my first taste of being in the front line of attack by association.

The Conservatives, now under David Cameron's leadership, were beginning to grow in confidence and attack more effectively. The guns were out for GB. Right-wing activist Paul Staines, blogging as his alter ego Guido Fawkes, launched a campaign attacking me personally for the public sector work that Opinion Leader did. He, and other Conservative bloggers picked up on the citizen engagement work that OLR had done. He accused government departments of hiring OLR solely because of my work with GB. . . and implied that the work that I conducted for GB was a quid pro quo for the government citizen engagement work.

As anyone who has bid for Civil Service contracts will verify, nowadays – quite rightly – everything is tendered to within an inch of its life. Knowing a minister, let alone the Chancellor and PM heir apparent, would be a hindrance rather than a help and place the potential contract under even closer scrutiny. It was true that much of the time that I put in for Labour was pro bono, as it had always been. Like most political activists, whether drafting leaflets or knocking on doors, I gave my time willingly out of support for the cause.

Furthermore, many of the costs associated with my political work were paid by the Labour Party or by a sympathetic organisation such as the Fabian Society. Nonetheless, the story ran. This was a tense and difficult time and GB was impatient with anything that might adversely affect his forward march. On one occasion after a particularly nasty piece, claiming ludicrously that Opinion Leader had charged £153,484.38 for a one-day seminar, had run, GB burst into our weekly meeting and exploded, 'You're in the eye of the storm. What are you doing about it?'

Although other Team GB members were kind and sympathetic, I was offered no support to counter the media savaging that I received, and its damage to my business that now employed more than a hundred people. My colleagues at Opinion Leader, whose excellent and pioneering work was being unfairly criticised, were unbelievably tolerant. Chair of Chime Tim Bell wrote to Theresa May pointing out that when he had worked for Mrs Thatcher at Saatchi, Saatchi's biggest clients were government departments, with that side properly tendered for and kept separate from the political work, just as we managed projects at OL.

I was hurt, both by the accusations themselves and also by GB's less than supportive response. I had seen him treat others harshly but, up till then, I had always been made to feel valued. After much agonising and, following discussions with Viki, my ever tolerant business partner, I decided to step down from my role as CEO of Opinion Leader and stopped working on any public sector clients, to avoid making either GB or Opinion Leader Research vulnerable to further attack. Instead I focused on my corporate role as joint chair of Chime's research division. Meanwhile, sadly, GB shelved the listening programme – it looked to be more trouble than it was worth. . . Citizens were not going to get their say after all.

IN OR OUT?

As we approached the time of the likely transition to No. 10, GB continued to press for me to be available as a full time employee. I considered it carefully and wrote a paper weighing up the pros and cons of making the move. The advantages of becoming an integral part of the team would be better co-ordination between research and strategy. The disadvantages were significant, though. For me personally, I was enjoying the work at Chime, where the business was growing fast. I would be sorry to leave.

I also had growing concerns about the way that GB's office was managed, which meant that moving across looked even less attractive. A few months earlier I had sent a note over to Ed Miliband and Spencer Livermore, which set out a communications strategy to take Team GB through to transition. However, I made it clear that I felt that the office, as currently structured, was not able to support this. The lack of a CEO or chief of staff had become a huge problem, and I noted that the team 'lacked direction and leadership, being under-resourced and unco-ordinated. There is no sense of a team working together towards shared objectives.'

Spencer, immensely able, was impossibly stretched and there was an over reliance on both the Eds and Douglas, all three of whom now had their own constituencies and ministerial jobs. Other key staff, such as the press function and Council of Economic Advisors, lacked line management and therefore clear direction, meaning that they were too often riskily 'flying blind'. There was a further problem with the many friends and supporters that GB listened to, who, in the absence of a clear line or disciplined message, were often adding in confusing or unhelpful suggestions. I felt that it would be hard to be effective in this environment, which GB showed no immediate signs of changing.

But the most overwhelming reason against moving in with Team GB was that, I believed, being inside the office looking out, rather than outside looking in, I would find it much harder to remain true to the voter's voice. The government's decision to stick with the

Dome was just one example I had witnessed of how easy it was to hear what you wanted to hear if you owned the strategic solution to a problem. In the end, I felt that my loyalty to Labour and GB was best served by affirming that my greatest loyalty was to the voter. I concluded that I would be more use out than in, and declined the move. This decision was reluctantly accepted. I genuinely think it worked well, and kept me more focused on the voters' views than I could have been on the inside. I believe it made me more useful to GB and the team. However, it also made me more vulnerable to office politicking, as we would see after the "non election".

TRANSITION AND BEYOND

We were all in high spirits at the special conference in Manchester at which GB was confirmed Labour Leader. Harriet Harman, whose campaign I had strongly supported, was elected deputy on the same day. GB hugged me warmly at the champagne reception afterwards 'Well done to you – you got us both in. You got two!' The train home afterwards was very jolly. Team GB was joined by Team HH and we took over a whole carriage. Tipped off that booze supplies on the train were low we despatched a crack team to the supermarket at Manchester Piccadilly station and toasted the future with plastic cups of warm white wine.

The run-up to transition had been the most intense period of work so far. We were in the field with focus groups weekly supplemented by quantitative polling. There was a constant flow of speeches and statements from GB's office to mine – I would read through and offer comments. The important ones would be tested in focus groups, including the powerful old school motto, 'I will try my utmost', that GB used to great effect on the day he entered No. 10. I discussed this work in regular meetings, with GB twice a week, with the policy team, the media team and a strategy group convened by Ed Balls which met every Wednesday evening.

After becoming leader, GB continued to seek the voters' views at every turn, calling frequently and emailing most mornings to share new thinking for policy ideas, speech lines or other initiatives. I had checked focus group reactions to his first Cabinet, to the government of all the talents concept, to his healthcare policy, initiated by senior surgeon, now health minister, Professor Ara Darzi, and to education policy, as well as monitoring voter reaction to GB's handling of the flooding, terrorism and other disasters that met his first few weeks in office. Over the summer, I holidayed with my family in Greece and spent much of the fortnight reviewing first drafts of his Labour conference speech – his first as leader.

NOT THE ELECTION

I was lucky not to be criticised publicly as others were when team GB turned on itself in the aftermath of the non election fiasco. However, I know that I was criticised privately, specifically (and wrongly, as I have discussed in Chapter 12) for failing to warn GB about the rising importance of inheritance tax as an issue with swing voters. GB had decided that it was this that had caused the anti-Labour/pro-Conservative surge in that fateful week in October. I also know that, although the programme of polling and focus groups continued, it was never again received by GB with the same enthusiasm. The voter had stood in his way. The protestation GB made in his interview with Andrew Marr, effectively calling off the general election, 'I have not been influenced by focus groups and opinion polls', was more a prediction for the future than a statement of how GB had handled the past few weeks. My contact with him dwindled from frequent meetings and daily calls and emails to next to nothing.

I have thought about this a great deal, and I am honestly not sure what I could or should have done differently in the autumn of 2007. I remain of the view that GB would have comfortably won an election had he called it then. However, the possibility of a shrunken majority, given Labour's collapsing poll lead, made this hard advice to insist upon, especially as GB's own expectation had been a triumphant landslide. With hindsight, the phantom 2007 election was actually lost earlier in the year, when the centrepiece of the Budget intended as a launch pad for electoral success was a cynically received tax cut, disastrously funded by losing the 10p start rate. And, had the voters' disdain for inheritance tax not been ignored in favour of the tax cut, the Tories would have been deprived of their opportunity that autumn. Given my recommendations at the time it was an irony that this formed the basis of the attack on me. It was an unhappy time in Team GB.

By Christmas 2007, the office was in total disarray and Spencer had resigned. Stephen Carter's appointment, announced in January, seemed to me to be a positive move. However, Team GB was now a dysfunctional family at war with itself. An aggressive new internal media briefing operation – the source of which I do not know for sure – was launched to undermine Carter, as he grew close to GB, and, rightly, sought to discipline the numerous formal and informal advisors that endlessly and variously bent GB's ear. Anonymous 'No. 10 sources' endlessly briefed negative stories to the media to undermine him: 'No. 10 advisor accused of loose talk and naivety', 'No. 10 advisor earns more than PM' and so on.

I tried to ignore this unpleasant cloak and dagger behaviour, but soon found myself personally embroiled. As well as seeking to destroy Carter directly, the anonymous briefers – clearly people working in and close to No. 10 – aimed to destabilise all his working relationships. I began to read in the press how Carter was planning to sack me: 'Carter reviewing the position of Gordon Brown's long serving opinion pollster, Deborah Mattinson'. I called him up and asked what was going on. He was aghast. 'This was categorically nothing to do with me. Please can I ask you to trust me until you have reason not to?' I believed him. By autumn 2008, the briefings finished. Carter had left.

DRIFTING TO THE END

David Muir, a chirpy adman, fellow Scot and old chum of Douglas's from Edinburgh University, had been brought in to No. 10 a few months after Stephen Carter. I had first met David during September 2007, when we were hastily hiring ad agency Saatchi and Saatchi to accommodate the likely autumn election. He emailed me at Christmas inviting me for lunch and I was tipped off that he was probably to join the team, which he eventually did after Easter 2008. New to politics, but a hard worker, he dropped his own family plans to spend days in August consoling GB, by now a miserable and isolated figure, and working on the conference speech. He and I tested many versions of the speech.

As others drifted out of favour or moved on, David Muir for a while acquired the power base of the 'last man standing'. Meanwhile, I grew more and more concerned about my own role. My limited contact with GB had shrunk to almost nothing. I only ever saw David and was entirely reliant upon him to get the voters' views across. In early 2009, I sat down with David and took him through a note, setting out the task ahead and expressing my concerns about how the research programme had evolved. I spelt out that we were suffering 'a lack of clear strategic direction, lack of funds, and lack of integration of the research team in the decision making process'. I asked David to be very frank and honest as I believed that GB needed to have direct and personal contact with a pollster – if it wasn't going to be me, I would volunteer to step aside. He looked me in the eye and told me that he was certain that GB wanted me to continue.

Shortage of money had now become a major problem. Labour's finances were in dire straits and no one was making the case for research. The only way to get the vital work done was for me to donate the full costs of all the expenses associated with the focus groups as a declared party donation. This I did for a series of focus groups during spring 2009. My contact with GB continued to be only occasional. I was, however, still asked to present to political Cabinet meetings from time to time. This was a very mixed blessing as my presentations were edited and I was usually only asked to talk about the Conservatives – there was no appetite to share the reasons for Labour's dwindling poll share with political colleagues. By now it was not even talked about inside No. 10.

In desperation, in June 2009 I drafted a note for GB and asked Sue Nye, who I trusted completely, to hand it directly to him. By then Labour's poll share had slumped to the low 20s – worse than when I had first become involved with Labour in the 1980s. I wrote, truthfully, however, that I still believed the situation to be retrievable because voters were not persuaded by Cameron, and still held views of GB and of Labour that were positive, if recessive.

I addressed GB's leadership style head on. He had recently

endured media mockery after the disastrous 'grinning YouTube' incident, where an uncomfortable video performance was released by No. 10, making him a laughing stock. I was concerned that the advice he was now getting was encouraging him to take Cameron on in a personality contest which I felt he was bound to lose. I wrote: 'You are a lighthouse leader: people look to you to show the way and tell them what to do. This is a very attractive leadership proposition in the present times but does need to be executed with extraordinary discipline, and a focused sense of purpose.'

I reminded GB that his previous popularity had been derived from what we used to call the four Ss: that he was 'strong, straight talking, serious, and solid' and that 'the economic crisis should have showcased these skills. . . but instead our March poll showed that "your impressive leads on those most salient attributes have all turned into worrying deficits"'.

I went on to suggest that GB needed a 'Big Moment':

> something disruptive that will make people look at you again, and remind them of how they used to feel about you. This might take the form of a very striking announcement or policy shift. Whatever it is must be true to the three tests above. In particular it should symbolise your direction of travel – it must be something you really care about.

I made recommendations about communications strategy and the need to be more disciplined to reflect a more single minded message, and that less would be more on policy too, suggesting coming up with a small number of concrete policies that would symbolise GB's approach and deliver tangible benefits attractive to middle ground voters on the economy, health and new politics.

I had just completed the last ever focus groups that I would run for GB. I had been shocked by how switched off people were from everything that the government did. There was a settled view that the country was in a rut and must change to move forward. GB personified this stasis and was depicted like a carthorse ploughing the same furrow over and over, or a tethered bear, angry and frustrated but trapped. Once again I stressed the need to inject a sense of purpose and dynamism into the government, through GB's own demeanour. Voters wanted change: 'Most of all, you need to show now that you really understand the urgent desire for change that the public feels. This means pledging some specific and tangible achievements within a very short time phase – e.g. manifest completion by the autumn, to show you mean business.'

GB neither replied nor even acknowledged receiving this. It was to be the last note I wrote for him.

AFTER THE SUMMER

On 4 June 2009, as the polls closed on the disastrous local elections, the 10 o'clock news buzzed with breaking news: James Purnell, Blairite Cabinet minister, had resigned, making a devastating statement that 'GB's continued leadership makes a Conservative victory more likely'. Text messages pinged into my phone: 'Can GB survive?'. As I and others speculated, Peter Mandelson, now fully rehabilitated in GB's Cabinet, hit the phones and rescued GB from certain disaster, persuading, cajoling and threatening Cabinet colleagues to stay put or else. The possible mass exodus dwindled away. GB was safe. Peter's reward was a promotion that elevated him in all but name to the number two slot. It also put him in charge of campaign strategy. David Muir, increasingly distanced, now simply stopped returning my calls. I approached Peter, who did not respond either.

My dilemma now was whether formally to step down. The personal advantages of doing were significant as it would again free me up again to work across a wider commercial and public sector portfolio. It would also liberate me from the frustration of reputational association with something over which I had no influence. Two factors held me back. First, and most importantly, I was reluctant to allow the Tories the opportunity to make mischief out of my resignation, accusing me of being yet another 'rat leaving a sinking ship'. Continuing in name for the few months left seemed a small price to pay. The second reason was less worthy. Frankly I was scared that if I publicly disassociated myself, Peter Mandelson and the No. 10 spin machine would try to prevent the Tories making a positive story about my departure by attacking me in the press. I would read articles about my own deficiencies that would justify my departure and position it as a sacking. I bit my lip and stayed put in name only as a Labour pollster, and watched the final months of the GB era unfolded.

It was a sad end to many years serving party and politician, but, as the disastrous election campaign unfolded, a relief to be watching the activities rather than to be part of them.

15. A broken relationship

DISGUST AND DISENGAGEMENT

In summer 2009 I ran focus groups with swing voters in the landlord's living room above a pub just outside Luton. News of the expenses scandal had broken a couple of weeks before and press and TV news could talk of little else. Alison, 42, a hairdresser with three teenaged children, was emphatic: 'It's a complete racket . . . they're all in it for themselves. If we did what they've done we'd be in prison.'

David Muir, GB's Head of Strategy for the past year, was sitting behind me listening in on the discussion and taking notes. He stopped writing and clicked the top of his pen in and out in an agitated fashion as everyone rushed to agree.

Disgusting! They're all disgusting, really.

Yet, on probing further, page after page of individual MPs' misdemeanours, so lavishly detailed in the media and pored over by the Westminster Village, had gone almost unnoticed. These voters had picked up very little and were unable to quote a single specific example of wrong doing – even the celebrated moat clearance or duck house. Only Sarah, 44, an admin officer with a recruitment agency, divorced with two children, thought she vaguely remembered something: 'Wasn't there someone who got caught watching porn and we'd paid for it?'

Alison thought it was actually someone's husband, but didn't know whose. No one seemed very sure. I asked if they felt that any individual politician was particularly to blame. Were any better or worse than the others? Was one party coming out of it all ahead of the others? Then the $64,000 question: did the governing party take a bigger slice of responsibility for everything, as many Westminster commentators had suggested, just because they are there, in control and could have done something to stop all this?

Sue, 36, a part time worker at Debenhams, living with her boyfriend, grew impatient with this line of questioning: 'Honestly, I can't be bothered with any of them. They're all as bad as each other – a complete waste of time.' This 'plague on all your houses' sentiment, confirmed by many opinion polls at the time, was a source of relief at No 10. On his way home that evening, David Muir sent me a text message: 'Phew!' He had feared an angry onslaught targeted at Labour as the party in power, and braced himself for a drubbing. We had delayed this set of focus groups twice to let things die down a little from the early feverish revelations.

Paradoxically, the reason behind voters' refusal to play the party blame game hinted at a deeper, underlying problem. The truth was worse than No. 10's worst fears. I wrote in my debrief note the next day: 'There was less anger towards politicians than we have often seen in the past. This is because these voters are now totally switched off from politics. They are no longer listening. They are no longer watching. Their deep cynicism has led to total disengagement.'

Of course, voter disengagement did not start with the expenses scandal. In the 2005 election, turnout remained stubbornly low at

61 per cent despite the closer contest that would tend to indicate greater attention from the electorate. During the campaign, voters told me how bored they were. More than half of those polled in one survey chose the word 'dull' to describe the campaign. Going to vote had to do battle with that evening's *EastEnders* for its share of people's time – and all too often it lost out:

I feel lethargic about it all.

Those leaflets and all that – it all goes straight in the bin.

I know they say you should vote but quite honestly Thursday's always a busy day for me – and I like Thursday night telly.

One explanation was that voters felt that, although the contest in 2005 was closer than it had been in 2001 or 1997, it was not exactly gripping. As they saw it, there wasn't much to choose between the main parties. Polls showed that just 7 per cent claimed strong support for any political party. Back in the 1960s that figure was 45 per cent. Less than a third thought that the main parties really did stand for different things, compared with 84 per cent in 1987.

THEY'RE ALL THE SAME

Are all politicians 'the same'? One of the first presentations that the Shadow Agency researchers Roddy Glen and Leslie Butterfield prepared for Neil Kinnock back in the mid-1980s was called 'Beyond the Pale'. It used the visual device of a rectangle divided into three blocks. The right hand block was labelled 'Right Wing Beyond the Pale'. The left hand block was labelled 'Left Wing Beyond the Pale'. Roddy and Leslie showed how effectively Mrs Thatcher had positioned the Conservative Party bang in the middle with her popular policies like council house sales. Labour, with its warring militant factions and its loony left was firmly on the left and 'Beyond the Pale'.

One of the triumphs of New Labour was its importing of Clintonesque 'triangulation': political positioning that, at its most basic, avoided the extreme edges of the left–right spectrum, and at its most cunning stole the opposition's clothes. So while TB talked up public service reform and choice, GB planned a market friendly economy and Peter Mandelson talked of being 'seriously relaxed' about the super wealthy. David Cameron's early embracing of pro-green rhetoric and later his acclaim for the NHS, 'the embodiment of fairness in our society/we recognise its special place in society so we will not cut the NHS', were all examples of the parties avoiding being 'beyond the pale' and huddling together in the voter-friendly centre ground.

This solved a problem but created a new one: voters were left feeling that little was at stake in an election. Political parties converged as a homogenous mass, all driven in the same direction by their leaders, with little differentiation and little real debate. Local political activists felt excluded from this top-down process. My colleague Graeme Trayner and I conducted a study for the Power Inquiry – Baroness Helena Kennedy's Commission established in 2004 to explore how to revive our democracy. Our interviews with local members of all the main parties showed them to be suffering from low morale, feelings of powerlessness and lack of influence. They were beginning to question the point of all that sitting around and sounding off in community centres and church halls. All the major parties have seen a significant decline in membership since the 1990s. If the members weren't interested, who would be?

The reaction to the expenses scandal, the increasing lack of political choice and voter disengagement share a connection that is, at its heart, the premise for this book. All too often, the Westminster Village has one set of preoccupations, while the electorate has another. Ordinary voters neither know nor care about the 'he said, she said' gossip and process stories that are the obsessions of Westminster politicians and journalists. Countless times I have ventured forth to meet focus groups in Swindon, Nottingham or Bolton with a list of questions designed to test opinion on the latest Westminster fixation. What have they picked up in the news lately, I ask. The question always provokes a flurry of responses which almost never relate to Westminster's burning political issue of the day.

In 2007, during the transition from TB to GB, while the media filled page after page with profiles of GB, his team, his policies, his family, his old school friends, and amidst endless speculation about whether or not he would make a good PM, groups of voters in Gravesend could talk only about missing three-year-old Madeleine McCann and the 'appalling' 2012 logo. On the Monday that followed a weekend of febrile debate after the 'non-election', not one voter mentioned it spontaneously in their self-generated list of 'top ten news items'. On prompting, a few had picked up on the story, they just hadn't thought it particularly interesting or newsworthy.

Too often political commentary seems to be in code, a riddle of insiders' speak couched in bewildering jargon. Its focus is process rather than outcomes. It is alienatingly cliquey. Assumptions are made that astonish any ordinary voter who happens to notice (and of course, many don't). In a focus group I ran after Charles

Kennedy stepped down as Lib Dem leader, one indignant voter told me how he had watched Nick Robinson on the BBC *Ten o'Clock News* talking about the 'open secret' of Kennedy's alcoholism. He was furious: 'So everyone knew about this open secret? How? It's outrageous! Everyone knew – apart from the poor idiots who voted for him!'

The start point for the gulf between Westminster and voter is information. The media usually presumes a level of knowledge that voters just do not have. I tested different news coverage approaches to international political stories blind amongst BBC viewers. I discovered that they preferred *Newsround*, not realising it was a kids' show. The reason? Because this was a news programme targeting primary school-age children it assumed it was telling a story from scratch and provided vital background information. Quite simply, many media stories require knowledge of people and policy that most voters do not possess.

Asked what politicians do, faces go blank. Back in October 2000 I ran focus groups for Ann Treneman of *The Times*, who was writing a piece about how people saw the role of the MP. We found no awareness at all of how the Westminster machine worked. The whipping system, the relationship between the Commons and the Lords, the job of the select committees: all were a mystery to voters, who saw just two things: the PMQs rabble and the road-show that moves into town during an election campaign. Neither had or have any positive impact on their lives.

The Hansard Society's annual political engagement audit published in March 2010 found that people thought that politicians were least likely to be doing the things that they most wanted them to do: representing the views of local people in the House of Commons, and holding the government to account, and most likely to be doing the things they least wanted them to do: furthering their own career and personal interests, representing the views of their political party or presenting their own views via the media. The focus groups confirm this:

> They're feathering their own nests, that's all.

> They're out there saying vote for me, vote for my party – just looking out for themselves really.

POSITIVE POLITICS

In early 2008, a few months after Gordon Brown became Prime Minister, I drafted a review of voter attitudes to Westminster entitled 'Positive Politics'. GB had had ambitious plans to review the role of the MP, including a ban on second jobs and a review of expenses and pay. After the non election, this project, which would have needed some good will from colleagues to get through Parliament, went on to the back burner. I was extremely worried about sidelining voters' growing concerns. I wrote:

> Because people don't know what politicians actually do, they find it impossible to judge whether or not they are doing it well. The problem is compounded because, while voters do 'get' what government is meant to do, they do not see any real accountability, they mistrust the communications that they are fed, and are deeply sceptical of targets and statistics. As we have seen, they no longer even trust their own experience, discounting that as an isolated fluke: 'I've been lucky' syndrome.

This was a year before the expenses scandal broke, but people were already convinced that all politicians were in it for their own financial gain, with some being actually corrupt, while others were merely 'on the make'. A Populus poll at that time showed that the Labour government was felt to be 'about the same' on 'guilty of sleaze' as the last Tory government. People believed that politicians were milking the system:

> We pay for their houses, their wives' and kids' wages, even their hairdressers and their meals out. It's a complete joke!

> They're all as bad as each other – all in the same deal – no one will ever sort it out – why would they? They're on to a good thing!

This was also about lack of empathy. Most voters believed most politicians to be 'out of touch with how ordinary voters live their lives'. Later in the 2008 report prepared for GB, I noted that 'the widely held view is that MPs are extremely wealthy and lead unusual cocooned lives. Thus the start point is that they are not expected to understand how voters live their lives (or to care)'. A month or two before, when the credit crunch first hit the UK, voters were furious that politicians did not seem to understand the immediate and devastating impact that soaring prices of the 'three Fs', food, fuel and financial services, was having on their lives. At this stage the media were also ignoring the story, save for 'technical' stories on the economic pages. The public were outraged:

> It's alright for them, they don't know what a loaf of bread or pint of milk costs because they don't have to – but I do.

> They only ever think about themselves, not the likes of us.

Voters do not believe that what happens in politics and government makes any difference to their lives. In March 2010, the Political Engagement Survey published by the Hansard Society found that fewer than one-fifth of those questioned voted Westminster into the top three 'institutions that influence my everyday life'. Just 17 per cent agreed that what the Prime Minister does 'impacts on my everyday life'. Six out of ten said that they knew 'not very much' or 'nothing at all' about politics.

The expenses scandal was debated by the Westminster Village as though it was just about politicians' remuneration. I say that this is another example of the political classes missing the point. Voters were clear that the row was not just about pay, but also about what politicians did to earn that pay. It was about value as well as cost. As Angela in Luton put it, in a focus group in 2008: 'It is honestly money for old rope – they swan about, flipping their houses, busily going to and fro first class – then they turn up at the Parliament to get together with their mates.' Helen agreed: 'Nice work if you can get it.'

For most voters, looking at what they see of politicians' work, it seems like very poor value indeed.

BREAKDOWN OF TRUST

After the 1997 election, polling by MORI showed that trust in government ministers had doubled overnight. Blair's 'servants of the people' pep talk to his new, keen-bean MPs was capable of reducing focus groups of swing voters to tears. The disappointment voiced five years later when those great expectations were not realised was not about lack of delivery in the NHS or education, nor even about Iraq; it was about the dashed hope of finding a different way of doing politics. That was the broken promise which triggered the collapse of trust.

Put simply, politicians are trusted less than any other profession – the police are four times more likely to be trusted, trade unions twice as much. Even the media are trusted more. MORI found that political trust dropped to an all time low after the expenses scandal. Only 13 per cent trust politicians to tell the truth – the lowest score in the survey's 26-year history. The Hansard Society's 2010 survey grouped voters according to their attitudes. The research arrived at eight different voter types. The largest group – a quarter of the electorate – was called the Disengaged/Mistrustful. The next largest group were known as the Detached Cynics. The Disengaged were the least likely to be certain to vote, with just one in four saying they would. Only half of the total sample said they were certain to vote.

So political reputations have been in decline since the early days of New Labour in 1997. At Opinion Leader Research, the business I ran for more than a decade, we regularly conducted 'reputation audits' for big companies to help them monitor how they were seen by customers and other stakeholders. One question that correlated strongly with a positive reputation was a high score for 'I'd be happy for my son/ daughter to work for company X'. One of the most telling questions asked by Hansard's recent study was 'How proud would you be if your child became a. . .' Being a politician trailed in the bottom three, just a little ahead of estate agent or tabloid journalist. Being a doctor came top with a score four times higher, being a head teacher scored three times higher, being a solicitor or business person scored more than double.

In 2009, Opinion Leader ran a briefing session for senior commercial clients entitled 'Has trust gone bust?' Research presented that day set out the qualities that engender trust in any institution.

Top scores were: customer service, financial probity, reliability and 'admitting mistakes when things go wrong'. Small wonder, perhaps, that trust in politicians has dropped off the scale.

The OLR research also showed that opinion leaders and public alike agreed that 'apparent loss trust is really a loss of deference. We no longer assume that a figure of authority is trustworthy, they have to demonstrate it.' How do they do that? Again the empathy/in touch point shines through. We concluded that successful organisations 'walk in their customers' shoes', demonstrating a real understanding of customers' needs, hopes, fears and aspirations. We showed how, in the economic climate of the time, successful businesses like Tesco, with its broadening of the 'every little helps' theme to being Britain's biggest discounter, successfully hit the spot, as did Marks and Spencer's focus on 'wise buys'. The research concluded:

- Trust is strongly linked to personal relationships and feeling emotionally connected.
- Customer service builds trust. M&S are good with their customers. The £10 dinner has provided a quality service that people can identify with and which speaks to their needs.

The research also demonstrated the increasing importance of strong leadership, with people looking for clear direction, honest and straightforward communications and a degree of hope and optimism:

- In a society where faith and family are not strong there is a need for some leadership which people can trust.
- Honesty from a CEO. Coming clean and shooting straight goes a long way.

The political parallels are obvious and challenging. On the eve of the 2010 general election the big question was whether the coming campaign could address any of these points in voters' minds. Pundits were predicting lowest ever levels of engagement in the campaign and lowest ever turnout too: on 6 April, the *Daily Telegraph* predicted 'the lowest turnout of modern times ... as voters stay at home because of the MPs' expenses scandal'. In the event, the turnout improved a little on that of 2005, but was still relatively low.

Another telling finding from the Hansard Society work was that voters on the receiving end of most political activity – that is, those people living in the all-important marginal seats – were even more likely to be cynical. In ordinary constituencies, 49 per cent of voters agreed that 'MPs spend time furthering their personal interests', while 61 per cent of people in marginal seats agreed that this was the case, suggesting that all that foot leather burnt tramping the streets campaigning and canvassing was actually counter-productive, flagging up voters' views on the emptiness and self-seeking nature of modern campaigning.

Certainly this seemed to be borne out by the Harlow voters. I asked our focus group panel in Harlow – the UK's fifth most marginal seat – to bring along an object to sum up their expectations of politicians. Danny held up a DVD: 'I've brought the Jim Carrey film *Liar Liar*'. John brought along a book with a paper jacket that he had made himself. The title, hand drawn by John, was '101 Expenses Fiddles' by Ben D. Truth MP. Natasha opened her handbag and produced a tired-looking piece of fruit: 'I've brought a mouldy pear. When you buy it in the shop it looks very fresh and appealing, but very quickly it turns bad. I hope I'm wrong but I think I'm gonna be right.'

16. The opposition

This book's aim is to provide an insight into the world of politics through the eyes of the voter. Since most of my work over the past twenty-five years has been about voter interaction with Labour politics, so the Labour Party has been its main focus. But, as any voter will tell you, rightly or wrongly, politics is an adversarial game: it's a contest. I could not do justice to the voters' tale without spending some time looking at how they see the opposition.

I started writing this chapter, as the 2010 campaign began, with my eye very firmly on the Conservatives. For most of the twenty-odd years that I have been polling and conducting focus groups, UK politics has been a two-horse race. Labour's main rival, as we approached the 2010 general election, was the Conservative Party. On 15 April, as the first UK leaders' debate drew to a close, all that changed. Election campaigns traditionally favour the smaller parties by putting them under the spotlight. It had always been assumed that the debates would be helpful to the Liberal Democrats by placing them on an equal footing to what the Westminster Village often describe as the 'two main parties'. Nobody predicted the scale and scope of the change.

Yet, with hindsight, the ingredients for the electoral upset that was to come were all in place long before the debate. The backdrop was a powerful anti-politics sentiment. Voters yearned for change and were out of love with the government and its leader. However, the Conservative Party had failed to really capitalise on this mood, not consistently breaking through the 40 per cent poll share threshold that would place an overall majority comfortably in its sights. David Cameron polled ahead of his party, but, as the focus group work consistently showed, had not 'sealed the deal'. Voters found him likeable but lacking substance. A strong performance by Nick Clegg was all it took to catapult the 'third party' up the poll rankings and transform the election.

I THINK. . . I SAY. . . THE TORIES OVER THE YEARS

One week before the election was called, I convened my Harlow panel of swing voters for the first time – all residents in this two-way Lab/Con marginal. They were previous Labour voters and now undecided. I wanted to get a sense of how the Conservative Party had changed over time. I had prepared an exercise I often use with commercial clients to help understand the personalities of brands. If this brand could speak, what would it say to you? And if it could think, what would it be thinking? Based on the assumption that the party leaders themselves were the embodiment of the party brand, I again divided the group into pairs and gave each a photo of every Conservative leader from Mrs Thatcher right up to the present day. Each leader had an empty thought bubble and an empty speech bubble coming out of their heads. Showing what they knew about each leader, our Harlow voters filled these in.

Given the relative youth of some of the panel, it said much for the enduring imprint that Mrs Thatcher has left on the Conservative Party, and on the nation, that she was by far the leader with the clearest image. People had a strong sense both of what she stood for and what she had done. The photograph we used showed an airbrushed and immaculate Mrs T, crowned by a golden helmet of hair, bedecked with pearls and diamonds, smart and trim in a 1980s-style shoulder-padded navy blue suit.

The Harlow voters, many of whom would have been only children when the photograph was taken, imagined her saying:

> With me everyone could buy a house. . . and I have stamped on Arthur Scargill.

> I'm not scared to make changes.

While she thought:

> I'm always right.

> I won't let anyone cross me, I am the Iron Lady!

And, a more contemporary:

> Girl power!

I recalled old SCA work from the Thatcher era, where Mrs T, at the time a more polarising figure, many of whose powerful negatives have softened over the years, redefined not just her own party but also political leadership, heralding a new, more presidential style. As a middle class, rather than an upper class, Tory, her appeal lay in her instinctive understanding of middle ground voters, exemplified by council house sales, but also by her fervent patriotism, especially during the Falklands war, successful union bashing, and tough talk on benefit cheats and 'scroungers'.

With the exception of David Cameron, the other Conservative leaders had rather less incisive images. John Major was best known for his second, less successful, post 1992, term of office, rather than his first, where simply not being Mrs Thatcher gave him a licence to be there.. The Conservative Party brand did not progress in his time, becoming merely a very watered-down version of Thatcherite Toryism. Voters recalled him struggling to hold his government together:

> I want to keep everyone in my party happy as I have a small majority.

> Trust me, we are united. . . I hope they don't put the knife in any deeper.

William Hague was best known for being prematurely promoted, and somewhat at sea. Nothing of his party positioning or polices had left a lasting impression:

> Whose advice shall I listen to? I'm lost in this world.

> I'm the new kid on the block with fresh ideas. . . but where are the ideas?

Almost nobody recognised Iain Duncan Smith or could offer any thoughts about his contribution to Conservatism. I told them his name to act as a prompt. After a moment's collaboration, Sadia and John wrote: 'IDS – I sound like a boring sexual disease.'

Michael Howard's thoughts and speech bubbles mostly remained empty too. Keen to write something, Denis and Alicia used his photograph as a prompt and put: I'm the face of experience. . . old hand. . . God I'm old!'

Only with David Cameron did the group return to something approaching the clarity achieved by Mrs Thatcher. His speech bubbles were earnest, perhaps a little pleading:

This is me. I'm here to help. Trust in me. Believe!

I will bring this country back to the forefront as the world's capital. I will save this country!

Give me a chance, I'm here to help.

While Cameron's secret thoughts were a less positive mix, some smugly assured, others less confident:

I can do this, I'm sure I can. I just need to make you realise and understand it's gonna take time.

I so know I'll be the next Prime Minister! This is a walk in the park!

I'll say anything to get into power. Toe the party line.

Bring it on. The future's bright.

Since Thatcher and Cameron were really the only Conservative Party players, but presented such differing leadership styles, I asked the group who they would prefer as leader, if the choice was between those two. All except Denis chose Mrs Thatcher without a moment's hesitation. Her forthright approach, determination and 'can do', combined with her understanding of the middle ground voter, part instinctive, part born out of her own background, to create a winning formula.

> ALICIA: She did what she said she was going to do. David Cameron just gives you promises, you don't know what he's really like.

> LORNA: I think she really did make changes. She actually did things.

> DANNY: I'd go Thatcher, just because of how bold and bolshie she was.

> NATASHA: Because she's been in that environment, living above a shop, she could say, 'Well, I know how to look after the family purse, so you can trust me to look after the country's purse.'

Just Denis, the biggest fan of David Cameron in this focus group session, made the case for him, and how he might solve Britain's problems, using a contemporary football analogy:

> I think David Cameron can do the same, if he's honest and says, 'Look at the crisis we're in,' like David Gold and David Sullivan did with West Ham [on coming to terms with the club's financial crisis post the collapse of the Icelandic banking system]. He needs to say, 'This is what we face, guys; get used to it.'

WHAT WOULD A MARTIAN THINK?

Moving right up to date, I wanted to get a sense of how they saw the Conservatives at the start of this crucial election contest. I asked them to imagine that a Martian had landed, and was bemused by all the election activity. I divided the group into four pairs and asked each to work up a description that they could use to explain what the Conservative Party was all about: how it differs from Labour, who it represents and what policies it stands for. David Cameron would not have been unhappy with the general drift of the observations; the Conservatives were now positioned firmly in the highly sought after 'new' space, embodying the change that most people wanted to see:

PAIR 1: Young and fresh.

PAIR 2: A party looking for a new start.

It was also a party conspicuously trying to target a broader group of voters. For many years I had found that in word association exercises the first thing that voters would write down for the Conservatives was 'for the rich'. There had been a persistent underlying unease that the Conservatives were a party who looked after vested interests: wealthy people, big business, and were out of touch with how ordinary people lived their lives. Up until Cameron, the Conservatives leaders through the years of New Labour had done little to dispel this.

PAIR 1: Focusing on high percentage of middle class.

PAIR 2: Conditioning themselves to all classes – trying to help.

However, some of the policies that people associated with the Conservatives harked back to a more traditional Conservative set of values:

> PAIR 3: Building individuals' wealth by introducing lower taxes.

> PAIR 4: Take down the unions.

There were some positive image associations:

> PAIR 3: Portray a family image.

But also some entrenched negatives remained:

> PAIR 4: Snobbish; not from the 'real' world.

Sadia explained:

> Because of their background, they're not from the real world. Most of them went to public school so you do wonder if they know anything about the working classes or how they work...'photogenic' is another one: good image, good PR... I called it 'family cloning': they try and put this image out there of the perfect 2.4-children stereotypical family.

CONSERVATIVES VERSUS NEW LABOUR

Tony Blair is often described as a lucky politician. Certainly he was lucky in terms of the opposition he faced throughout his leadership.

2001 was the first election that my colleague Graeme Trayner had worked on. He recalls:

> The Tories never broke through at all. The electorate had made an
> early judgement that Hague wasn't up to the job... that speech as a
> sixteen-year-old, the baseball cap, the fourteen pints. Philip Gould
> [pollster to Blair through the 2001 campaign] was paranoid about
> the Labour lead but the Tories were just never on the radar.

In focus groups that I ran for BBC's *Newsnight* through 2001 in Luton, where there were two marginal seats, voters concurred with this view, seeing Hague as weak in his attempts to shed the Tory's patrician image. In a projective exercise the drink that Jacky, a deaf communicator, chose for him was 'a glass of water. No substance there, just weak,' while Bob, a site manager, added, 'Lager. The drink for the boys. He's trying to be one of the boys.'

'Is he one of the boys then?' I queried.

'No,' came the reply. 'I don't think he's got a good enough idea of what the everyday person wants... of what they'd expect.'

Now the desire to occupy a broader positioning was meeting with greater success:

> They used to be more for the top end but now they're trying to
> help everyone, be more for the common man, whereas it used to be
> Labour for the working classes.

> They focus on a higher percentage of middle class people as a
> whole, not the higher end, but they used to be more upper or upper
> middle... They're trying to cover a wider range of people than they
> used to.

But David Cameron had clearly not entirely shaken off the Hague image of the toff trying to get on down with the people. When asked what sort of car the Tory leader would be, a typical response was Danny's: 'He'd be a Jaguar, but he'd want you to think that he was a Ford Mondeo.'

TORY CHANGE: OPTIMISM AND FEAR

So, if the Conservatives stood for change, what did that change mean? Again, I divided the group into pairs. Each pair was given a set of scissors, pens, cardboard, glue and four magazines. I asked them to make up a collage representing how they felt about what the Conservative Party offered with words and photographs cut from the magazines.

Twenty minutes later each pair showed off their handiwork, sticky scrapbooks of cut-out photos and headlines, supplemented with handwritten slogans where the magazines had not provided the bon mot. They talked through their work. The first thoughts would have put a spring in the step of the Conservative leader, reflecting the best of his personal positioning – a fresh start. Words like 'fresh' and 'new' featured in every scrap book, as did vibrant spring colours.

> We've gone fresh, young and glitzy, because they want to project this image, they always want to be on TV. He's kissing his wife there, everyone's smiley and happy. It feels fresh across the board.

> New, change – we've put cleaning products on there to represent a fresh clean start.

Importantly, this flagged up a clear differentiation between the party's overall image and Labour's. It highlighted how, after thirteen years, Labour looked tired and stuck in a rut. GB, when he became leader, had failed to be the change messenger himself. Was Cameron's gamble that it was enough to simply not be GB's Labour paying off?

> All these things like fresh deals, new starts, healthy, new. . . it just doesn't come across like that with Labour at the moment. . . we're all down in the dumps if it stays the same.

> It would be difficult for them to say that they're fresh, because it just feels like they've been rolling on. The Budget we've just had wasn't fresh. There was nothing they were saying that was new.

However, there was a serious flaw. The Conservatives' positive fresh image was ill defined. The Harlow voters knew what it was not, but not what it was. They could call to mind no tangible policies or specific pledges to help them flesh out this brand of change. Instead voters were left to draw on what they had always imagined that Tories stood for:

> I would say that they look towards individuals to build their own wealth, and they look to lower taxation, that's a Tory theme, and they want to build up small businesses.

This included was a strong, traditional positioning on families, too:

> Family values, people sitting down and eating at the table together, working things out together.

'I think that's a good thing,' Denis, married with three kids, asserted quietly. 'I think family values have gone out of the window with both mums and dads going out to work.' This presumption derailed the positive consensus building up and identified a dangerous gender gap. Alicia argued with Denis: 'Mums and dads both have to work! The economy being what it is!'

Further discussion predicted danger lurking if Cameron did not define what kind of change the Conservatives would bring. The voters' collages revealed the genuine anxiety they felt as they contemplated change at a difficult time for the economy. In the absence of reassurance from the Conservatives, again, they filled the gaps themselves.

Words like 'terror', 'scary', and 'fear' featured heavily in the scrapbooks that they had prepared. There were also concerns about the task ahead: had the Conservatives created unrealistic expectations? There was a big focus on finance with every collage featuring photos of cash, piggy banks, pound note signs and other shorthand signals denoting the critical challenge of Britain's economy.

The flying pig represents lies, Katie Price because it's all fake, to look nice for the screens. 'Everyone is scared' because, well, we don't know what is going to happen.

We put a lot of money on ours, as money's really important. A picture of lottery tickets, because we feel like it's going to be a bit of a lottery, a bit of a gamble.

I'm nervous – how much is this going to cost me? What challenge will they take on first? How will they manage? How will it affect me? Oh dear, they suffer from a lack of experience.

REBRANDING A SKODA

In the days after the first leaders' debate, Westminster Village was in a frenzy. The campaign had been turned on its head. Clearly the Lib Dem leader, Nick Clegg, had 'won' the debate, looking at the instant polls broadcast immediately after. His performance had also pushed his party into second place in most published polling over the next few days, relegating Labour to trail third.

Our Harlow voter panel had been keeping campaign diaries, where they recorded what they had noticed and evaluated each party's campaign. Week on week, the Lib Dems' score almost doubled to 6.29 average, from 3.67. People had noticed Nick Clegg, often for the first time. As Lorna put it, 'I must say, I think this is a big thing. Maybe three weeks ago if you asked 100 people who he was, at least 40 per cent would have had no idea. I think people knew the party name but they wouldn't have known his name or picture until now.'

I thought that 60 per cent recognition was in fact a generous assessment. In any event, while Nick Clegg now provoked excited positive reactions, his offer was not without problems for this group of voters. They were concerned about what his party might do. They associated the Liberal Democrats with almost nothing: no awareness of Lib Dem views on electoral reform, for example. Just one policy area stood out, a potentially worrying one for this middle ground group of voters: immigration. There were vague recollections of Nick Clegg favouring an amnesty for illegal immigrants – generally regarded as a disastrous move.

They'll all come over knowing it'll be OK in a couple of years.

They still felt that they did not know enough about his approach to the economy and to taxation.

Like Cameron, Clegg's personal image was running significantly ahead of that of his party. We explored their views further with some projective techniques: what kind of car, or animal, would he be, and would the Lib Dem party be? Here we saw the difference between the two. While Clegg might be 'up and coming, like a Kia', the party might still might be a 'bendy bus – great idea but not very practical' or, as an animal, 'a poodle. . . I wouldn't be seen walking down the street with one'. Even Clegg himself was 'a Skoda – been rebranded but I'm still not sure that I'd want one'. The jury was out but at least the voters were sitting up and noticing, more than the man who, just a week before, could have walked down the streets of Harlow unrecognised might have dared to dream of.

WHO CAN OWN CHANGE?

People had been clear that they wanted change, something fresh and new on the political scene, and suddenly there was something fresher and newer than David Cameron. The adjectives that had previously been attributed to Cameron and the Conservatives, 'youthful', 'fresh', 'new', 'different', were now being used to describe Nick Clegg and the Lib Dems, while Cameron was attracting some of the more world weary words that would have automatically been used to describe GB and Labour: 'tired', 'trying', 'lost', 'argumentative'.

It seemed that Cameron was now paying the price for his conviction that simply not being Gordon Brown would be enough. He had taken a conscious decision not to define his offer too closely and to wait for the government lose the election. This had seemed to be the less risky approach. Yet it was still a gamble, and a gamble that Blair had not been prepared to take back in 1997, but then he had had the benefit of the years of graft put in by Neil Kinnock, transforming the party into electability, chucking out unacceptable policies, even unacceptable party members.

Eighteen months earlier, during the 2008 Labour Party conference I gave a briefing about the Conservative Party to Labour candidates and trade union campaigners. I concluded that the Tory leader, while undoubtedly having some attractive qualities, had not clinched it with voters. The Conservatives had not won over the electorate, even though Labour and GB were at their lowest ebb. I pointed out that 55 per cent of people felt Cameron was 'lightweight' and focus groups had accused him of 'being invented by a marketing department'. The bottom line was that people did not know what he stood for and he was not ringing true. The famous bike/limo/papers anecdote stuck because it symbolised this.

In part, the problem was that he had not successfully 'detoxified' the Conservative Party, as he had vowed to do. A Labour-supporting friend recently suggested to me that Cameron was not doing very well, and may end up being the Tories' 'Neil Kinnock'. I was outraged. Looking back and remembering how much work Neil put in to create an electable party, expelling party members who broke the rules, painstakingly reviewing every single policy with the voter firmly in mind, transforming the party machinery, I found it hard to see any parallel at all.

It seemed to me that the Conservatives had tried a short cut approach to Labour's long trudge back to government after years in opposition. Elected to lead the party in 2005, David Cameron believed that simply not being GB's Labour Party would be enough. Was he rerunning the 1987 rather than the 1997 general election? It looked like a quick slick of paint rather than a more fundamental overhaul. As the campaign unfolded and the voters gave their verdict we could see that this was not going to be enough.

17. The popularity contest

'This may have the feel of a TV popularity contest,' began GB in his opening statement to the second leaders' debate of the 2010 general election. He went on, 'If it's all about style and PR, then count me out. But if it's about the big decisions, if it's about judgement, if it's about achieving a better future, then I'm your man.' As he drew to his conclusion, he boldly acknowledged his poor personal standing with the public: 'Like me or not, I can deliver that plan.'

It may be that Team GB believed that this acknowledgement was the only strategy left as GB approached the final fortnight of the campaign with his personal ratings in decline. But it begged a bigger question: would it ever be possible for a politician who is not regarded warmly by the electorate to win an election?

WHAT ARE POLITICIANS LIKE (NOWADAYS)?

In Chapter 1 I outlined the voters' pen portrait of a 'typical politician', drafted in focus groups in 1985. They described an articulate, self-seeking toff:

- Upper class
- Male

- Pinstriped suit
- Drinks champagne
- Rich
- Drives a Rolls-Royce
- Worked in the City
- Reads *The Times*
- Went to Eton
- Holidays in Barbados
- Lives in a mansion
- Confident
- Arrogant
- Good speaker
- Southern

Twenty-five years on I wanted to know what had changed. I asked my swing voter panel in Harlow to conduct an identical exercise and they wrote:

- Lives in a big detached house (but not a twenty-room mansion)
- Eats out in London restaurants
- Reads the *FT*
- Able to persuade people
- Worked in finance
- Articulate
- Determined
- Two faced
- Shady
- Loving loyal wife
- 2.4 kids
- Always looking out for Number One

- Drinks whisky or G&T
- Drives Bentley, large Volvo, or maybe environmentally friendly car chosen for their image
- Tries to get on to *Have I Got News for You*
- Labrador owner
- Smartly dressed
- Becomes football supporter in the run-up to the election
- Does charity work in the constituency and talks about it a lot
- Out of touch
- Children in private schools

Comparing the two reveals some startling similarities but also a number of crucial differences. Both profiles depict someone well to do, although as time has passed the politician is expected to be more ordinary: affluent middle class rather than upper class: living in a nice detached house, not a mansion; drinking spirits, not champagne. The skills set remains similar too: being persuasive and articulate clearly matters.

Other changes are significant. Now we expect to see the candidate's life in the round. His whole life – and it is, voters assume, likely to be a 'he' – his 'loyal, loving' wife, his 2.4 privately educated children, even his choice of pet is up for scrutiny.

The most important change, however, is the creeping cynicism that pervades even this simple set of descriptions. In 1985 voters were matter of fact, and, on the whole, non judgemental. Now, the profiles are peppered with negatives: the typical politician is 'shady' and 'two faced', and 'out for number one'. Authenticity scores points, lack of it loses them. As a rule, politicians' motives are presumed insincere. . . his car is chosen for 'its image', he does charity work or even attends a football match purely to make a vote-winning point. His publicity seeking extends to a willingness to go on TV shows like *HIGNFY* to be the butt of comedians' jokes. It's worth it to raise his profile.

Another interesting difference is how little party affiliation differentiates nowadays. Back in the 1980s the generic politician profile closely matched that of the Tory politician, while the Labour profile was different: working class, stroppy, and with a trade union background. I probed on this with the Harlow group: would this have been different if you'd been describing, say a Conservative politician, rather than a Labour one? Scott told me: 'I think the person I was describing was primarily a Tory. . . but they've all become very similar now.' Michael agreed:

> Yeah, they're all too similar now. I used to have this impression that Labour was funded by the unions. Michael Foot had that scruffy persona and Harold Wilson was with his pipe. . . far away from Tory or Liberal. . . You could see them as a sort of working man's party. But now it's like Cameron and Brown. . . they're not alike in the way they look, but in their appearance, in their clothing. I see both as being in Savile Row suits.

THE IDEAL

My start point for the next line of questioning was to ask what the job of the MP should be. I set out in Chapter 14 how little voters know about what politicians actually spent their time doing, but I wanted them to spell out their ideal. What did they actually want politicians to do? Unfortunately, it quickly became obvious that the voter knew so little about what possibilities the role might offer that this task proved impossible.

However, the group did have a clear sense of the attributes they believed a successful politician would need. These grouped into five areas: personal integrity, willingness to work hard, being 'in touch', being a good communicator and having relevant experience.

Personal integrity was a powerful counter to the reputational damage caused by expenses and an essential 'hygiene factor'.

> MICHAEL: They need to be sincere and honest.

> NATASHA: Honest – able to be in the public eye, to cope with scrutiny.

Willingness to work hard is important, too, given the specific demands of the job. This should be proven in advance, with the would-be politician earning the right to be there.

> MICHAEL: It's a long job, they're up till three or four in the morning in the Commons. I'd employ two people to do the job if needs be.

> TRACEY: Someone who has worked hard, and established themselves through their hard work rather than having it handed to them on a plate.

This hard work should yield relevant experience which is partly about specific qualifications but also about maturity and wider life experience:

> Good education, that's life education, not necessarily academic – having done a bit of everything. You wouldn't want to employ someone who is twenty.

Proven financial and economic background – not necessarily as a banker or accountant, but to be able to understand the economy.

Intelligent and well educated but with human experience behind them.

Being 'in touch' with the voter was more about how the politician behaves, than where he comes from.

JOHN: Being a person of the people.

SCOTT: Down to earth.

But voters also want politicians who are motivated by a sense of 'higher purpose': to inspire and motivate the rest of us. There was regret that this sense of vocation was often missing nowadays:

SADIA: People do it as a job now but it should be done with a passion.

MICHAEL: Be able to inspire people.

SADIA: Come up with ideas to add a bit of spice to our lives, thinking outside the box.

TRACEY: There needs to be substance there, more than just an image.

But strong communications skills are vital in the modern era:

SCOTT: They must be a charismatic speaker.

TRACEY: Articulate.

LOCAL MATTERS

Having local credentials was something of a recurring theme. Most people want their MPs to live locally, to spend most of their time locally and to know all about local issues. While a high profile figure who is significant on the national stage has some appeal, they would prefer their MP not to do any other jobs (in or out of government) They see the MP as an individual, who, although adhering to the overall creed of a particular party should be most strongly motivated by the local community's needs, and, importantly, accountable to them.

> MICHAEL: They need to work on the local side because at the end of the day they are only there because local people voted for them.

The importance of 'local' had been made clear to me by my first Labour focus groups, conducted during the critical by-election in Fulham in 1986. The resulting campaign featured billboards and window posters designed by ad man Trevor Beattie, who would go on to produce some of Labour's most memorable campaign advertising. The campaign was single-minded in positioning Nick Raynsford as the only local candidate – a family man who lived in the constituency and was raising his three children there; who really understood local people's issues. Hundreds of posters, all displayed in homes throughout the constituency, proclaimed 'Nick Raynsford lives here!' Dramatising his strong local roots won Raynsford the historic victory that was one of the turning points in Labour's long journey towards 1997.

The ideal MP would always champion local causes. The Hansard

Society's 2010 Audit of Public Engagement confirmed that people felt that MPs should spend the majority of their time in the constituency, not in Parliament. It also confirmed that people see the MP's primary job as listening to and helping local people. This means standing up for local causes in the face of big government, big business, big anything. He must be someone who manifestly understands individual constituents' needs – and cares. He is someone who is not driven by personal gain or influenced by vested interests but motivated by a greater cause.

LIVING UP TO THE IDEAL

So how do real politicians measure up to these demands? I used an array of photographs to prompt the Harlow group to evaluate individual politicians, past and present, from all three main parties. Many familiar faces around Westminster had simply failed to cut through and were not recognised by anyone; these included Chris Grayling, Chris Huhne, George Osborne and Alan Johnson. A guessing game ensued:

SCOTT: Is he the Health Minister?

SADIA: Isn't he Welsh?

Others were infamous, rather than famous. Peter Mandelson was one of the best known, albeit for the wrong reasons:

MICHAEL: Well, he's done everything wrong, hasn't he? Didn't he get someone to buy a home for him and claimed it on expenses?

TRACEY: He was sacked twice by the government.

George Galloway would also not be pleased by his claim to fame:

NATASHA: The cat man! [*peals of laughter and recollections of* Celebrity Big Brother]

Ann Widdecombe had also descended into caricature:

MICHAEL: Another pantomime Dame.

SCOTT: An extremist nutter.

TRACEY: Yeah, an extreme Catholic who doesn't believe in contraception – she doesn't talk to the country I live in.

The politicians whose reputations were positive and enduring had all challenged the status quo bravely. They were seen as their own people, not slavishly following a party line, willing to speak out for what they believed to be right. They had also come across to the Harlow group as truly authentic, unafraid to be themselves even if this meant being unconventional. They were 'risk takers' like Mo Mowlam, who was known by everyone:

SADIA: She just stood for everything that is right and good.

TRACEY: What she did in Northern Ireland was extraordinary.

Or, less well known but generally positive, especially with the women, Clare Short:

SCOTT: She had the same kind of thing as Mo Mowlam – just stood up for her principles.

JOHN: She was willing to take on the media with her Page Three challenge.

And some even reinvented themselves successfully after sticky starts, like Michael Portillo:

TRACEY: Did he do a job swap TV programme with a single mum? He really went up in my estimation after that – I think they should do more things like that.

SCOTT: He did a really good TV programme on humane killing. Ten, twenty years ago you wouldn't have had Portillo in there but now he's changed. He's likeable.

HEROES AND VILLAINS

I was curious to take this further and see what, if anything, voters admired most in politicians they knew, and what they liked least. I asked the group to nominate three political heroes and three political villains. They immediately pushed back on this task. Michael protested, 'I'd just like to say that I have a problem with the word "hero" for this.' Sadia agreed: 'Yeah, none of them are exactly Mother Teresa, are they?' However, they all sat down and worked through the task, first of all producing the following heroes list: Churchill (4 votes), Thatcher (2), Bevan (2), Obama (2), Mandela, Franklin, Lincoln, Shirley Williams, Kennedy.

I queried why nobody currently in the House of Commons had been chosen, and Tracey explained, 'You need time to judge people and see the impact they had.' But Obama had snuck through because, as Sadia put it, 'He's the first black President and he's trying to move things forward, and he's not bad looking for a politician!' Scott concurred: 'Yes, the razzmatazz that Obama brings to American politics, that's what we all love. It made him an inspiration. . . Tony Blair had that years ago.'

This prompted me to ask why Tony Blair hadn't made it on to the hero list. Sadia explained, 'I think if he hadn't done the war. . . He could have been one of our best Prime Ministers. He seemed to run the country quite well. He put a good face on the country. His mistake was the Iraq War. . . If it hadn't been for that. . .'

After discussion, the group were able to identify the criteria that united their political heroes: the ability to inspire, the ability to cope with adversity and the ability to bring about positive change. Ideally these laudable aims needed to be illustrated by a tangible outcome – back to our old friend the symbolic policy:

MICHAEL: Creating wonderful things like the NHS.

Sometimes the politicians were themselves the personification of the change they brought about:

SCOTT: Obama. Change the face of American politics – he has done that, literally.

TRACEY: Thatcher. Being the first woman PM.

Two other personal characteristics were felt to be vital too:

NATASHA: Doing what they say they will do.

SCOTT: Staying human, in touch with the common people.

The villains list provoked even more animated conversation. The voters' villains were: Peter Mandelson (3), Hitler (2), Saddam Hussein (2), George Bush (2), Robert Mugabe, Nick Griffin, Blair, Thatcher, Gordon Brown and 'any expenses git'. Peter Mandelson had the dubious achievement of being seen as a greater villain than Adolf Hitler, Saddam Hussein or Robert Mugabe. However, the darling of the Westminster Village was more a figure of fun to the voter than a figure of evil, despite the other unquestionably sinister villains in whose company he found himself. He provoked knock-about humour amongst the group. I raised an eyebrow and John explained, 'He's a sleazeball.' Scott added, 'I kind of strangely like him. He's like a lion with a lamb. He can't help himself. That's who he is.'

Then the others piled in, everyone with a point of view:

JOHN: He's like the baddie in a pantomime.

SCOTT: No! The pantomime dame.

MICHAEL: He's the Child Catcher in *Chitty Chitty Bang Bang*!

Many of the other villains' qualifications were more obvious but I also queried George Bush:

NATASHA: Because of Iraq.

> SADIA: He was very narrow minded.

And Tony Blair:

> NATASHA: I actually had him as a hero, then crossed him out and
> put him as a villain. I was thinking about the war...

Mrs Thatcher was the only person to make it on to both lists:

> TRACEY: Because I think she was brutal, heartless, divisive.

> JOHN: She could be both a hero and a villain.

A DIFFERENT MODEL OF LEADERSHIP

Our discussion on heroes and villains had moved us from the sphere of
the ordinary constituency MP into a wider discussion about leadership.
Two weeks later, back in Harlow, I asked the panel to develop this theme:
what are the qualities of a good leader? I asked them in the first instance
to think more widely than political leaders and to consider the leadership
styles of men and women that they admired from other walks of life.

They tackled this by constructing 'Frankenstein' leaders out of
component parts:

> SADIA: The balls of Mrs Thatcher, media friendly like Clegg, family
> man like Cameron, calm like John Major, honest like Vince Cable,
> good all-round knowledge like Gordon Brown.

> TRACEY: I'd vote for him!

They brainstormed around the topic, agreeing that other possible transplantable parts might be imported from a range of well known leaders:

- Innovative like Theo Paphitis
- The delegation and people skills of Richard Branson
- Decisive like Alan Sugar
- Shrewd like David Miliband
- Deal making like Duncan Bannatyne
- Able to talk to a wide range of people like Nick Clegg
- Charismatic like George Clooney
- Tough like Alex Ferguson

More than twenty years earlier, researcher Roddy Glen had conducted some focus groups to explore leadership for the Shadow Communications Agency. He had concluded that effective leadership was especially vital for a political party at a time of transition, as Labour was then, both to unify its mission and to personify the party's qualities, creating an easy shorthand for the electorate. He produced a similar wish list of leaders' qualities. In his debrief he made clear that likeability was not a prerequisite. With Mrs Thatcher as the dominant role model at the time, he identified what he described as the 'admiration paradox' where, Mrs T's qualities made her an admired leader although no one would want her as a friend. Neil Kinnock's persona was the opposite.

Researching leadership styles amongst swing voters twenty years later, as GB was preparing to set out his stall in 2006, I found that 'empathy' characteristics like 'listening to the public' and 'understands what ordinary life is like' mattered much more than they had done then; they were some of the highest-scoring attributes. The world had changed and we had seen very different leadership styles in Tony Blair and Bill Clinton, more open and informal. This mirrored the changed politician pen portraits at the opening of this chapter. In 1985 politicians were allowed to be distant figures of authority; now we were demanding more accessible, rounded personalities.

In 2002, Opinion Leader Research ran a briefing session on leadership for senior clients. The survey that we ran then grouped leadership characteristics into three typologies. The first was the Rottweiler: a 'power' leader who is authoritative, is clearly 'the boss', and is tough and consistent. This was Margaret Thatcher or Winston Churchill's kind of leadership. The second, the Puma, was a visionary, inspiring enthusiasm and goodwill, popular, but leading from the front. Example pumas were Tony Blair, Bill Clinton or Richard Branson. Finally, came the Dolphin: a 'social' leader achieving their goals through consensus and participation, being persuasive and motivating. Princess Diana and Kofi Annan were held up as examples of this breed.

Not surprisingly, the research concluded that most successful leaders were a mix of these different attributes, and clearly different situations demanded different approaches. However, the public believed the that most successful leader overall was mostly Puma, demonstrating vision and the ability to motivate (68 per cent); then Dolphin, persuasive and consensual (21 per cent) and with a relatively small amount of grit; the Rottweiler element was scored at just 5 per cent.

A POPULARITY CONTEST?

In the research I carried out for GB's personal campaign in 2006, we found that strength mattered a lot more than likeability – in fact it was twice as important. Experience was a high scoring attribute, too. While continuing to develop GB's '3D persona', especially the empathetic qualities like listening, we seized on these findings and drew comfort from them.

GB's campaign tried again to focus on his experience and strength during the 2010 campaign. By the third leadership debate, after the unfortunate Mrs Duffy incident, they attempted to disregard likeability as 'style', while claiming that GB had 'substance'. He did indeed have substance – more so than the other candidates, but he lacked the vital puma qualities of enthusiasm and vision and the dolphin quality of persuasion.

So, how to answer the question posed at the beginning of this chapter? Is it possible to be a successful politician nowadays without attracting some level of public warmth? My judgement would be that it is not. It may have been back in the 1980s, but in the transparent world in which we now live, we make far greater demands on would-be politicians, and especially on political leaders. This highlights the paradox that underlies politicians' reputations. Voters are less forgiving than they were back in the 1980s. They are cynical, disengaged, sometimes angry. But these negative feelings derive in part because voters still have a touching faith in the potential of politicians' positive motivations. It is a popularity contest, and the stakes are high.

18. The 2010 campaign

The Harlow panel of swing voters were settling down for a nice snooze at the start of the 2010 election campaign. Despite living in one of the most fiercely contested marginal seats in Britain, during what promised to be one of the most closely fought election campaigns for decades, they were just not very excited. On our first meeting I had asked them to bring along items to sum up their views of politics. Their choices included a hairdryer (all that hot air) and an empty bottle (it's all so vacuous). The plan was to ignore as much as they could and get on with their lives.

By contrast, the Westminster Village was very excited indeed. In the weeks that followed, the political parties gave us the leaders' debates, manifesto launches, Cleggmania, Bigotgate, the wives' fashion show, Gary Barlow and an Elvis impersonator, countless photo opportunities in schools, factories, and old folks' homes, and poster campaigns which were instantly and hilariously subverted on the internet.

Meanwhile the press and broadcast media commissioned up to five opinion polls a day, hired experts in every conceivable policy area, in body language, in fashion, in US politics and in communications. We heard from business leaders, playwrights, impersonators, comedians and pollsters who wrote, broadcast, blogged and tweeted 24/7.

So did the people of Harlow nod off or did they wake up and take notice? Did the campaign make any difference?

All twelve were asked to complete weekly diaries detailing what they noticed, that they liked, and what they didn't like as the campaign wore on, and we met up once a week to get an in-depth view of how it all impacted on them.

This is the story of their campaign.

WEEK ONE

Our first campaign focus group met the day after GB's visit to the palace. The starting gun had been fired but voters had not yet thought much about the national campaign, although local activity was already making a splash. I asked if anyone had picked up on the National Insurance rise that Labour were proposing. This had dominated the previous week's media coverage with the Conservatives dubbing Labour's plan a 'tax on jobs' and lining up top business leaders to denounce it.

The panel's response was muted. There were murmurs that it had been Easter weekend – as Michael put it, 'not a good weekend for politics'. Scott agreed: 'I was busy with the family all weekend too.'

Most people, anticipating the next few weeks, were already switching off a little, expecting to be moved as far as mild irritation by any campaign activity that they could not escape.

SADIA: I've an awful feeling I'm going to be annoyed by it.

SCOTT: If they start doing that kind of he said/she said stuff, that really gets my back up.

NATASHA: Negative campaigning – oh shut up!

The panel's diaries

They noticed that they were in a very active marginal seat, with Robert Halfon, the Conservative candidate, proving particularly hyperactive. Almost all the initial diary observations were about the local, rather than the national campaign:

> SADIA: Election, election – we are officially in overload! You can't get away from it, it's through your door, on posters, on telly, everywhere!

> SCOTT: Bill Rammell [Labour] and Robert Halfon [Conservative] on the front page of the *Harlow Star*.

> ALICIA: A giant flag in Nazeing, where Robert Halfon lives.

> ANGELA: The Conservative Party very proactive in my community... sitting on the roadside with their signs.

> LORNA: Lots of houses on my route to work with Conservative placards.

They liked some of the local campaigning they had seen. Nick Clegg, his profile suddenly rising thanks to campaign coverage, was the only national politician to get a name check.

> DENIS: The Bill Rammell leaflet was a good memory jogger of what has been accomplished locally by him for the people. Very direct.

> ALICIA: Robert's flag.

Scott: Nick Clegg saying the Tories and Labour have blocked the Lib Dems on something.

Sadia: Nick Clegg on *Question Time.*

In one of the few mentions of national media coverage that week, Tracey had picked up on *Newsnight*'s coverage of marginal seats and liked this:

> They are visiting marginal constituencies and looking at what is going on; this first in the series was at the country's most marginal – Croydon. Harlow is also a marginal, and Bill Rammell has a majority of just 97, so I'll be following this *Newsnight* series with some interest hoping that they come to my town!

They disliked some of the local campaigning tactics and a few snippets of policy that they had picked up so far:

> Angela: The Conservatives waving to you as you drive by them in slow moving traffic. Somewhat embarrassing, I thought.

> Sadia: Our local candidates sitting on roundabouts and on A roads. . . they look so desperate.

> Lorna: Married people to get extra money. If you're single you are just losing out because you haven't met that special person to marry or can't afford to get married.

> Tracey: Rumours of death tax to fund elderly care, increases in NI, the tax breaks for married couples (what's the point?).

Tracey, who had so enjoyed the *Newsnight* story about Croydon – a bit like Harlow, felt overwhelmed by the national news coverage:

> The broadsheets and the BBC news website have blanket election coverage already. . . I'm bored by it! I want to stay well informed and find out what real policies are for all the parties, but there seems to be a mountain of information to wade through in order to feel that I'm looking at all the suggestions and options. I doubt if I'll ever get to grips with all of that, and it's likely to increase as election day draws nearer. Unless something jumps out of the news at me, I feel pretty ignorant.

And giving each main party marks out of ten the Conservatives started the campaign in the lead, with Labour in second place:

Conservatives 6.17
Labour   5.50
Lib Dem   3.67

WEEK TWO

This was the week of the first TV debate. Only one person, Paul, had watched the debate all the way through, switching from TV to radio halfway through 'to get a different perspective'. Angela 'had it on but was doing other things as well'. The rest had followed the story in the media, mainly the TV news, or the internet after the event.

Interestingly, the group's initial discussion focused more on Gordon Brown's performance than Nick Clegg's. Generally the format was not felt to play to GB's strengths, and most comments were critical.

Paul, the eager beaver who had opted for a multimedia approach, explained what he had learned from his experiment: 'The only difference really was that Brown came over better on the radio.' Alicia had also been listening to the radio and had an explanation for this: 'I heard Brown talking on the radio afterwards about how he thought he'd done. He said he thought he should have been smiling at people more. He hasn't got the right body language, he's used to being in the background.' Angela thought so too: 'It might sound silly but I hate the way he speaks... that thing he does with his mouth.'

Lorna was the first to introduce the topic of Clegg's rise to fame, picking up on media coverage afterwards:

> I was working when it was on TV, but I saw the news and read about it on the internet. The main thing I took from it was how this outsider as they put it has come in and given hope... a lot of people who wouldn't have voted, or people who might have voted Liberal but thought they wouldn't get elected are now thinking 'Ooh, maybe I will'. I think it's really stirred things up and made people have a think.

As the media were now talking up the prospect of a hung Parliament, I asked the group what they felt. I suggested an exercise, in pairs, drafting 'birth announcements' for a hung Parliament. It revealed considerable anxiety underneath the initial novelty.

DENIS AND ANGELA:
We are pleased to announce the birth of a hung parliament
The Queen announced she was not amused
Weighing in at twelve stone times three
Two are joined at the hip

Parentage: very debatable

We are expecting a lot of changing and a lot of hot air!

DANNY AND LORNA:

We've got a stork carrying an unknown

A chain that's been broken, which is being fixed by everyone, all working together

And a question mark

PAUL AND ALICIA:

We're proud to announce the birth of twins

Two different personalities:

One is loving and giving and tries to please everyone

And one has its own ideas and sticks to them

One's poo doesn't stink; the other's smells of roses.

In the discussion that followed, the panel worried away about what a hung parliament might mean. They were not clear and felt others would not know either:

ALICIA: People aren't really sure what a hung parliament is.

Rather than empowering voters, a hung parliament, they felt, was likely to disenfranchise them in favour of scheming politicians:

DENIS: It makes a mockery out of voting. . . you haven't got a say! It makes a mockery of the whole system.

Pressed to consider any advantages, my questions were met with initial silence. Finally Denis ventured, 'I suppose it might force them to work together for the benefit of the country as a whole.' Alicia was the first to challenge this view: 'But they're so different.' Her views were based on local experience: 'We've got one in Harlow, and it's useless. . . it shouldn't be allowed because it just doesn't work. They just can't work together, can they?'

The panel's diaries
They noticed Nick Clegg had stolen the show by the weekend when the diaries were completed. But even at the height of 'Cleggmania' he was competing with local activity, which was still making as much of an impact as any of the national parties' efforts.

> TRACEY: There's been an awful lot about Nick Clegg's success on the live TV debate.

> LORNA: The Lib Dems had a very good week last week and it looks as though they might be in the running again.

> ANGELA: The Conservatives are out in force in my local area.

> ALICIA: Local Conservative vans everywhere.

They liked Nick Clegg. There was effusive praise for and support for challenging the notion of a two-horse race. This energised the campaign and fuelled their interest. Local campaigning, however, continued to get almost as much mention, with the Conservatives the most visible, but Labour's Bill Rammell defending his turf hard and to some effect.

> JOHN: Nick Clegg seemed so confident in the debate.

LORNA: It has made it more exciting, and probably making people stop and think twice. Maybe all the people who would like to vote Liberal but think it is never worth it might change their mind.

ANGELA: I like the fact that the Lib Dems are now a challenge to the other two.

ALICIA: It was good to see Bill Rammell on my doorstep, finding out personally his views and his goals.

Several panellists had noticed and were critical of the media tirade against Nick Clegg. They also disliked arguing and 'scoring points' in the debates. Even apparent attempts to collaborate or find common ground were mistrusted. GB attracted mixed reviews.

TRACEY: The way the knives are out for Nick Clegg because he did so well. I don't like this personal mud slinging.

JOHN: David Cameron and Gordon Brown seemed to spend more time trying to score points off each other... Gordon Brown sucking up to Nick Clegg like a playground bully when the worm has turned.

PAUL Very impressed with Gordon Brown in Week 2 – more confident – looks like you could trust him with future plans during the recovery

ANGELA: Sounds silly but I thought Gordon Brown was so strange on the debate programme – like a rabbit caught in the headlights of a car.

And giving each main party marks out of ten, the Conservatives remained narrowly in the lead but all three parties were converging with the Lib Dems replacing Labour in second place.

Conservatives 6.57

Lib Dems   6.29

Labour   6.14

WEEK THREE

By week three everyone in the panel was a little more engaged. Nevertheless, most felt that this campaign, although more interesting than they might have expected, had not exactly taken the nation – or Harlow – by storm. 'I feel like nobody debates it,' Michael observed. 'You go to work and nobody actually talks about it. I remember ten to fifteen years ago, people used to discuss it but now they're more interested in Wayne Rooney's groin, you know? Nobody ever talks about the politicians.'

Natasha wondered if this was because it was a sensitive issue for some: 'People feel uncomfortable talking about politics.' She also wondered if young people were particularly uninterested: 'The younger generation, myself and my friends have no interest in it. . . I mean I know it affects me more, having a child, but a lot of my friends have no interest in it whatsoever.'

The local campaign, especially that of Conservative candidate Robert Halfon, still dominated the conversation, as it seemed to dominate the constituency. The Conservatives were on the streets, on the doorstep, even in B&Q.

There were mixed views about how 'presidential' the national campaigns had become with each party seemingly reduced to a one-man show.

> PAUL: I think that's what's lacking at the moment. Especially David Cameron doesn't seem to be bringing in any members of his own party – he seems to be doing it all on his own.

Some regret was expressed at how personalities were dominating rather than issues and policies.

> NATASHA: They're being very celebby, aren't they? I don't think it's necessary.

This might have been a strong area for GB and Labour to develop but, amidst views that GB was trailing Clegg and Cameron in the debates, he was not seen to have effectively carved out the anti-celebrity, substance-over-style niche for himself: 'He's no better or worse than the others,' Michael commented: 'Why doesn't he take a lead? He could say, "You carry on talking about my hair and my silly smile and my bad eye. We're going to talk about the policies."'

Given that everyone was claiming that they were eager to concentrate more on the parties, as well as the leaders, and on the policies, I proposed an exercise where the group prepared mini manifestos for each party based on what they knew about that party's policies and likely style of government as we moved towards the final week of the campaign. I also asked them to pretend to be the campaign team, advising the party in the final week or so of the campaign.

The Conservatives' mini manifesto

Style of government Fresh, new, quite confident. Wanting to make a change, to show they were the new party in charge. To use their experience to put right what they think Labour has done wrong.

Advice for the campaign The best way to try and win the vote of the working man is to have a policy on working tax credits because they're planning to take money away from that.

Plus have a policy on immigration, increasing the money going into the NHS and have a time scale for bringing the troops home from Afghanistan.

In the last party political broadcast, it really looked like he (DC) had made a connection, he came over so well. He was out on the streets, talking to people, with his sleeves rolled up. Doing more of that would be good – be seen to connect more with people.

The Liberal Democrats' mini manifesto

Style of government A bit deluded – a lot of these ideas can seem great, but it's all going to cost and the economy can't bear that cost.

We don't know how he (NC) would stand up on the world stage – we don't think he's strong enough or has the experience. Cameron's got experience of running the party, but Nick Clegg's just been thrust into the limelight suddenly.

Advice for the campaign Not to argue or bicker, just to smile. See more of Vince Cable, because people seem to like him. Clegg's doing well, but it would help to bring in others like Vince Cable, who's a bit older.

Be clear on immigration policies and on benefit policies. They need to explain where the money's coming from.

Labour's mini manifesto

Style of government A sorry style, suffering. It's been very difficult after thirteen years, we're in this mess. He's got to apologise for making these errors. It's a very high hill he's got to climb. We can't see that it'd be radically different. A smug government.

Advice for the campaign Just keep pressing the idea that they've saved the economy and that we are pulling out of recession.

Talk about good things that they've done for the health service, reducing waiting lists and such like.

It would be good if they had a new leader, but maybe it would just be better if they had someone younger like David Miliband there by Gordon Brown's side.

More help for childcare and single parents.

Keep stressing the policy over image thing. Hammer the policies not the cosmetics, because it should come down to the nitty gritty of what they do, not image, but unfortunately that's the world that we live in.

The panel's diaries

The Lib Dem momentum was the main topic, with the debate again a showcase for Nick Clegg. Local campaigning now seemed to have receded a little and it was the national story that was dominating the conversation.

> TRACEY: Nick Clegg does seem like a credible alternative to Brown/ Cameron and not just hype.

> NATASHA: There is a definite shift in popularity – the Lib Dems are about the idea of change and a fairer government.

NATASHA: The likelihood of a hung parliament is increasing.

They liked that the TV debates had enlivened the campaign and changed the dynamic. Some had caught up with the debates after the event. Still the events themselves were felt to be a little dry.

TRACEY: I've now watched the first and the second TV debates – I think it is excellent that there is this forum to hear what the party leaders have to say, although my attention span doesn't quite stretch to ninety minutes and I mentally switch off by the end.

NATASHA: I liked the way that David Cameron came across in the Sky debate – he defended himself against Gordon Brown's accusations and came back well with the leaflet that Labour handed out with the false claims.

They disliked that the detail of the campaign – the policies or 'substance' – was hard to unpick. And most of the group were now quite troubled about the implications of a hung Parliament.

TRACEY: Perhaps it's just me but I find it hard to actually remember what the individual party policies are. . . It's all washing over me rather than me actually absorbing this stuff: the spectacle/cut and thrust is more interesting than the detail.

LORNA: No one will say what they will do if there is a hung Parliament.

JOHN: A hung Parliament would never agree on anything and nothing would ever get done.

Giving each main party marks out of ten, the Lib Dems had now moved into top place, with Labour sliding down further into third.

Lib Dems	6.71
Conservatives	6.57
Labour	5.57

WEEK FOUR

By week four, the enthusiasm spiked by the first debate had waned a little. We had to nag the panel to complete their diaries, and only half did, mostly submitting them late.

In the focus groups, one topic dominated the initial discussion of the week that had passed: 'Bigotgate'. Everyone had seen it and no one thought it was a pretty sight.

> TRACEY: Gordon Brown's bigot remark – that was a bit of a downfall for him, wasn't it?

> SCOTT: How he reacted on the Jeremy Vine show, when he was listening to it too – he really shot himself in the foot.

Events like this tend to cut through when they reinforce a previously held view. While the Westminster Village were drawing dark conclusions about how the incident reflected GB's 'bullying character', instead the Harlow voters were reminded of a different 'truth' about GB: his unfitness for the modern telegenic age. Sadia put her finger on it: 'I think he's alright as a person and he's not been given much of a chance, but a silly mistake like

that. . . if you're on the campaign and you're wired up to mics. . .'
Scott agreed: 'In the modern day, when there are so many cameras
around, and microphones, it's just very naïve.' And Danny piled
in: 'When Gordon Brown's under pressure he just can't cope.'
Scott continued: 'In the modern arena he just doesn't seem to be
the kind of person who copes very well – he's an old fashioned
politician, maybe fifty years out of date.'

The killer was the contrast with his opponents. Sadia said, 'David
Cameron wouldn't get caught like that, he's just too slick.' Or his
predecessor, said Scott: 'Tony Blair would never make that mistake.'

Other campaign activity was much less noteworthy. The final
debate had failed to produce a startling outcome, and not many
had bothered to watch it at the time or catch it later. Few were
discussing the campaign with friends, family or colleagues either.
Local campaigning was still the most striking thing, especially
Robert Halfon's, notable for its ubiquity, although the roadside
activities remained controversial.

> DANNY: He sits there behind a big placard talking on his phone
> and a woman stands five feet behind him giving it hell for leather
> – it's embarrassing!

> TRACEY: It's impossible to ignore but there's no substance to it – it's
> just a man sitting by the side of the road.

Harlow Voter Panel Campaign Awards

The end of the campaign was in sight, so we decided to create our
own Harlow Campaign Awards. I invited everyone to review the
whole campaign and vote for the winners and losers.

Best campaign Liberal Democrats.

> DENIS: Because they came from absolutely nowhere, so they must have had a good campaign.

But the discussion that ensued focused more on the Conservatives, damned by faint praise.

> SCOTT: All Cameron had to do was not mess up. . . not do a Bigotgate and be defined by a mistake.

Worst campaign This was unanimous: Labour. This was all about GB's own persona, unpopular and unsuited to 2010 politics.

> SCOTT: In modern times, they need a modern politician. He should be able to speak to people younger than me, who haven't the attention to listen to him. They want things immediately, they want things in bullet points. He just doesn't come across like Nick Clegg or David Cameron or even Tony Blair.

> DENIS: I think it's significant that they haven't put his face on the leaflets.

Even GB's impassioned speech to Citizens UK on the final Sunday before polling day, praised by the media, failed to hit the spot and took the group back full circle to Bigotgate.

> TRACEY: He seems to have more of a genuineness and a personal integrity that the others haven't got. . . if anyone was going to make a mistake like this Bigotgate thing it would be Gordon

Brown because he's not so savvy as the others at handling the media.

Best debate Again, this was unanimous: Nick Clegg, although already there were hints that Clegg had peaked too soon.

> SCOTT: If people had voted that night [of the debate] he would have had a very good chance, but as the weeks have gone on. . .

Best ad Significantly, given the low-key role of paid-for media, memories were sketchy here.

> ANGELA: The Conservative one – the grinning one.

> DANNY: Is that the one that looks like a Labour one, with Gordon Brown and it says this man's going to make you pay. . . yeah, I like those.

Best broadcast Party political broadcasts, agonised over in party HQ's had made even less impact. The Cameron shirtsleeves film was the best known of a very anonymous bunch.

> SADIA: The only broadcast I've seen was a Tory one.

> DENIS: I tend to turn them off.

> TRACEY: The only one I remember was the Conservative one with David Cameron – it was a nice sunny day. . . I can't remember a word of what he said but he came over well.

Best manifesto Very little of the contents of each of the manifestos had been noticed. When filling in their award voting forms, many left that topic blank. There was a short discussion about the Lib Dem manifesto and whether it was affordable, leading to a rare discussion about dealing with the deficit.

> SCOTT: We were talking about this the other day and how many policies that they all mentioned without putting any costs against them. . . and they were saying that the Lib Dems had the least amount of uncosted ones so I've put the Lib Dems.

Best policy Again, the panel struggled to name anything and several forms were left blank. This election was not about policies and few had cut through.

> SCOTT: The Lib Dems giving you the first £10, 000 tax free.

> ANGELA: Immigration – deploying people to areas where they need the skills like in Australia.

ANTICIPATING THE OUTCOME

Finally, as we were now two days from a result, I asked everyone to think about how they would feel given the different election outcomes. None of the options for a majority government held real appeal.

Labour was for most the worst option: 'same old, same old'. Voters would be surprised and, for the most part, very disappointed with this outcome, as it did not satisfy their urge for change – now overwhelming. Yet a Conservative or even Lib Dem winner also failed to hit the spot. While either of these did promise change, there were powerful misgivings about both. The Conservatives were felt to be only touting the 'not Labour' line, with no positive programme to sell, while the Lib Dems were just too much of a leap in the dark. While both offered change, neither version of change held a strong appeal.

We also explored reactions to the two possible collaborations: Con/Lib and Lab/Lib. This is where the effect of relegating policy to an also ran can be seen most vividly. Instead the Harlow voters' decisions were based on the reputation of the party brands. Therefore Lab/Lib was rejected out of hand as it was felt that the two parties had so little in common that this was a combination that would never be made to work. The cultural rather than the policy gap was too great:

> SADIA: You've got Labour who have been there for years and the Lib Dems who are new.

> SEVERAL: It won't work.

By contrast, the Con/Lib Dem combo was judged as ' a good team to work together', their 'newness' winning out over any policy differences:

> DENIS: Both working at the same goals, both fresh.

The panel's diaries
Again, local campaigning – especially Conservative campaigning – took the greatest share of voice. Bigotgate was the top national event, along with some comment about the Lib Dems 'peaking too early'. They noticed:

> ALICIA: Placards up, different villages next to each other voting for different parties.

LORNA: Mr Brown caught on mic calling a lady a bigot.

NATASHA: News reporting that the Lib Dems may have peaked too early as recent polls are showing a decline.

There were a couple of positive comments about GB's Citizen UK speech, otherwise it seemed as though voters were struggling to see any positives at all, and were definitely zoning out again.

SADIA: The increased passion that GB is showing, he is starting to show that there is more to him than his serious/miserable persona.

NATASHA: Nothing to comment on – it's been a busy week for me, so I've not noticed much.

For dislikes, nothing was really cutting through apart from Bigotgate.

TRACEY: I watched the third TV debate but my attention had well and truly gone after about forty minutes. I feel a bit electioned out and just want Thursday to arrive so we can get it over and done with and know a result.

LORNA: I disliked. . . the amount of leaflets that I am getting through my door on a daily basis.

Marks out of ten show the Conservatives back in top position, despite little of their campaign getting noticed. Labour, after a bad week, was in third place, but the Lib Dems were dropping back also.

Conservatives	7.3
Lib Dems	5.0
Labour	3.2

THE OUTCOME

The panel met two days before Election Day, and I asked them to second guess the outcome. The group was split down the middle, with half predicted a narrow Tory victory and half predicting a hung Parliament.

Those predicting a Tory win were right locally, at least. In Harlow, with its Labour majority of less than 100, an effective Conservative campaign on the ground (notwithstanding Robert Halfon's highway lurking) achieved a relatively easy win.

Nationally, however, by creating a hung Parliament, the voters had spoken and had managed to blow a raspberry to all of the main parties: Labour was punished for being the incumbent, with an unpopular and old fashioned leader, when change was top of the voters' wishlist. GB finally found his voice in the last few days, after a disastrous campaign, but it was too little, too late. Yet the Conservative brand of change, never clearly set out, failed to fire the public imagination. People flirted briefly with Nick Clegg, the new kid on the block, but in the end were not impressed by his offer either.

Now, as politicians disappeared behind closed doors, we all awaited the final outcome.

19. Conclusions

This book tells two parallel stories.

One is the story of New Labour's rise and fall seen through the eyes of the voter. It charts what Labour had to do and what Labour had to ditch to get noticed in the first place, and then what else it had to do to win back sufficient trust to succeed in 1997. We see how, with more voter acclaim than it had dared to dream of, Labour began to believe its own hype and stopped listening to voters, ultimately with fatal consequences.

But this is not just a story about the ups and downs of one political party over another. As the Labour Party, first under Tony Blair and then under Gordon Brown, relinquished its hard won electoral success, and David Cameron struggled to reinvent his party, albeit with less time and a lot less determination than Neil Kinnock had had in the 1980s, a much more far-reaching attitudinal shift was taking place. Voters had stopped trusting politicians and politicians and voters had stopped listening to one another.

That is the other story. There are no winners in the tale, only losers. Despairing politicians call it 'anti-politics'. But voters are not anti politics; rather they are anti politicians, anti political parties, actually anti the whole of Westminster. The gap between Westminster Villagers – politicians, policy wonks, commentators and journalists who live, eat and breathe their own breed of politics – and everyone else has never been greater.

These two stories have the same conclusion – politicians and those around them must never, ever sever the connection with voters. When *they* lose that connection, they lose.

A DYSFUNCTIONAL RELATIONSHIP

Reviewing the last twenty odd years, I'm struck by two changes that have conspired to make the relationship between voter and politician more dysfunctional now than ever before. The first is how the Westminster Village has changed. It has become more rarified; increasingly made up of politicians and journalists who have a very single minded focus on political process. The army of special advisors and assistants, which that more than doubled in the Labour years, has become the alpha gene pool for new MPs from all parties. Journalist Peter Oborne in his book *The Triumph of the Political Class* traces how this group tends to lack experience of life outside Westminster before working there, and, once there, spends less and less time in the company of 'civilians'.

At the same time, as I set out in Chapter 17, voters want more from their politicians. No longer content for them to be the remote and one-dimensional figure that Mrs Thatcher typified back in the 1980s, voters now demand to see politicians in the round: to know about their backgrounds, their families, their hobbies, their homes – to get to know them as people. Unsurprisingly, many politicians fail to live up to this kind of scrutiny. Fearing failure, some cannot resist sacrificing authenticity in favour of a more saleable back story.

The tools of the trade in Westminster have changed, too. Modern campaigning techniques, which in more innocent days helped Labour to reach out to the voter, have morphed into the dark arts which Labour's Lord Mandelson is credited with perfecting. This is fitting; in some ways he is the personification of this book's central theme: adored by the Westminster Village yet reviled by voters. The clarity and professionalism he brought to communications became known as spin: now a shorthand for politicians' lies. The quest for visual symbols of the candidate's purpose has become the hollow photo opportunity. Modern party campaigning, aided by the media, fuels cynicism and mistrust by failing to understand the voter, failing to manage expectations and then failing to deliver, seeing the campaign as an end in itself. All three main parties emerged from the 2010 campaign with their reputations in a worse condition than when they entered it.

But the voter is not without blame in this unhappy saga. Always ready to complain, but unwilling to roll up their own sleeves, the electorate has colluded with the political classes to create a world of Peter Pan politics: where the voter lives in a perpetual child-like state and never grows up. Voters must take some responsibility for their alarmingly sketchy knowledge of how politics and government works. It is a problem. And most voters know only too well that the services they seek come with a price tag attached: often more than they are prepared to pay. Yet insist on them they do, and the brave politician who points this out will be punished at the ballot box. Small wonder, then, that so many politicians shrink from the honesty that emerged in our Harlow focus groups as one of the voters' top political attributes.

Just when it seemed that the relationship had hit rock bottom, back in 2009, the expenses scandal broke, confirming the electorate's worst fears about politicians living in a different world – a lavish world – at their expense. In this chapter I want to spend some time reflecting on the causes of the dysfunctional relationship between voter and Westminster, before going on, finally, to present the voters' recommendations on how to fix our politics, and consider what next for Labour.

A BREED APART

Politicians are seen by the public as a breed apart. Like fairy tale goodies and baddies, they are never ordinary. Often they are villains: on the make, incompetent, immoral, out of touch. Very rarely they transcend this, acquiring instead a fragile heroic status. Then they are lauded for being 'their own people', inspirational, passionate and courageous. The romance of good and evil is enhanced because of the mystique surrounding the job itself.

People have very little idea about what politicians actually do. When I asked the Harlow panel to come up with an MP's job description, it quickly became apparent that their knowledge of the role was so sparse that even defining it as it currently exists would be an impossible task, let alone changing or expanding on it. Typically, the job of the MP is interpreted as either self seeking campaigning (why would 'vote for me' be anything else?) or half hearted and unqualified social work. This leaves the voter to fill in the gaps, usually with a negative story, helped by a media with an incentive to create a short term sensation with little regard for the longer term consequences.

As I described in the earlier chapters of this book, involvement in party politics is an unusual pastime, and the people who do it tend to be unusual. Perhaps because of that, the practice of local party politics often places emphasis on process rather than outcome and on talking rather than doing. It is a rare local party that would actually do something practical and useful that reaches out to the community such as Battersea Labour's old folks Christmas dinner.

Political party members tend to be homogenous and not very representative. Despite considerable effort, there are too few young people, too few from black and ethnic minorities and far too few women. Educated middle class middle-aged males, usually white, on the other hand, are over-represented. The Labour Party is particularly metropolitan, too; one-third of its members are now in London.

One well-trodden path to becoming an MP is to come up through this local party hierarchy, dutifully attending and speaking out at meetings, maybe becoming involved in local politics, then being adopted as the local candidate. It is not exactly a template for normality, but arguably is more so than the other, increasingly common, route of the favoured son: top university, work for a political party or politician followed by a candidacy in a suitable safe seat often fixed with the help of trade union connections.

Both of these, especially the latter, result in the much despised 'career' politician, someone who has scarcely worked outside politics. Such politicians start off with little knowledge of the wider world and, while they may become experts in how Westminster works, have few practical skills or broader life experience to offer as they progress.

For Labour, the trade union link, at least historically, had the virtue of encouraging some MPs who had come up through the wider Labour movement and who had at some point in their past done 'proper' jobs. However, as we have seen, the trade unions themselves have sometimes struggled to keep pace with the changing world: too few women, too few service industries workers, too few people working in small businesses. Now fewer Labour MPs have a union background, and those that do tend not to have worked up from the shop floor, instead being recruited as professional union officials; they then go on to become professional politicians.

Despite the exciting development of open primaries, there is little reason to suppose that the Conservatives, now the biggest party in the House of Commons, will be any better. Open primaries, whereby anyone can apply to represent the constituency on behalf of the Conservative Party were only practised in a handful of constituencies in 2010. Instead the *Guardian* found that, as well as drawing heavily on the advisor/researcher Westminster community as a resource, both for MPs and for the new Cabinet, one out of ten new Tory MPs come from a management consultancy background – a group of professionals thought by many to have no practical experience in anything at all.

These problems are compounded by the Westminster modus operandi, when a candidate finally arrives there. A long-hours culture persists, although working hours and votes have improved thanks to the tireless efforts of a small number of Labour women, who were derided for it at the time. Many MPs will still find themselves working most weekday evenings. In the case of those with out-of-London constituencies, they are also many miles from home. The demands can be significant, especially for those who supplement their income with external work. Ironically the argument in favour of this is that it keeps politicians connected with ordinary life, but most will be employed in the wider Westminster Village: journalism, lobbying, political consultancy and so on.

So the Westminster-based political class lead lives that are vastly different from those whom they purport to represent, with different aims, different views, different attitudes. The 'vortex' issue of immigration is a good illustration of this. Politicians secure in their jobs and their creature comforts cannot envisage feeling threatened and resentful towards immigrants in the way that many voters do.

When immigration is talked about in the Westminster Village it is picked around gingerly, wrapped in the safety of policy abstraction. By contrast, the voter uses emotional language, increasingly visceral as he or she warms to the theme.

GB's encounter with Gillian Duffy became the defining moment of his 2010 general election campaign because it showcased two interrelated fatal flaws: GB's inability to communicate with ordinary voters and his lack of empathy with how they see the world, manifested by his shocked response to her (rather mild) question about immigration.

GETTING CLOSER TO THE VOTER

When I first started working with Labour back in the 1980s, like the hundreds of communications professionals who volunteered their time for the Shadow Communications Agency, my motivation was to help the Labour Party to update its pitifully inadequate marketing and media. Getting closer to the voter revealed that good communications was not nearly enough and, after defeat in 1987, Neil Kinnock began his radical transformation of the party and its policies. Tony Blair took the project on. He listened and seemed to have an almost instinctive understanding of middle ground voters, as well as an unerring ability to persuade the Westminster media to spread the word on his behalf.

But Blair's problem was that, once in government, it became selective listening – he heard what he wanted to hear – first demonstrated when voters' protests about the Dome went unheeded. It was argued to be a relatively small expenditure to create a positive symbol for the future. Voters' inability to evaluate and contextualise the amount spent derived from previous political sleight of hand. This was the same sleight of hand that over-sold and double-counted public service investment. When things were going so well, it must have been difficult not to believe all those headlines. Voters began to complain that it would be better to promise very little and deliver than promise everything and fail. Their voices were not heard; the lesson was not learned.

Listening is crucial, but is only half of the story. An honest conversation between politician and voter is needed too. In the early New Labour years, expectations for improved public services had soared. Unfortunately, delivery proved harder than achieving a headline about spending money – especially when the money boasted about was not always there to spend. Rightly, Labour had addressed the 'what's in it for me?' question with middle ground voters. But in the absence of a frank exchange with voters about the challenges of funding public services this simply heralded an unsustainable consumerist approach to politics.

GB took this head on, and making the case for a tax rise to fund the NHS was a rare example of political honesty. Although successful in turning public opinion, arguably it was an intervention that came too late. By the time the funds could flow though into service delivery, voters had already made their minds up that public services had failed. 'I've been lucky syndrome', where the disillusioned voter had lost faith to such an extent that they no longer trusted the evidence of their own experience, was an inevitable consequence of poor expectation management, and it was now too late to reverse the trend.

Spin had become a byword for government complicity. The spinners were now better known than most politicians. Already a negative talking point, the Iraq War gave spin a sinister new dimension. Tony Blair had hoped that this might be an example of strong leadership winning out, and that the popularity hit would be short term, with respect growing for his principled position. This was not to be. The so called dodgy dossier brought dishonesty in politics to a new low, with the government judged to be not simply talking up its achievements but actually lying.

A SECOND CHANCE

When GB took over in 2007 there was a real opportunity to address some of this. His weakness, being less of a slick communicator than either his predecessor or his main opponent, was also one of his strengths; he was 'unspun' and straightforward. The voters were clear that they wanted change, and GB had the chance to be that change. The preparation that went into his leadership positioning should have equipped him well, and in his first few months he exceeded the expectations of Westminster Village and voter alike.

But all too quickly he stopped listening. After the doomed non-election, GB lost the stomach for voter feedback; it was no longer serving up a very palatable message. Instead, he retreated into his No. 10 bunker – the dream home had become a prison. Turning to a succession of flavour-of-the-month advisors, chopping and changing as he went, he now gave the impression of drift and lack of direction. The voter and the voter's priorities, so uppermost in GB's mind in the run-up to transition, were now sidelined.

The financial crisis was a potential turning point – a jolt that could cause the voter to look again at GB and the government. To his credit, GB acted bravely in bailing out the banks. However, the opportunity to have an honest conversation with the voter was passed over. Alistair

Darling had been the first to come clean about the scale and nature of the economic problem, only to have the 'forces of hell' unleashed upon him. Later Darling had proposed addressing the growing deficit with a message along the lines of 'our cuts will be better than their cuts', but denial of any need to make cuts at all was the brief from on high. GB preferred to seize the opportunity for a dividing line attack of the Conservatives' cuts versus Labour spending.

It was hard to watch this happen and not conclude that politicians listen closely to voters when they want to get elected, and rather less closely once they have been.

WHAT ARE POLITICIANS WORTH?

When news of the expenses scandal broke, the emphasis in Westminster was on MPs' remuneration. We were treated to page after page about their pay and their expenses. It was powerful stuff – although the focus groups revealed that much of the tantalising detail obsessed over in Westminster and the media passed ordinary voters by. They also revealed that a vital ingredient had been missed out of the Westminster media post mortem: how we value something is contingent not just on what we pay but also on what we get back. The real problem with MPs' pay was that most voters looked at what they got and found it to be very poor value.

As I have pointed out, it is difficult to underestimate how little people know about what politicians actually do. They know little about how Parliament works, almost nothing about the work of select committees, about why we have political parties and how 'the whip' operates, or about the role of the local MP. And what they do know they don't like very much.

Political campaigning rarely enhances political reputation, yet, living as we do in the world of the permanent campaign, it is everywhere, all the time. Negative activity, personal attacks and fear stoking, while achieving a short term goal, annoys and turns off voters in exactly the same way as Prime Minister's Questions, televised from Parliament, does. At the start of the election campaign this is what our Harlow panel dreaded, and were preparing to switch off from.

Positive campaigning can also be problematic. Over promising is a powerful temptation as politicians strive to sell their product. Even the benign 'vote for me' message is an irritation; while politicians and their helpers earnestly believe they are working hard for a noble cause, voters will look at what they are doing and see it as self-seeking and the emphasis on talking not doing that highlights the strangeness of politicians. In Harlow in 2010, Robert Halfon, the local Conservative candidate, took up a position by the side of one of the major A roads into town, and he sat, for days on end, with a female party worker signalling his presence to passing motorists, whereupon he would wave his 'Vote for Change' banner and smile. He won, despite voters' utter bewilderment – what was the point?

DEMISE OF THE MEDIA

Westminster media and Westminster politicians feed off one another. Each justifies the other's existence. They obsess over the same gossip and insider stories and assume that everyone else shares the same knowledge base and appetite for more. Even I, a political anorak by anyone's standards, baulked at the *Guardian*'s four to six page coverage each day during the 2010 campaign. Political journalists' particular passion is for process stories: how things are done behind the scenes, rather than why, and involving a cast of characters that are completely unknown to all but other Westminster Villagers. (How often have I had to find a tactful way to explain to a politician that it didn't matter if the focus group members saw them arrive – as they wouldn't know who they were anyway?)

Fewer and fewer people now read a national newspaper. Recent data shows we spend on average fifteen minutes a day reading one compared to three hours a day watching TV. Our Harlow group all got their news from the TV (the more so since the debates took off), and from the internet, using mainly broadcasters' websites. The *Sun* had backed every general election winner since 1979, but, to its fury, its influence faltered in 2010.

As distanced from ordinary voters as politicians, Westminster media can read them wrongly. During 'Bigotgate' the media talked up how the incident had proved GB was a bully. Yet, as our voter diaries and discussions show, the problem was different: the voter saw GB as a slightly sad, old fashioned politician, ill equipped for the modern world and unable to cope. That, along with the sense that GB was not prepared to listen to voter concerns about immigration, is what they took out of the Duffy affair. These things they knew already – 'Bigotgate' confirmed them. Media attempts to paint GB as somebody that they did not recognise went ignored.

Media coverage that demonises politicians helps to perpetuate and validate the voters' disappointment in politics. The Harlow panel were angered by the right wing press's attempts to smear Nick Clegg after his success in the first debate. Ya boo behaviour, personal attacks and political point scoring may have a short term benefit, but longer term it only serves to undermine all politicians and create the 'plague on all your houses' mood that predominates, reflected by the voters' unforgiving verdict on 6 May 2010.

PETER PAN POLITICS

There is no doubt that some politicians have played fast and loose with the electorate's good will, and that is the price that all now pay. Through my work over the years, I know many politicians personally. A few I would count as friends. In truth, I would judge that many from all political parties are thoroughly decent people, extremely hard working and genuinely committed to a higher cause. I feel sorry that they have to deal with this backlash of voter disappointment, but deal with it they must.

However, I believe that the rest of us, the voters, also have a crucial role to play if we really want to mend our democracy. Voters in focus groups have often admitted to me that they want to 'have their cake and eat it'. But voters are smart – they know that they cannot. Recent views on dealing with the deficit are a good example, where voters seek reward without sacrifice, yet know in their heart of hearts that this cannot be possible. They will punish any politician who speaks the truth, buy into promises that they suspect cannot be kept, and then point the finger of blame when it goes wrong.

This is Peter Pan politics: politics where the electorate never grows up. Instead the voter is indulged like a spoilt child by politicians desperately seeking their favour. They are offered gifts, made promises, sometimes lied to. Peter Pan politics creates a never-never land where politics is something that is done by politicians to voters, with voters only needing to take responsibility for casting their vote – and sometimes not even bothering to do that. There was a good deal of talk about high turnout in May 2010. Yet it was only 65 per cent, significantly down on elections in the 1970s and 1980s. Still one voter in three opted not to bother.

There are many causes of the loss of faith between voter and politician. One of the most powerful is also a potential source of hope: people feel let down because their hopes were so great. Voters hold dear a romantic notion of the ideal politician. The bar is high: it's Nelson Mandela or Barack Obama, individuals who are driven by noble ideals and by public service, never personal gain. It's individuals who achieve lasting and positive change, often against difficult odds. It's individuals who are in touch with the popular mood, but not afraid to show leadership by challenging it. If a voter holds most politicians up to this benchmark for scrutiny they will be found wanting. Yet this yearning is surely something that politicians and political parties could and should harness.

TIME FOR A CHANGE

So much of this is about voter and politician keeping in touch with one another. Focus groups are a unique way of doing that. They have been unfairly maligned during the New Labour era, perhaps because they are too easy for politicians to ignore when the findings don't suit them. Yet they remain a valuable route to truthful insight. There is perhaps no better way for a politician to hear the public's views, in their own voice, without being in the room too. With a politician present, the exchange becomes distorted: voters are either intimidated into politeness, holding back their real feelings, or angry and outspoken, seizing the opportunity for axe grinding. Either way, politicians end up with a false sense of where the public are at, overestimating voters' interest and underestimating how wide the gap between them has spread. They also underestimate the desire for change.

This book tells two stories. One is about party politics, how the New Labour story begins and ends. As I write, the end has arrived, and the Conservatives and Liberal Democrats are now working together in coalition. The implications of this may be very far reaching. As we have seen, voters loathe the adversarial nature of British politics. They long for politicians to work together constructively, and, especially on big issues and in moments of crisis, they favour a pooling of talent from across party boundaries – a so-called 'National Government'.

GB's 'government of all the talents' was a conscious effort to meet this need but did not cut through as he failed to lure any really big hitters from other parties, or really to demonstrate different outcomes. It also ignored the need for cultural rather than structural or procedural change. Anticipating a hung Parliament as one of the outcomes from 2010, voters' biggest anxiety was that rather than collaborating constructively, politicians would bicker and point score behind closed doors, pursuing narrow partisan interests instead of the national good. It remains to be seen whether the Lib Dem/Con coalition government can succeed in overcoming these challenges.

The other story is about the voter's relationship with politics and politicians more generally. As we drew towards the end of campaign 2010, our Harlow panel, while remaining typical swing voters, had, after attending numerous meetings, begun to take more notice than they would otherwise have done, growing more confident about expressing their views and debating their corner. They had started to become lay experts. It was time to try an experiment.

I decided to bring all twelve together for an extended session on the Monday after the election, and to work with them to develop some solutions to fix the problems that they had so clearly identified. Rather than a focus group, this was to be a Citizens' Jury: an extended session where there would be plenty of time for deliberation, debate and discussion. I would provide information to consider, ideas generated by experts in academia and think tanks to fuel the voters' imaginations, and plug the gaps in their knowledge.

I identified four challenges for Team Harlow:

1. How can politicians better represent their constituents?
2. How can people be encouraged to take more interest in politics?
3. How much should we pay politicians. . . and what should they do for the money?
4. What can the media do to connect politicians and people rather than divide them?

And I was eager to hear their views on the final outcome of Election 2010, as events were unfolding by the minute: how did they feel about the LibCon coalition, and what were the implications for Labour's future?

20. What next?

WEEKEND IN LIMBO

It was the weekend after the general election on 6 May, and we were in the limbo land of a hung Parliament, as many had predicted. The Harlow panel filled in their diaries. I asked them, as usual, to note down what they had noticed, what they liked and what they disliked, but also what they felt about the result and what they hoped would happen next.

They noticed, obviously, that the result was a hung Parliament. The immediate presumption was that this placed the onus on Clegg and Cameron. They also knew that turnout was up a bit, and that some polling stations had failed to cope. A few noticed that GB had found his voice towards the end of the campaign – sadly too late to make a difference.

> SADIA: The pressure is now on the Lib Dem leader to side with one of the two larger parties.

> DANNY: How calm David Cameron is: he is handling the hung Parliament situation very well.

> JOHN: I was a bit surprised when they showed the queues of people

locked out of polling stations, but the turnout was only about 65 per cent. Apathy rules OK I think!

PAUL: Gordon Brown's performance improved over the week.

They liked that Nick Clegg was apparently honouring his earlier statement that he would talk first with whichever party gained the largest number of seats. Cameron and Clegg were both praised for their statements in support of the national interest.

SADIA: Nick Clegg's statement that whoever gets most seats should be given a chance at power showed integrity and strength, I felt.

DENIS: Nick Clegg and David Cameron's speeches after the vote were probably the most honest response we have had from the political parties during the campaign.

They disliked the result itself. Whichever party they leaned towards they had ended up disappointed. Some disliked the uncertainty. Many disliked the media coverage in the immediate aftermath, especially criticism of GB for staying on at No. 10. Sympathy for the underdog was already kicking in.

ANGELA: I disliked that although the Lib Dems put up a good fight it was not enough to persuade people to put a cross in the box.

SADIA: I don't like the way that some media are slating GB about going back to Downing Street and remaining PM until things have settled.

TRACEY: Someone's got to be nominally running the country while the inter party negotiations are going on for goodness sake!

LORNA: I disliked that no decision has been made, no one has a clue what's happening.

While they thought that the result was predictable (indeed they *had* predicted it) most were still disappointed. They were also now feeling impatient for some kind of resolution, even if it was not the one they would have originally chosen.

ALICIA: It was predictable, no big shock.

SADIA: Mixed feelings – I'm not surprised, but disappointed that the Lib Dems didn't do a lot better.

TRACEY: Apprehensive. I want a stable government to steer us through troubled economic waters even if it's colours that I didn't choose...

DENIS: The exit polls were pretty accurate and the result was an anti-climax.

The panel were unanimous in their desire for a speedy resolution, and, consistent with their views in the last focus group, generally felt that some kind of LibCon arrangement would be the most attractive outcome. Putting the country first was the top priority...

PAUL: I hope that the Conservatives and Lib Dems will join together.

John: That the Conservatives will get into No. 10 with a few Cabinet positions for Liberal MPs.

Denis: Only one phrase comes to mind and that is 'for the good of our country'. Politics has to take a back seat and common sense has to prevail!

Tracey: That politicians can put aside their differences and work together in the tough times ahead. . .

TALKING POLITICS WHILE THE POLITICIANS TALK

The following Monday, 10 May, I was heading up the M11 to Harlow for the final session with all twelve of our swing voter panel – a Citizens' Jury where their challenge would be to come up with their own ideas for mending the broken relationship between voters and politicians. I had arranged to meet Sue Matthias and Dan Hancox, who had both been helping me pull the book together, at Bounds Green tube station to drive up together. As I pulled over to collect them, news was breaking on the radio. GB was about to make a live announcement outside No. 10: he was resigning as Leader of the Labour Party.

It was four days after the general election but there was still no government. Lib–Con talks had been going on all weekend without resolution. Earlier that day Labour had briefed that they also had held secret talks with the Lib Dems over the weekend, and that the Lib Dems were now requesting that formal talks should start. Sue, Dan and I listened to events unfold as we drove up. GB spoke from the steps of No. 10. He was prepared to stand down if that would ease the development of a Lab–Lib arrangement to govern.

I had booked a conference room at The Green Man, a local Harlow hotel, to get a space large enough to house all twelve panellists. Once there, with teas and coffees poured, and greetings exchanged, I gauged reactions to these developments.

Tracey, like us, had listened to the news as she drove over to meet everyone. She explained what had happened to the rest of the panel:

> Gordon Brown said he's resigning as leader of the Labour Party, in time for the conference in September. . . I'm not clear if he's resigning as PM or not.

> PAUL: Is that the same thing?

> TRACEY: I don't know who's Prime Minister any more! [*All laugh*]

I asked whether they preferred the idea of a Lib–Lab coalition, now presumably back on the cards, as opposed to a Lib–Con arrangement. A show of hands revealed an overwhelming majority in favour of the latter, with only Sadia and Tracey preferring Lib–Lab. I asked why.

> ALICIA: Well, they were saying that if it was Lib–Lab there won't be enough seats to make the 326. . . and they [Libs] work better with the Tories, so. . .

> LORNA: I just think that the Conservative and Liberal Democrat policies would benefit me more. . .

JOHN: I just don't see how you can get a Labour government staying when they've been trounced in the polls? It seems to go in cycles – after ten years they become megalomaniacs, all of them. And even if Labour change their leader, they'll have the same policies.

DENIS: The power is in the Lib–Con option and anything else would be demeaning to the voter.

NATASHA: I agree. I voted Tory and they didn't quite get a majority, but I'd feel cheated with Lib–Lab.

DENIS: I think there'd be a revolt!

WHAT DO WE NEED TO DO NEXT?

As a preamble to this session, at the end of our last meeting, two days before polling day, I had asked the group to come up with some initial ideas for improving politics and the way politicians behave. They wrote:

- Honesty – if we're in a bad state, say we're in a bad state
- Be more visible, as in coming round more often – you want to see them in businesses and in nursing homes not just two weeks before an election
- And to listen
- And to be innovative
- Be accountable – I think it was Nick Clegg's idea to be able to sack them – why should you have to wait four years?

- Their education and background is often so different – that makes it hard for them to relate to people
- We thought that maybe they should have to live in the constituency

WHAT KIND OF CHANGE?

Based on these thoughts and other points that the panel had made during our conversations over the past few weeks, I identified four areas for possible change. For each, I had prepared a list of the issues or problems, many identified by the voters themselves, and also some possible solutions to feed in after the voters had had the chance to develop their own ideas. To help the panel overcome the limitations of their own knowledge, and to be more creative, I had drawn on a range of experts' published views, including the IPPR's 'A Future for Politics' paper drawing on ideas from six different think tanks, published in November 2009, and Meg Russell's excellent Fabian Society pamphlet 'Must Politics Disappoint?'

We divided the panel into four groups of three and gave each one question to start them off. After twenty minutes or so, we moved everyone on to tackle a different problem and build on the ideas generated by the previous group. This way everyone had a chance to tackle each area. Halfway through, we fed in the issues that we had generated and then some of the solutions as a starter for ten. (These are in Appendix IV on pages 339–44.)

At the end of the three-hour session, each group presented their ideas, edited down to a shortlist of ten. Finally, each panellist was given ten 'votes' and invited to nominate their top ten ideas. After some bustle and horse trading the group arrived at their suggestions for each topic, and, finally, their recommendations for ten ways to rebuild our relationship with politicians.

Q1. How can politicians better represent their constituents?

1. Simplify the system
2. Tell the truth – even if the truth is ugly
3. More forums and websites for listening to public opinion
4. Equality and diversity of representation – fewer middle class men
5. Annual job appraisals
6. Follow through on their policies
7. Modernise Parliament
8. Politics should be more balanced between the national and the local
9. You shouldn't be a minister and an MP
10. Proper training for MPs should be compulsory – and introduce an 'apprentice' or junior MP to work in the local area.

This first series of recommendations reflects the voters' desire for representatives to be more accountable as well as more representative. Their demand for a simpler system confirms a degree of discomfort with their own levels of knowledge about the process.

One of the most interesting points, 'you shouldn't be a minister and an MP', as well as the training/apprenticeship idea shows how the voters believe that the job is a big one and needs full time concentration – a point echoed in the section on the MP's role and remuneration. Of course this begs the bigger question of how we resource the Executive but certainly our Harlow panellists feel that constituencies with a minister for the MP have been short changed.

Q2. How can people be encouraged to take more interest in politics?

1. Re-brand and localise the title of MP e.g. as 'local representative' or similar
2. Make economics a compulsory subject in schools
3. More honest and factual information disseminated
4. More openness about political options and voting – more discussion
5. Simplify policy issues for young people
6. Use programmes like *Newsround* to open up politics to young people
7. Better political education
8. Make politics more fashionable
9. Local events like street parties to boost the sense of community spirit
10. More good literature on the subject – read Deborah's book! (hurrah)

This list of priorities reveals the voters' hunch that ignorance is the biggest barrier to greater public involvement. A by-product of this more rarefied Westminster Village is to make politics even less accessible. The more politicians spout jargon with ease, the more ordinary voters see politics as an exclusive activity only for those who can display specialist knowledge. There are also concerns about the unfashionable 'geekiness' of politics, especially as a barrier to young people's involvement.

Q3. How much should we pay politicians and what should they do for the money?

1. Pay politicians twice the national average wage, i.e. £50,000

2. Be accountable to voters and sackable
3. Politicians must live in the constituencies that they represent and have strong links there
4. Expenses should be subject to public scrutiny and transparency and published locally
5. Politicians should have normal holiday allowances (four weeks)
6. Job descriptions should be clarified
7. MPs be held accountable to those job descriptions
8. Make being an MP a full time job – no outside work at all
9. MPs should spend less time in London – they should investigate electronic voting and video conferencing
10. Where second homes in London are necessary, they should be one-bedroom flats

Westminster Village might look at this list and feel that this is the voter being punitive: punishing politicians for expenses and other misdemeanours. However, the discussion surrounding this had a rather different tone; most of the remuneration package ideas were an attempt to normalise the MP rather than admonish. There was also a strong urge for modernisation, reworking the role to take advantage of new media and communications, and again stressing the need for local links.

Q4. What can the media do to help connect politicians and people rather than divide them?

1. Focus on policies not politicians' private lives
2. Present policies clearly and concisely
3. More politicians versus the public debates on TV
4. More leaders' TV debates – not just during an election campaign
5. Better information on how policies affect you should be made

available with monthly results and achievements published by
MPs in local newspapers

6. Media should cover more politicians, not just the party leaders
7. Debates should be made more gladiatorial
8. Use multimedia especially digital channels for politicians to put
their points over
9. Newspapers should be made to express any bias they have openly
10. Media should highlight positive work done by MPs especially
in their local constituencies

Local accountability features in the media recommendations,
too. These also make a plea for the media to provide a more basic
information service.

The Harlow voters' Top Ten ideas

1. Better political and economic education from a young age
2. Make being an MP a full time job
3. MPs to follow through on their policy promises
4. You shouldn't be an MP and a minister
5. Media should focus on policy not politicians' private lives
6. More politicians versus the public debates on TV all the year
round
7. Better information on how policies affect you should be made
available, with monthly results and achievements published by
MPs perhaps in local papers
8. MPs to spend less time in London – investigate electronic
voting and video conferencing
9. Simplify the system
10. Introduce an 'apprentice' or junior MP to work in the local area

Reviewing these lists, developed amidst heated debate with real energy and enthusiasm, I am struck again by the high minded ideals reflected by many of the suggestions: the voters' avowed appetite for the truth, however unpalatable, their concern about unrepresentative representatives; their determination to discipline both the MP's role and remuneration.

The 'Top Ten' list of priorities reinforces the need for better information: many of the ideas in the winning list are about education and information dissemination, aiming to achieve the confidence necessary to take part in the debate. The others tend to be about the role of the MP, and how he/she can become more accountable and more connected to constituents.

In my view, the Harlow panellists, each one of them a typical swing voter with no specialist expertise, have come up with some insightful suggestions and innovative ideas: 'apprentice' MPs is an interesting thought, as is the idea of rebranding the MPs' role to be more local. Some of the ideas, like banning MPs from taking additional jobs including ministerial posts, beg wider constitutional questions, but all are worthy of consideration.

Over the weeks, and culminating in that final Monday night session, our Harlow voters had really engaged in the events of the election, giving their time and their careful thought both to the state of our politics and the state of our party politics. The only remaining question is whether anyone would listen. . .

ENDGAME

While the Harlow voters were putting the world to rights, politicians continued talking behind closed doors. Finally, twenty-four hours later, five days after the general election, the end was in sight.

Although the Lib–Con coalition had not yet been agreed, GB now stood on the steps of Downing Street, Sarah looking on, and announced his own departure. I shed a tear, just as I had done watching him arrive there three and a half years before. His touching and dignified speech 'and as I leave the second most important job I could ever hold, I cherish even more the first: as a husband and a father' reminded me of why I had admired him so much in the first place. He is a hugely talented and fundamentally decent man.

Events moved fast and an hour later David Cameron was at the Palace with the Queen, then making his own way down Downing Street with his wife, Sam. He stopped to speak before entering, announcing his plans for a coalition government with the Liberal Democrats. We would learn more about this the following day, when he and Nick Clegg, now Deputy Prime Minister, held a joint press conference in the Rose Garden behind No. 10.

The Harlow panel had been discharged on Monday evening as the project was drawing to a close but now I was eager to find out their final thoughts on the outcome. I contacted Dan and we emailed and telephoned as many as we could contact during Thursday. Their responses, trickling in through the day, were remarkable in their consistency.

Despite no one getting the result that they had really wanted, almost everyone was happy with the final outcome. The majority, in fact, were more than happy, seeing this as the kind of collaboration that they had always hoped politicians would make in the national interest, putting party tribalism aside.

JOHN: Hopefully a fresh approach to solving the country's problems.

Scott: I'm quite excited by it – I think it could be the chance of something new.

Danny: Really good and positive outcome, young fresh and promising.

However, their optimism was tinged with doubt, especially from those who were least keen on the idea of a Conservative government:

Angela: I'm hopeful but apprehensive.

Scott: I just hope they're not playing games.

There was also consistency about what was needed to make the coalition work: compromise and keeping focus on the national, rather than the party interest. The jury was out on how achievable this would be.

Danny: Be strong, work hard together and always think of Britain.

Scott: Compromise, put the country first, make it work no matter what... hard to say if it will work, it's a big job.

Finally, I asked them all to think about what the Labour Party should do next. Listening to their advice it is easy to forget that Labour had been in power for the past thirteen years, won three elections and, in the end, did well enough in the fourth that no other party could claim an overall majority. The Harlow voters, even those who themselves voted Labour in 2010, were recommending a very substantial rethink. GB stepping down was no more than the first small baby step on the road to electability.

ANGELA: They need to make themselves a younger party – more polished like the other two. Their policies did not work, they will need a complete change.

SCOTT: Go right back to basics.

JOHN: Gordon Brown stepping down was a start. They need a new, younger approach.

TRACEY: They need to rebrand themselves as an alternative to Con/LD.

DANNY: Look at the opposition and take notes.

Danny's last point was interesting. Throughout the campaign, voters told us they wanted change. As the incumbent, Labour could never provide that change. Conservative change seemed superficial, too reliant on simply not being Labour. Clegg's Lib Dem version of change held brief appeal that fizzled out – his change was a leap too far.

But now, together, these two were, in Danny's mind, Labour's opposition, setting an example that Labour must learn from. Could it be that the elusive 'new politics' had been achieved by this coalition? Had the Lib Dems accelerated the agonisingly slow modernisation of the Conservatives, while they in turn had legitimised the insubstantial Lib Dems?

ANOTHER FRESH START

Hours after the Rose Garden press conference, where David

Cameron and Nick Clegg had wooed Westminster and voters alike with their energy, their camaraderie and their fresh, different approach, the Labour leadership contest kicked off.

Surrounded by a small group of supporters David Miliband stood outside the House of Commons and announced his candidacy. The following Saturday, brother Ed had challenged him – soon to be joined by fellow Team Brown member Ed Balls, then Andy Burnham as well as John McDonnell, the left winger who tried to make a stand against GB. Then finally, as an act of resistance against the middle aged, middle class, male homogeneity of the other candidates, the first black woman MP, Diane Abbott, also threw her hat into the ring.

The debate is starting as this book goes to press. I hope that whoever wins truly understands the scale of the task ahead. It is absolutely not 'steady as we go', and a switch at the top is not, in itself, enough, especially if one of the front runners win – all are strongly associated with what has gone before. It is time for a change as radical and far reaching as the changes that were made in the 1980s and 1990s. It means being honest about mistakes made. It means really reconnecting with voters like our Harlow panellists, and rehabilitating our politics by carefully considering the suggestions they have made.

Interestingly all of the Labour leadership candidates are talking about the need to listen more to voters. Some are citing attitudes towards immigration as an example of Labour not listening enough, eyes wide, as if they have just heard about the topic for the very first time. But talking about listening is not the same as actually listening. Yes, voters stopped listening to Labour because Labour stopped listening to them. How did they know Labour had turned a deaf ear? It was because of what Labour did (or didn't do), not because of what Labour said. The imperative now is to listen long and listen hard, and then respond with courage. Or voters will continue to feel that they are talking to a brick wall – and the future Labour leader may as well be.

Appendices

1. The Budget has had a fairly neutral impact on floating voters. In terms of the specific measures most felt that they would be worse off, but only marginally, resulting in a sense that it was not very positive but 'could have been worse'.

The most striking measures were:

- 2p tax cut
- Abolition of 10p rate
- Increases in child tax credits and child benefit
- Fags and booze up
- Petrol and tax on bigger cars up
- Inheritance tax threshold lowered
- Pensions

But overall, the feeling was 'gives with one hand, takes with the other' with the net result that, after a certain amount of fiddling around, nothing much had changed:

In the end it was a bit of a non-event.

The difference is only pennies when you add it all up.

Voters found it hard to say which groups of people might be better off; the women thought that lone parents would be:

You're being penalised for being a normal family.

2. More worrying was the sense that the Budget had been presented somewhat dishonestly, being positioned as one thing, than revealed to be another when the small print was read. Both groups felt this strongly, especially the men:

He dressed it up then minute by minute it all unravelled.

All spin!

This referred mostly to the 2p/10p switch, and concerns around lower-paid workers, expressed in the pre-Budget focus groups, were confirmed.

This mood reflected two other problems: that GB did not have fresh ideas, and was resorting to 'sleight of hand' to create a story; and/or that GB (who is universally felt to be very clever) thinks the electorate are stupid.

He's a cute customer: very shrewd and canny – and if you were dumb enough just to believe the headlines he'd have fooled you.

3. Women knew very little about the Conservatives' response,

while men thought that Cameron had managed reasonably well in a difficult task.

Men were aware of the challenge facing the opposition leader on Budget Day and concluded that he had done OK:

> He did as well as anyone could, really – and he's always going to get the sympathy vote for that one.

4. Views of GB were fairly consistent with recent weeks. Strengths (women were more positive than men) include: family man, honest and straightforward, intelligent, good Chancellor, has conviction, while the weaknesses are: not fresh and different enough, lacking the rounded image needed to be PM, too dour and lacking in positive energy and enthusiasm, not clear enough about what motivated him beyond being PM.

> We desperately need fresh thinking, someone to come along and freshen things up – but he's been around for ever.

> He's a money man.

5. Views of Labour are hard to differentiate from views of Blair.

There is a strong sense that the party (having promised so much) is mired in sleaze and that it will be hard to move on until Iraq is properly dealt with. There is also concern that the party is divided.

But residual strengths – for (ordinary) families, down to earth – are still under the surface.

The biggest challenge for Labour (other than addressing the weaknesses above) will be convincing that they have something new and different to say.

I can't believe they have any new cards to play.

They're getting very stale.

6.   The women's views of Cameron were consistent and fairly negative, while the men were more positive.

Strengths are: young, fresh, enthusiastic family man; weaknesses are: trying too hard, being insincere.

Both groups are concerned by the thought that he is very like Blair. The men, however, cut him more slack and felt that he is beginning to gain in confidence and grow into the role, although they are also more likely to be turned off by his 'toff' image.

7. Both groups have no real sense of the modern Conservative Party beyond Cameron.

They identify a tension between old school (crime, immigration) and the new school (environment – which they heap scorn upon). They are not sure that anything has really changed yet.

They need to oust the old guard – don't know if they have.

That green stuff really annoys me. It's the new thing to be PC about – all rubbish.

8.   Both the statements tested worked really well, especially the partnership government note. This worked well because it was so specific. Both groups thought that it would transform the current negative relationship between voters and government:

Us and them, out of touch, they don't listen, they don't care what we want, they're in it for themselves.

The new role for MPs is extremely popular – so much so that voters doubt that any politician would do it – but they are convinced that it would mean a better quality of representative more focused on the job.

Government offices in supermarkets and shopping malls seemed a fresh new idea, as was cutting bureaucracy.

People getting involved in services is a positive:

- The idea of Citizens Juries is well received (although the terminology needs explanation as it implies a connection with the legal system).
- People are outraged that there is not already a right to petition Parliament.
- The right of recall was not understood and needs clarification as a mechanism, but may have appeal.
- Voters may be reluctant to volunteer as governors due to lack of time and fear of lacking expertise. Persuading employers to give time off for civic duties might be popular, as would a campaign to persuade people that they do have the skills.

The language in the 'mission statement' worked well too, especially the patriotism.

It made me feel really proud.

But people do feel that there is more wrong than right with Britain and this needs to be acknowledged (although they do not argue with the central premise).

However, this needed more specifics. Both groups commented that they would like to see more explanation about how this ideal would be achieved – and some accountability measures built in.

Both groups were bemused about who might propose either, especially the first – it would be totally unexpected and, they felt, very popular.

Whoever wrote that should be Prime Minister.

I'd be really chuffed if it was Gordon Brown.

II. TAKING STOCK: WHERE VOTERS ARE; HOW THE GOVERNMENT IS SEEN; CONSIDERATIONS FOR 2008 (DECEMBER 2007)

Overview

This note summarises voters' current views: they remain negative about the condition of Britain and have become somewhat negative about the government.

They believe it is 'time for a change', but do not see that the new government is moving in enough of a different direction. They are not getting a clear message from the government about its intentions.

GB is the personification of the government – much more than TB was as there is currently less of a sense of team. While he has enduring strengths, he is still seen as rather one-dimensional – he is not yet making a personal connection with voters either with what he says or what he does – and seems rather downbeat and negative himself.

Cameron, by contrast, seems high energy, and is cutting through personally. However, he continues to have strong and persistent weaknesses. It is vital to develop an ongoing attack on him, reminding people of these negative attributes.

We need to start the New Year showing a change of pace with signpost initiatives that flag up our longer-term objectives.

We need better message discipline, and to focus on visual as well as verbal messages especially for GB – enabling him to connect better with voters.

We must develop distinctive trademark themes illustrated by symbolic policies that speak to people's main concerns. This needs to include some visible quick wins.

We should also be developing a voter route-map from now to spring 2009. This needs to set specific challenges and objectives, and should include the development of an overarching unifying mission that can join up the themes to a central vision.

Voters' views

Voters continue to feel extremely unsettled and negative about the condition of Britain. Their concerns focus on perceptions that street crime is rising, discipline and respect have broken down in schools, and public services are under strain. They are particularly anxious about the NHS being able to deliver if they need it.

While the economy is not top of their lists of worries, it is an underlying anxiety that can easily rise to the surface – many voters, especially those in battleground seats, feel that their family economy is vulnerable: they may have a big mortgage, be dependent on two incomes, have credit card debt, and worry about their children being able to afford to buy their own home.

They feel that government is unfair to people like them –

absolutely not on their side. Instead, they think that government only looks after the undeserving needy (especially immigrants), or the rich and powerful – while people like them work hard, pay high taxes and get little back. Government seems like poor value for money.

They judge government by how it treats people like them and their families. They are cynical and their start point is that government is trying to hoodwink them – and that all politicians are 'out for themselves'. Party brands are more contaminated than individual politicians or leaders are.

How voters view the government

Against this backdrop of anti-political malaise, the mood is strongly 'time for a change'. During, and immediately after, transition there was at worst open-mindedness, at best hope that GB's new government could deliver the change they feel that they and Britain needs.

However, in the past few months, voters believe that the new government has faltered, bogged down by events and errors. They do not know what it stands for and there is no sense of the direction it is heading in. It is not connecting with them – they do not hear any of its messages.

GB is the principal character here, as they know very few members of the new Cabinet and do not yet see a team effort – thus GB personifies the new government. His personal ratings have been relatively resilient during this period: he is still seen as competent, strong on the economy and hard-working. He is felt to be more sincere in his aims than most politicians are. People still remember the government's early days where they noted several important contrasts with the old regime:

- GB's highly committed personal working style e.g. cutting short a holiday in the UK to attend to foot and mouth
- More focus on domestic rather than international agenda
- Straightforward and unglitzy/unspun
- Nice family and wife – who seem not to be 'on the make'.

However, the transition did not achieve a more 3D image for GB than he had at the Treasury: people still feel that they know little about him, and he does not make a personal connection with voters.

- In fact, he often seems evasive – not answering the question, not looking at the questioner, both in interviews and in the House (the interview conducted after Benazir Bhutto's death is a good example of this – GB appeared to be looking down throughout).
- The other main vehicle that GB uses to convey his ideas, the set-piece speech, serves to add to the sense of alienation: most voters have never sat through a formal lecture and it is an unfamiliar setting – one that could only exist in the strange world of politics. In this context they see GB as a lonely figure reading from notes behind the barrier of a lectern.
- This problem is compounded by the language that GB uses: often abstract, complex and impersonal.
- And GB's demeanour and body language often seems defensive and closed – he seems tired and unhappy.

Thus the hoped-for change to the voters' agenda has not materialised: there is no knowledge of what the new government stands for, and how that manifests itself in concrete policies. Instead, the government appears buffeted by events, not setting the agenda, weary and running out of steam. Voters still talk mainly about pre-transition when discussing the government as this is what they know about. Further, there is a concern that 'talking' rather than 'doing' is to the fore as the government seems fixed on 'talking projects', launching reviews and inquiries which seem to offer layers of bureaucracy rather than real solutions.

These problems are compounded because Cameron, while still suffering from the same weaknesses he has always had – naivety, inexperience, being out of touch, being all talk and PR stunts, and no action – has some powerful strengths against this backdrop of desire for change: he seems fresh and different and he seems hungry for the job: full of energy and enthusiasm.

And he is making a more personal connection with voters than GB is, using his informal, personable style in more familiar settings – out and about with people, using colloquial language and personal anecdotes.

It will be vital to stage a co-ordinated and persistent attack on Cameron in the next few months – working the perceived negatives to maximum effect.

How can we shift gear?

We must get back on the front foot and demonstrate GB's understanding of the voters' agenda and his desire to bring about the change that they want to see.

- While emphasising the acknowledged successes of the past ten years (the economy, child tax credits, nursery education), it might be that we can build on these successes towards a new theme – e.g. what I always set out to do was to create a stable economy for Britain that could enable people to run their family economies. . .

- This will be especially important if there is a belief that the world economy poses a threat to the UK.

We need to have a combination of 'signpost initiatives' that demonstrate a change of pace and new energy and some longer-term ambitions that we can be judged on over time. It is crucial that GB is seen to be leading his team on this and that they are following – showing a joined-up government, a united team – all heading in the same direction.

We need to remember some of the discipline from the Treasury – resisting the temptation to tell a new story every day, instead finding the most compelling language and repeating it and repeating it.

We also need to find new ways of communicating the message – liberating GB from the static speech format – he needs to be out and about more, in informal settings, with colleagues and with members of the public, and in informal interview settings such as GMTV and BBC Breakfast. He needs to use the same, warmer personal approach even if it is a more formal set-piece interview with a less friendly interviewer.

Moving forward

We need to develop a new overall theme with specific underpinning of 'symbolic' policies. The agency can help with the voter-friendly language. We then need some 'quick wins' that bring about change that people can see straight away.

Possible areas might include:

- A stable family economy: building on existing reputation but turning it to family budgets (the family economy?), specifically helping with first-time buyers – an identified pressure point, or with council tax –the most resented tax after IHT.

- Reliable public services: developing some hard and fast guarantees (GP access, health MOT, hospital hygiene, nursery provision, elder care) – or your money back?
- Education for life: education that links to the world of work – especially apprenticeships.
- Discipline for young people: Community National Service – make it compulsory?
- Safe communities: more police – you get the mobile phone of your local bobby.

Developing an overall theme

Right now, this matters much less than just getting on with it, and being visible – talking and acting on the things that voters are really worrying about.

However, over time it is important that initiatives coalesce around a unifying theme that can be the hallmark of the government. A variation of the Britishness theme may work well here – there is an appetite for patriotism – but we feel some distance from being able to make such claims at the moment. Nevertheless, it will be important to have a route map that can take us from where we are now to where we need to be, by, say, spring 2009 in terms of voter attitudes.

III. DEBRIEF NOTE ON TWO FOCUS GROUPS HELD IN HARLOW, 19 MAY 2009

1. Overview

Unsurprisingly, the expenses furore has damaged all parties and confirmed voters' belief that politicians are greedy and self-interested – the effect is much worse for Labour, as they 'should know better'.

- Responses so far are inadequate, especially from GB.

Labour's message on the economy has cut through for men, but not women.

- 'Growing our way out of a recession' appeals to men, although they are unaware of any specifics.

Defence is not a major issue, but people are concerned about Britain losing the nuclear deterrent.

Cameron is felt to be taking the Conservative Party forward with energy and vigour. They do not yet love him, but they are impressed.

By contrast, Labour lacks direction and has lost sight of its values. GB seems out of his depth.

2. Who we were talking to

- One group of eight men and one group of eight women in C1C2
- Aged 30–50
- They were swing voters who voted Labour in 2005 and 2001 but are unlikely to vote for Labour now

- They have not ruled out voting Labour altogether
- In general, the male group identified more strongly with Labour than the women.

3. Expenses

The expenses affair has confirmed the views people already had of greedy, self-serving politicians, and cuts across party divisions.

- When asked what they recalled, excessive mortgage claims stand out as particularly damaging, while other expense claims seem more petty.

No party is perceived to have dealt effectively with the issues.

- Cameron's 'pay up or stand down' message is the stronger of the two. In general, responses are seen as slow and reactive.

It has been more devastating for Labour.

- Men in particular feel betrayed by Labour, as it's the sort of thing expected of the Tories, but Labour values should govern decent behaviour. It is especially corrosive in the current economic climate.
- It destroys what was left of 'public service ethos'.

Moving forward, any regulatory body would have to be clearly independent and have a strong reputation.

- Politicians obviously can't be trusted to regulate themselves. At present there is no real sense of contrition, and the issue requires a broader review.

- Opinions differed on what the reforms might look like – some thought MPs earned enough already to pay for most things themselves, others that they should just be more strongly regulated.
- This leads to bigger questions about the role of MPs and what value they provide to taxpayers. Healing the relationship will require a much greater rethink.

4. The economy

Labour's headline message has cut through with men, but not women.

- The men had a headline sense of Labour strategy (grow not cut) and agreed with it but knew no specifics.
- Women had no sense of what we are doing at all.
- The Tories don't have a clear message. But they are associated with youth, change and more dynamism, which were attractive to the women in particular and may hold the promise of future strategy.
- Most feel things will get better – we may be past the worst.
- People don't believe it will be worse in a year's time. The fear expressed in previous weeks has subsided.

GB's experience still counts for something.

- Although women also wondered if he should take the blame.

There's a feeling that undeserving banks got off the hook while other sectors go to the wall.

- Men eager to see investment in jobs, especially manufacturing.
- There's an appetite for tougher regulation of the banking sector.

5. Defence

Both groups showed strong underlying anxiety about abandoning Trident.

- Men felt it made Britain look weak, and is an important bargaining chip.
- They did not agree with the argument that there should be a choice made on defence policy, despite the economic situation.
- Women were more open to the 'mountain' argument.
- Defence cuts are easier to make for Tories than Labour, as defence is a traditional Tory strength.

6. Views of the parties

Conservatives

There is little love for the Tories and little real evidence of change (except Cameron in the case of the women).

- Still, as always, seen as rich, City banker, patronising, condescending, with a vested interest in courting ordinary people. The animals that women likened DC to were generally strong and aggressive – he seemed like a bull ready to charge for government. As a drink, he would be something classy and

expensive – a continental lager or champagne (although this does hint at a lack of substance – like a spritzer)
- The men were less inclined to the Tories. They saw DC as a fox or a snake. In terms of drinks, he was thought to be a letdown – an overpriced beer or a shandy that looks better than it tastes.

And there remain big questions over whether he can take his party with him.

- The men described his relationship to the Tory Party as if he is the tip of an arrowhead. He is the strong and visible public figure backed by the rest of the party. However, the rest of the party are not well known, and there are some doubts about them because of this, as well as doubts about whether they are really with him.

DC feels contemporary, 'normal' and is a good, decisive communicator.

- He comes across as a people person, but can appear a bit too sleek and smarmy.
- Women thought he'd be a 'modern' husband and hands-on dad – they felt he'd be good fun to go out for a drink with. The men also thought he'd be good company, but didn't feel they'd be able to trust him, and couldn't imagine him as a real friend.
- He seems enthusiastic and youthful – although some doubt whether there is anything more beneath the surface, and feel he may be too eager to please.

Labour
GB is a decent man out of his depth.

- He is a Mr Magoo character, well meaning but clueless.
- Many accepted his abilities as Chancellor, but felt him to have failed in the top job.

He is temperamentally unsuited to leadership, and not a people person.

- He comes across as awkward, old fashioned, tired and out of ideas.
- Many people thought of him as being like a bear or a badger – gruff and defensive.
- The men could see him as the sort of friend you could trust, but not as necessarily as someone fun to share a few pints with.

GB seems poorly advised and indecisive.

- People believed he listens to flattering courtiers. One man commented that while GB would not let you down, his friends probably would.
- His relationship with the party is very different to the arrow pictured for Cameron. GB is seen as lost in the crowd. He does not provide the kind of direction DC does.
- Imagined as an animal, GB is like a horse ploughing the same furrow, a large dog chasing its tail or a tethered bear – strong but angry, frustrated and impotent.

7. Conclusions

We urgently need to demonstrate that GB is in control, and Labour has not abandoned its core values. Pressing on with the economy message is a good place to start – we need to keep going with 'grow your way' but also show how this helps hard-working ordinary people. We should also consider visibly tighter regulation of banks.

We should also act fast on expenses, widening the remit of our concern to the broader MP role, setting out what value people should expect to get from their representatives.

Cameron continues to have vulnerabilities, especially the taint that the Conservative Party image brings. People doubt that he can take them with him and we should seek to expose this.

By contrast, GB must appear strongly supported by a united party. His focus must be on setting out what GB's Labour looks like.

8. Summary of projective exercises

Women

	Labour	*Tories*
Animal	Pig (2), dog, hamster, sheep (3), meerkat	Dog, wolf, cat, bull, snake, fox, lion, giraffe
Beer/ drink	Heineken (2), Foster's, lager, ale (3), Stella	San Miguel, sparkling wine, Stella (2), European beer, Guinness, wine, brandy
Car	Vectra, Beetle, Ford (2), old Mini (2), Fiesta, dodgy old banger	Porsche, Mondeo, sports car, Jaguar, Mercedes sports car, 4x4, Skoda

	GB	*DC*
Animal	Bear, meerkat, snake, dog, badger, sheepdog	Bull, puppy, cat, mynah bird, eagle, Doberman, cheetah
Beer/drink	Alcohol-free lager, rosé, flat lemonade, dry wine, malt whisky, cheap lager, supermarket own brand beer, sherry	Brandy, something smooth, spritzer, bucks fizz, champagne, Tiger beer, something organic, nice red wine
Car	Three-wheeler, Mini, cut-and-shunt, Ford, Jaguar (2), Smart, Ford Orion	Audi, Jaguar (2), Ford, Range Rover, Land Rover, Smart, Porsche

Men

	Labour	*Tories*
Animal	Bulldog, chicken, sheepdog, bear, red setter, puppy, toad	Leopard (2), fox (2), snake, peacock, mantis, wolf in sheep's clothing
Beer/drink	John Smith's, Heineken, Foster's, IPA, flat beer, keg bitter, Tesco Value, Carling C2	Stella (3), Kronenbourg, Tetley's, premium continental lager, Foster's, cheap champagne
Car	Rover, Fiat 500, Mondeo, worn-out van, 1989 Volvo, Austin Allegro, Ford Escort, L-reg Mondeo	Lamborghini, Bentley, Porsche, Mercedes, BMW Z3, Audi, cut-and-shut Mercedes, DeLorean

	GB	*DC*
Animal	Bear (3), sloth, toad, plough horse, duck, donkey	Panther, squirrel, white tiger, fox, snake, lizard (2), toad, Jack Russell, hyena
Beer/drink	Newcastle Brown Ale (2), non-alcoholic lager, stout (4)	Stella, cocktail, Kronenbourg, mineral water, low-strength lager, Leffe, shandy
Car	Skoda, old Granada, pushbike, Scorpio, Allegro, old Rover (2), old Vauxhall	Ferrari, hot hatch, chauffeur-driven Mercedes, Sinclair C5, 4x4, Land Rover, Toyota Prius

IV. CITIZENS' JURY, HARLOW, 10 MAY 2010

Agenda

Warm-up and introductions

Discussion of outcome: what do they like? What do they dislike? What would they like to see happen next? Advice for each party? What do they think about electoral reform? Political reform? What would they like to see happen?

Introduction of four themes:
- How can politicians better represent their constituencies?
- How can people be encouraged to take more interest in politics?

- How much should we pay politicians and what should they do for the money?
- What can the media do to help connect politicians and people rather than divide them?

Group in four groups of three to take key issues and add to them, and rank them, then evaluate possible solutions and add to them... then share these thoughts with whole group

Then each topic is passed on to the next group who builds on what the previous group has done

Finally each group makes a short presentation of issues and solutions and the whole group votes

Then photos to be taken individually and collectively

Theme 1. How can politicians better represent their constituents?

Issues
- Politicians are not representative of the population – they are too middle aged, male, middle class.
- Politicians tend not to have done proper jobs, working in the Westminster Village.
- Politicians put party interests before voters' interests.
- Politics is about talking not doing.
- Politicians spend too much time scoring points from their competitors rather than doing useful things for their constituents.
- Politicians are not honest about what needs to be done.

- Politicians take voters for fools and don't understand/care what they care about.
- Too much politics takes place in Westminster rather than locally in our constituencies.
- Many politicians do other jobs as at the same time as being MPs.

Solutions

- MPs must have worked in other jobs/have specific experience before they can be elected.
- MPs must spend a set amount of time in their constituencies.
- Set a quota on age, gender etc. of MPs.
- Ban MPs from doing other jobs.
- Give more power to cross-party committees so that people from different parties have to work together more.
- Set MPs some specific objectives to achieve on their constituencies.
- Each constituency to have a panel like our Harlow panel to advise the MP on constituency matters – these should be selected randomly from the electoral register.

Theme 2. How can people be encouraged to take more interest in politics?

Issues

- People do not think that politics affects them much.
- People do not know much about politicians or politics.
- People do not trust politicians.
- People are led to believe that they can have it all in politics and don't want to think about it too hard.
- People think that politics is an expensive rip-off.

Solutions

- People to do a kind of political jury service where they are obliged to get involved in national or local decision making.
- *X Factor*-style TV show on policy issues.
- More direct democracy – referendums etc.
- E-voting in elections and on specific issues like where to make cuts.
- Tax breaks for political involvement.
- Opening up political parties so outsiders can stand – open primaries.
- MP must canvass views of constituents – e-voting and open forum meetings.
- Ordinary citizens to sit in on select committees and scrutinise all bills.
- Public review of electoral system.
- All schoolchildren to learn about politics, government and how they can get involved.

Theme 3. How much should we pay politicians and what should they do for the money?

Issues

- There is no job description for MPs; each interprets it very differently. Some work hard, some less so; some spend little time in their constituencies, some spend much more.
- MPs are unaccountable and mostly do not feed back on what they do – until election time, when they 'spin' their achievements to get re-elected.
- The consensus amongst many politicians is that they are underpaid compared with other senior people – also that they incur huge costs by having to run two homes.

- The consensus amongst many members of the public is that politicians are overpaid and on the make.

Solutions

- Job descriptions for MPs spelling out what is expected of them.
- MPs' salaries to be pegged to a similar profession.
- MPs' expenses to be signed off by constituents as well as officials.
- MPs to report back on what they have achieved to a specific template so comparisons can be made with other similar constituencies.
- Job shares to be allowed.

Theme 4. What can the media do to connect politicians and people rather than divide them?

Issues

- Media owners will promote their own views through their media outlets.
- Journalists and politicians are in cahoots.
- Journalists are allowed to run unattributed stories, meaning that politicians can plant ideas without any substantiation.
- 24/7 news cycle pressurises journalists to pressurise politicians for quick responses, and to chase short-term sensations.
- Media tend to simplify stories therefore sometimes ignoring the real issues or misrepresenting them.
- The media thrives on adversarial politics.
- The media build mistrust in politics and politicians by running negative stories about politicians' behaviour, never positive ones.
- UK press presents opinion as if it were news.

Solutions

- Stronger media regulation.
- Encourage more citizen journalism.
- Ban unattributed briefings.
- New commission to oversee relationship between politicians and media.
- Cross-party politicians to agree to work differently with the media.

Index of names